THE ARTS, EDUCATION, AND AESTHETIC KNOWING

THE ARTS, EDUCATION, AND AESTHETIC KNOWING

Ninety-first Yearbook of the
National Society for the Study of Education

PART II

Edited by
BENNETT REIMER AND RALPH A. SMITH

Editor for the Society
KENNETH J. REHAGE

19 NSSE 92

Distributed by THE UNIVERSITY OF CHICAGO PRESS ● CHICAGO, ILLINOIS

The National Society for the Study of Education

Founded in 1901 as successor to the National Herbart Society, the National Society for the Study of Education has provided a means by which the results of serious study of educational issues could become a basis for informed discussion of those issues. The Society's two-volume yearbooks, now in their ninety-first year of publication, reflect the thoughtful attention given to a wide range of educational problems during those years. In 1971 the Society inaugurated a series of substantial publications on Contemporary Educational Issues to supplement the yearbooks. Each year the Society's publications contain contributions to the literature of education from more than a hundred scholars and practitioners who are doing significant work in their respective fields.

An elected Board of Directors selects the subjects with which volumes in the yearbook series are to deal and appoints committees to oversee the preparation of manuscripts. A special committee created by the Board performs similar functions for the series on Contemporary Educational Issues.

The Society's publications are distributed each year without charge to members in the United States, Canada, and elsewhere throughout the world. The Society welcomes as members all individuals who desire to receive its publications. Information about current dues may be found in the back pages of this volume.

This volume, *The Arts, Education, and Aesthetic Knowing*, is Part II of the Ninety-first Yearbook of the Society. Part I, which is published at the same time, is entitled *The Changing Contexts of Teaching*.

A listing of the Society's publications still available for purchase may be found in the back pages of this volume.

Library of Congress Catalog Number: 91-066983
ISSN: 0077-5762

Published 1992 by
THE NATIONAL SOCIETY FOR THE STUDY OF EDUCATION
5835 Kimbark Avenue, Chicago, Illinois 60637

First Printing, 4,500 Copies

Printed in the United States of America

v

Acknowledgments

The National Society for the Study of Education deeply appreciates the efforts of all who have made it possible to bring out this important volume in its Yearbook series.

Bennett Reimer and Ralph A. Smith, the editors, together with their committee developed the plan for the book. Drawing upon contemporary thought with regard to aesthetic cognition, or aesthetic knowing, the chapters by Professor Reimer and by Professor Smith provide a convincing rationale for a far more significant place for the arts in our elementary and secondary schools than is the case today. This theme is elaborated from different perspectives and with great effectiveness by each of the other contributors, all of whom, like the editors, are distinguished educators with a genuine concern for education in the arts. To all who have written for this volume, the Society extends its sincere gratitude.

Professor Margaret J. Early, formerly a member of the Society's Board of Directors, graciously offered to assist with the editing of the manuscripts. Her perceptive comments and suggestions have been of enormous help. H. Jerome Studer, assistant in the NSSE office, prepared the name index and performed other important services so essential to the process of publication.

KENNETH J. REHAGE
Editor for the Society

Editors' Preface

In the Society's ninety-year history of publishing yearbooks, the arts have often been the subject of discussions, most notably in two yearbooks on music education (1936, 1958) and two on visual art education (1941, 1965). The present book, however, is the first entirely devoted to all the arts as a field of study. Various explanations are no doubt possible for its having taken almost a century for the arts as a curriculum area to receive such attention, but a compelling reason may well be that there has not been, until recently, a unifying concept sufficiently powerful and broad to encompass all the arts, to capture a sense of that which they all share as a defining characteristic related to their human benefit, and to require a role for education in the arts essential to the realization of that benefit. The concept that there is a special mode of cognition variously called aesthetic knowing, understanding, experience, and percipience by contributors to this volume may well provide the unity and educational relevance necessary to argue that the arts constitute a foundational school subject.

Venerable as the idea of aesthetic knowing is, it is being examined today with renewed vigor. This situation can be attributed to major shifts in thinking about the nature of knowledge and mind in modern philosophy, psychology, and education. In contrast to earlier behavioristic assumptions about human understanding and learning, which centered on describing overt behavior in terms of stimulus-response connections, contemporary viewpoints posit the existence of such mental functions as perception, memory, thinking, imagining, and problem solving in trying to understand human thought and action. These functions play strategic roles in the mind's processing and storing of information. And since knowing presupposes interpretive schemas, or conceptual frameworks, the word "cognition" can be said to refer to both knowledge and the mental operations that figure in acquiring it. Attempts to understand better the content and dynamics of mind have, moreover, persuaded theorists that artistic and aesthetic ways of knowing deserve a place among the significant forms of human intelligence. Insofar as one of the major purposes of schooling is the development of young people's cognitive powers, the provision of instruction in aesthetic cognition should, it follows, become an important part of that endeavor.

This volume discusses aesthetic cognition under four headings: the antecedents of contemporary thinking about aesthetic knowing and arts education; the nature of aesthetic knowing itself; the problems of teaching and learning; and curriculum change.

In Section One, George Geahigan reviews the discussions of arts education in the Society's previous yearbooks, providing an important perspective on current positions. Too often discussions of educational topics reveal indifference toward historical antecedents, and the editors wanted to counteract this tendency.

Section Two consists of three essays on aesthetic knowing from an educational point of view.

Bennett Reimer thinks it is now possible to claim a value for education in the arts that would place it at the center and not the periphery of school subjects. This claim, the cognitive claim, provides not only a convincing rationale for arts education but also a powerful set of organizing principles for achieving aesthetic learning.

Ralph A. Smith's essay may be read as a strong recommendation to supplement creative activities with expanded conceptual studies. Smith suggests that a humanities interpretation that is grounded in an adequate theory of aesthetic experience is an appropriate response to the needs of arts education today. His descriptions of an art-world curriculum and phases of aesthetic learning suggest ways to develop relevant conceptual frameworks for effective arts programs.

Although he strongly endorses the value of the new cognitive paradigm in arts education, Michael J. Parsons believes that we can no longer take for granted the nature, meaning, and value of art, or ways of teaching it. An interpretive paradigm of aesthetic cognition would be attuned to the social and cultural meanings that comprise a learner's cognitive stock, meanings that derive from both the world of art and from life generally.

The contributors to Section Three address a number of developmental and pedagogical issues that can influence the teaching and learning of art in school settings.

In explaining the impact of the cognitive revolution on our perception of children's art, Jessica Davis and Howard Gardner observe that, while child art has not changed over the years, our interpretations of it have. Moving beyond behaviorist orientations that ignored assumptions about the rational and imaginative functions of mind, cognitive theorists feature in their accounts the notions of symbolic understanding, schemas, images, and ideas.

David J. Hargreaves and Maurice J. Galton, two British writers, present a cognitive view of human development that encompasses both general and art-specific phases. Although they acknowledge that further research is needed, Hargreaves and Galton think that the teaching of the arts would benefit from an application of what is currently known about the nature of aesthetic growth.

Marcia M. Eaton provides additional support for the view that conceptual learnings are important in developing aesthetic understanding. Such learnings are relevant both to a clearer perception of the character of artworks and to an understanding of how our experience of works of art connects with other values we consider important.

The gift of the arts to the quality of life as lived and experienced is the theme of Mihaly Csikszentmihalyi and Ulrich Schiefele. In their view, schooling has failed to give adequate attention to the aspect of cognition they think is essential for cultivating the qualitative aspects of human experience. They give considerable credence to the often-stated belief in art's capacity to shape the human personality in positive ways.

In Section Four, John I. Goodlad reflects further on his perceptions of schooling and educational reform, topics that have preoccupied him over a distinguished career. Ideas about the arts held by school people—who tend to regard the arts as impractical and more a matter of the hand than of the head—discourage reform efforts, as do patterns of testing, traditions of schooling, and community expectations. Yet ever hopeful when it comes to the prospects of education, Goodlad thinks that something might be done after all given the current climate of dissatisfaction with the status quo.

It was the intention of the editors and committee members of this yearbook to make a contribution to the arts and cognition movement in contemporary arts education. Growth in the ways persons know the world and themselves is, after all, the point and purpose of schooling and education. If the young people who pass through our schools are to learn how to realize their full humanity, then opportunities for aesthetic growth must be provided. The development of artistic and aesthetic ways of knowing must become part of the basic education of all students.

The contributors to this volume suggest a number of ways this might occur. Accenting aesthetic growth differently, discussions weave back and forth between accounts of the nature of aesthetic cognition in the creating and performing of art and descriptions of responses to a completed object or performance. Attention, that is, shifts from one part of the aesthetic complex to another, from the artistic making of artworks to aesthetic responding within the society or culture in which such activities occur. The aesthetic learner is envisaged variously as a polymath of knowing (Reimer's four ways of knowing), as a child artist (Davis and Gardner), as a percipient respondent and art-world sojourner (Smith), aesthetic interpreter (Parsons), puzzle solver (Eaton), optimal experient (Csikszentmihalyi and Schiefele), and so forth. Despite a variety of viewpoints, it is noteworthy that contributors to this volume are more interested in articulating and strengthening the cognitive paradigm in arts education than in arguing among themselves. The message they most want to convey is that the cognitive paradigm in one form or another is one that the field of arts education would do well to ponder. All believe that arts education needs to be grounded in a broader conception of knowing than that which has ever held sway in American schools.

BENNETT REIMER
RALPH A. SMITH

Table of Contents

	PAGE
THE NATIONAL SOCIETY FOR THE STUDY OF EDUCATION	iv
BOARD OF DIRECTORS OF THE SOCIETY, 1991-92; THE YEARBOOK COMMITTEE; CONTRIBUTORS TO THE YEARBOOK	v
ACKNOWLEDGMENTS	vii
EDITORS' PREFACE	ix

Section One
Antecedents

CHAPTER

I. THE ARTS IN EDUCATION: A HISTORICAL PERSPECTIVE, *George Geahigan* 1

Section Two
Education and Aesthetic Knowing

II. WHAT KNOWLEDGE IS OF MOST WORTH IN THE ARTS?, *Bennett Reimer* 20

III. TOWARD PERCIPIENCE: A HUMANITIES CURRICULUM FOR ARTS EDUCATION, *Ralph A. Smith* 51

IV. COGNITION AS INTERPRETATION IN ART EDUCATION, *Michael J. Parsons* 70

CHAPTER
PAGE

Section Three
Learning and Teaching for Aesthetic Knowing

V. THE COGNITIVE REVOLUTION: CONSEQUENCES FOR THE UNDER-
STANDING AND EDUCATION OF THE CHILD AS ARTIST, *Jessica Davis*
and *Howard Gardner* 92

VI. AESTHETIC LEARNING: PSYCHOLOGICAL THEORY AND EDUCATIONAL
PRACTICE, *David J. Hargreaves* and *Maurice J. Galton* 124

VII. TEACHING THROUGH PUZZLES IN THE ARTS, *Marcia Muelder
Eaton* 151

VIII. ARTS EDUCATION, HUMAN DEVELOPMENT, AND THE QUALITY OF
EXPERIENCE, *Mihaly Csikszentmihalyi* and *Ulrich Schiefele* . . 169

Section Four
Aesthetic Knowing and the Culture of Schooling

IX. TOWARD A PLACE IN THE CURRICULUM FOR THE ARTS, *John I.
Goodlad* 192

NAME INDEX 213

SUBJECT INDEX 219

INFORMATION ABOUT MEMBERSHIP IN THE SOCIETY 223

PUBLICATIONS OF THE SOCIETY 225

Section One
ANTECEDENTS

CHAPTER I

The Arts in Education: A Historical Perspective

GEORGE GEAHIGAN

Of all the forces that have affected American education, perhaps the most immediate and enduring has been the drive towards universal mass education.[1] The rise of the common school movement in the nineteenth century and the rapid growth of the secondary school in the twentieth created enormous pressures to expand and diversify the curriculum to meet the needs of an increasingly heterogeneous student body. It was during these periodic phases of expansion that the arts were introduced into the public school curriculum. Music appeared first as singing and sight reading during the 1830s.[2] Art in the form of industrial drawing (which consisted mainly of exercises in copying abstract linear designs and schematic rendering of geometric figures) appeared in the 1870s.[3] Literature, which had previously existed as brief selections in primers and readers, became established as a high school subject in its own right under the guise of literary history and philology in the 1860s.[4]

Educators offered a variety of rationales for the introduction of these subjects into the curriculum. One involved an appeal to tradition: as one of the seven liberal arts, music had attenuated ties with educational practices dating back to the Greeks, and literature held a central place in the humanities. References were also made to the psychology of the period. Music and drawing were promoted by early educational reformers such as Pestalozzi for their value in developing mental faculties. And with the decline of Greek and Latin in the schools, literature also assumed some of the status of an

George Geahigan is Associate Professor of Art and Design and Head of the Division of Art Education, Department of Creative Arts, Purdue University.

intellectual discipline. There was, further, the appeal to practicality. Music played an important role in religious services and singing skills were needed in worship; the visual arts were thought to be useful for developing handwriting ability and in preparing students for vocations as artisans in the developing industries of the period; and literature was closely associated with utilitarian skills of reading and writing. As a romantic idealism took hold toward the end of the century, the arts were frequently promoted as a means of fostering ideals and promoting morality.[5]

These evolving and changing rationales were symptomatic of a deep-seated ambivalence about the significance of the arts and their value in American education, an ambivalence that persists to this day. Ever inclined toward the practical, American educators have tended to regard the arts as more enjoyable than necessary, as something to be attended to after the serious business of schooling had been finished. Herbert Spencer perhaps best epitomized this attitude when in 1859 he asked about the worth of different kinds of knowledge. On Spencer's view, pride of place went to the sciences as paradigms of useful knowledge. (Even knowledge in the arts, he believed, could largely be reduced to scientific knowledge, for example, knowledge of anatomy or psychology.) The arts were to be regarded as ornaments, something useful to be sure, but only as a means of occupying one's leisure time. Many educators would undoubtedly have agreed with Spencer when he claimed that insofar as the arts "occupy the leisure part of life, so should they occupy the leisure part of education."[6]

Such an attitude was reflected in the role assigned to the arts within the public schools. Although the arts became an enduring part of the curriculum, they were accorded only a miniscule share of curriculum time and educational resources.[7] The single exception to this has been the study of literature, in large part because of its ties to the language arts, the very core of the public school curriculum.[8]

Progressive Education and the Arts

The development of education in the arts has gone through several periods of change. Perhaps the most dramatic was the era of Progressive education. Progressivism as a reform movement can be traced to the 1870s. In the decades prior to World War I, it was a growing force among intellectuals and reformers, achieving its greatest impact upon American schools in the 1920s and 1930s. In the postwar period, Progressivism was a waning force before its eventual demise in the mid-1950s.[9]

Progressive education can be seen in part as a response to perceived problems within each subject area, and in part as a response to larger trends and movements that affected many areas of the curriculum. If the arts were less formal and rigid than some other areas of the school curriculum, they were by no means devoid of some of the ills that plagued educational practices in the pre-Progressive period. Instruction in the arts was sometimes marked by topics foreign to the interests of children, by analytical modes of teaching, by monotonous drill, and by rote memorization.

At the turn of the century, music education in the schools consisted principally of singing and sight reading of music, although instrumental music had gained a foothold in some secondary schools. The musical pieces that were sung and played came from a traditional repertoire that often had little appeal to students. Sight reading, which consumed much of the instructional time, was often undertaken through drill and rote learning without the corresponding musical experience that would have made the notation meaningful.

Art instruction consisted mainly of freehand drawing of objects—often plaster casts or three-dimensional geometric solids—and small painting exercises which focused upon the formal elements of line, value, or color. Although work with art materials invariably appeals to children, the focus upon realistic depiction or the formal aspects of a work of art could have had but little meaning or significance for many. Art appreciation lessons, when they were held, usually amounted to the teacher giving a brief lecture on some painting reproduced in black and white, or sepia. Students were expected to memorize isolated facts about the artist and the picture. Reproductions used in the classroom were often selected on the basis of their moral or literary value, rather than for any intrinsic interest or appeal.

Writing and English composition were largely taught through rote memorization of rules of grammar and rhetoric, rather than through the practice of writing itself. The study of literature was dominated by lists of classics which teachers felt compelled to cover in order to prepare students for college entrance examinations. Some of these works, while of undoubted importance in the literary heritage, held little interest for the general student. Instruction in literature often focused on historical information and the study of the language in literary works rather than upon the meaning and significance of these works for students.

In responding to problems such as these, Progressivism took the form of a series of different and sometimes contradictory reform movements, movements that appealed to different educational constituencies and resulted in a wide variety of educational practices. Three of the trends which most affected education in the arts were the social efficiency movement, the child-centered movement, and the social reconstruction movement.[10] All these movements were reflected to some extent in National Society for the Study of Education yearbooks of the period.

The social efficiency movement sought to reform schooling by making the curriculum more functional. Proponents of social efficiency attempted to do this by eliminating traditional subjects perceived to be irrelevant to the future lives of students, by establishing curriculum objectives on the basis of activities students would perform in future life, and by attempting to make teaching itself more efficient. Social efficiency proponents appealed to the emerging discipline of psychology, and in particular to the connectionism of Edward Thorndike, as a scientific basis for conducting research in and about the schools. It was largely through Thorndike's efforts that educational measurement and testing became established in the schools. The widespread use of IQ tests developed by Binet, Terman, and others to classify and group students is but one example of the prevailing enthusiasm for testing and measurement of the period.

The second of the reform movements, child-centered education, had a lineage that extended back to the eighteenth century and the writings of Rousseau. Child-centered educators sought to adapt the curriculum to the individual needs, interests, and abilities of students. In focusing upon the child, they also appealed to psychology for guidance, but it was the developmentalism of G. Stanley Hall, the functionalism of John Dewey, and the psychoanalytical theory of Sigmund Freud rather than the behaviorism of Thorndike that informed their practice. Child-centered educators promoted curriculum goals of self-realization and personality development through a curriculum that emphasized self-motivated activity. Early proponents of child-centered education such as Francis Parker and John Dewey gave the arts a major role in learning. Both recognized that children instinctively sang, drew, modeled, wrote, and spoke. Both believed these natural impulses should be exploited for educational purposes.[11] Many of the curriculum innovations of the period—William Kilpatrick's project method, and the core and broad fields curriculums, for example—were attempts to do away with traditional subject matter divisions and to establish purposeful activity as the basis for learning.

The social reconstruction movement was the third major force to affect the arts. Social reconstructionists sought to use the schools as a way of preventing or alleviating social problems in the society at large, an idea that had motivated educational pioneers since Horace Mann. Social reconstructionists focused on preparing students to function as reflective citizens in a democratic society. To accomplish this they argued for instruction in solving problems, for new curriculum content, and for an emphasis upon community life and participation in social activities within the school.

These reform movements affected education in the arts in different ways. The social efficiency movement had a fourfold impact. First, the movement pressured educators in the arts to rationalize the arts in practical terms. Educators were forced to point to ways that the arts could be of tangible benefit to students, for example by helping students make good use of leisure time. Much of the fortieth NSSE yearbook on art education, for example, was given over to an extensive survey of different visual art forms designed to show both their pervasiveness in American culture and their usefulness in commerce, industry, and the home. Literature, of course, could be justified because it fostered the development of reading skills. Second, educators were forced to recast the content of their subjects in more functional terms. One result was to give more emphasis in the curriculum to the applied arts and the popular arts, as opposed to the traditional fine arts. In the visual arts, commercial art and architecture, industrial design, and other areas of applied design were given more prominence as areas of study. English expanded to include media studies and in the 1930s the study of film. Third, the movement was responsible for beginning efforts to devise tests in the arts. Both the thirty-fifth NSSE yearbook on music and the fortieth on art contained chapters discussing measures of aptitude and achievement. The twenty-second yearbook on English composition was devoted principally to measurement.[12] But then as now educators interested in testing tended to focus on easily measured and quantified learnings, and to ignore higher-order cognitive skills, appreciations, and affective outcomes. For this reason, the testing and measurement movement had but a negligible impact upon teaching practices in the arts. Actually, the widespread use of IQ tests may well have had a negative impact upon the status of music and the visual arts in the schools. The overwhelmingly verbal character of these tests undoubtedly gave many educators a restricted view of intelligence that may well have blinded them to the intellectual capacities exhibited in artistic creation, performance, and response.

Of all the reforms, the child-centered movement had perhaps the most profound effect upon the arts. Instead of focusing solely upon content goals within each of their subject domains, educators were encouraged to view their subjects as instruments for promoting personality and social growth, for fostering the general well-being of students, and for encouraging learning in other subject areas of the curriculum. A wide range of new goals is thus reflected in the NSSE yearbooks of the period. Another effect of the child-centered movement was the introduction of new methods of teaching that were more attuned to the needs of students. In elementary music, rhythmical activities, singing games, folk dancing, marches, instrumental playing, and musical improvisation were added to the curriculum. New songs became part of the school repertoire, songs that were chosen for their beauty and appeal rather than because they illustrated a particular technique. Courses in music theory and appreciation were added at the secondary level. In the visual arts, freehand drawing and design exercises gave way to expressive activities in which children used art media to interpret themes and topics from their own experience. The range of art materials was dramatically increased so that children could choose a means of expression to which they were naturally attuned. In language arts and English, creative writing was introduced. The teaching of literature moved away from formal study and recitation toward more class discussion and the use of literature as a means of exploring the reader's own nature. Students were encouraged to read widely, and contemporary literature and literary works that appealed to juvenile interests supplemented the traditional classics.

If the focus upon student needs and interests had positive effects upon education in the arts, there were some negative outcomes as well. The emphasis upon activity in some instances became an end in itself. Activities were introduced into the curriculum simply because they were enjoyed, whether or not they made any genuine contribution to children's capacities to produce, perform, or respond to art. An overemphasis upon the immediate interests of children led in some instances to a neglect of the arts as organized bodies of subject matter. Random and haphazard experiences replaced any structured sequence of learning activities. The erosion of the arts as distinctive subjects was further exacerbated by attempts to correlate the arts with other areas in the curriculum. Often when correlation occurred, as in the project method, for example, the arts were treated as mere handmaidens, introduced to promote learnings in other areas of the curriculum rather than for any artistic or aesthetic ends that might occur. Educators were cautious about these innovations and well aware of the problems they presented to teaching and learning in the arts.

One further legacy of the child-centered movement should be mentioned. In using such slogans as the "whole child" and "creative self-expression," extreme proponents of child-centered education often appealed to romantic notions of artistic creation and response, or to psychoanalytic theories prominent during the early decades of the century. In the former instance, artistic creation tended to be viewed as a matter of inspiration or pure intuition, and the artist as an eccentric; aesthetic response was viewed as a matter of emotional seizure, uncontaminated by any element of reflective thought. Psychoanalytic theories tended to depict artistic creation and aesthetic response in terms of the workings of the unconscious mind— something to be identified with the irrational and compulsive.[13] Whatever insights such views contained, they also tended to oversimplify, and thus distort, the complex processes of artistic creation and aesthetic response. In doing so, they promoted some unwelcome stereotypes. Student involvement in the arts has often been tarred with the suspicion that it is a matter of deviant personalities engaging in compulsive behavior. Some educators have also regarded schoolwork in the arts as a form of therapy appropriate for students who were not succeeding in other areas of the curriculum. Such views also went hand in hand with a laissez-faire approach to teaching, an approach that has prejudiced many against education in the arts.

The last of the three movements, social reconstructionism, also had important effects on education in the arts. Educators in the arts were encouraged to view their subjects as a means of promoting democratic ideals and community life in the classroom. Appreciation of the arts was seen as a way of understanding social problems, the concerns of different social groups, and other cultures. Once again these changed goals had consequences in the classroom. One effect was to give further emphasis to group activities. In music, group performances were seen as a way of fostering social interaction, group cohesion, and community spirit. For much the same reasons, students in art classes did such things as collectively design backdrops and costumes for school plays and pageants. In the visual arts, handicrafts, folk, and ethnic arts were studied for the light they shed on other cultures and peoples, in many instances replacing study of the traditional fine arts. In English literature, study of the classics gave way to readings and classroom experiences organized around social problems and adolescent concerns. Such practices, whatever their rationale, often did little to foster genuine learnings in the arts. Once again, education in the arts was sacrificed to other curriculum goals.

As these various reform movements evolved and coalesced into the last phase of Progressivism under the banner of "life adjustment" in the 1940s, education in the arts could point to some genuine advances. But there were also some disturbing aspects to prevailing educational practices as well. In responding to the various forces that constituted the Progressive movement, the arts were justified on the basis of a wide range of educational goals. Often these had little to do with specific learnings in the arts, but rather with personality development or socialization of the young. Because they appealed to different educational constituencies, the arts maintained their place within the curriculum, but at the cost of their own cohesiveness as subjects.

Academic Reform and the Arts

The end of the Progressive era was marked by an undercurrent of criticism that gradually intensified as the second world war ended and the cold war began. Critics of education, often members of university faculties, were concerned about the erosion of traditional values and the lack of intellectual rigor in the public schools.[14] In the conservative climate of the postwar period, these concerns were taken up by a variety of constituencies outside the schools, troubled by a general perception that the United States was losing its technological lead over the Soviet Union, and by claims that the schools were being undermined by an inept educational bureaucracy. Much of the criticism focused on the teaching of mathematics and science, and much of the concern was about the development of the academically talented, rather than the average or below-average student.

If the teaching of literature did from time to time come in for some criticism from academics disturbed by the failure to teach traditional literary classics, education in music and art escaped the attention of most educational critics. But if the arts were not at the center of the ongoing controversy, there was a growing body of educators who were concerned about their condition in the schools, concerns that are reflected especially in the fifty-seventh NSSE yearbook on music and the sixty-fourth on art education.[15]

One perennial concern was with the status of the arts. Music and art had managed to retain only a marginal foothold in the curriculum. When they were taught at all (and many schools did not have programs in music and art), they were taught mainly in the elementary and junior high schools. At the secondary level, both music and art were elective subjects, taken by only a small fraction of students. Although literature had a secure place in the secondary school curriculum, it too was not immune to occasional challenges to its status as an essential subject. Creative writing, by way of contrast, never became established as a substantial part of the English curriculum. Even at the height of the Progressive period, English teachers tended to regard it as something to be taught after more basic work in language arts had been completed.[16]

Music and art educators were also concerned about a perceived problem of curriculum balance. Although some courses in history, theory, and appreciation in these subjects existed at the secondary school level, the overwhelming majority of music and art courses in both primary and secondary schools were performance oriented. Programs in music and art developed skills in singing, playing an instrument, performing in group ensembles, or practicing an art form, but did little to develop larger understandings and appreciations to accompany these skills. Most programs made little provision for those who would experience the arts primarily as listeners or viewers.

Educators in all the arts were concerned about the effectiveness of existing curricula. In attempting to secure a place for the arts in the schools, educators had subscribed to a wide array of curriculum goals. But educational goals not only justify practice; they direct it as well. Justifying the arts on the basis of their instrumental values tended to promote disarray in the classroom since some rationale could invariably be found for almost any kind of classroom activity. There was also a growing sense of estrangement between the content taught in the classroom and development of the arts as disciplines outside the public schools. In the visual arts, for example, a plethora of formula lessons were routinely used that had little to do with the actual aesthetic issues that preoccupied artists and critics. Literature study was largely oblivious to the concerns of the New Criticism which had come to dominate literary scholarship in the universities. Moreover, in attempting to serve different kinds of curriculum goals, education in the arts was often reduced to a series of random experiences. There was a pressing need for articulation in the curriculum from one experience to another, and from one grade to the next.

Educators were also concerned about the quality of instruction given by teachers who had inadequate preparation in the arts they were teaching. This was an especially acute problem in music and art where much of the instruction was the responsibility of the general classroom teacher who typically had little understanding of these art forms, but it was a source of dismay in English as well.[17]

For many, the need for educational reform was dramatized by the Sputnik launch in 1957, but well before that date reform efforts were underway in a number of mathematics and science curriculum projects that had been started in the early 1950s. These were initiated and directed by eminent scholars in the subject disciplines, rather than by public school educators. A milestone in the movement toward reform was the conference held at Woods Hole, Massachusetts in 1959, at which representatives from these projects met with interested psychologists, historians, and educators to discuss fundamental issues in science and humanities education. The report of the conference, written by its director, Jerome Bruner, was the enormously influential *The Process of Education*.[18]

Bruner's book was significant in signaling a renewed educational concern about knowledge and subject matter. Emphasizing that a fundamental problem exists whenever an excess of knowledge confronts students seeking to understand a subject, Bruner argued that subjects in the curriculum should be organized in terms of the structure of the discipline—those fundamental ideas and principles which underlie a subject and make it comprehensible. Conferees at Woods Hole contended that knowledge is related and that these relationships are best understood by experts within each discipline.

Bruner's discussion of readiness for learning emphasized the importance of translating subject matter in ways that are appropriate for children's stages of intellectual development. The book boldly hypothesized "that any subject can be taught effectively in some intellectually honest form to any child at any stage of development."[19] It went on to advance the idea of a "spiral curriculum," one organized in such a way that the same fundamental ideas and principles recur at different points in the course of a child's schooling. Bruner's description of enactive, iconic, and symbolic stages served to introduce many educators to Jean Piaget's postwar research in cognitive development.

Bruner's book was also significant in introducing many educators to emerging developments in cognitive psychology. His discussion of such topics as intuitive and analytical thinking, heuristic strategies, and the use of inductive learning sequences signaled a movement away from a behaviorist paradigm that had dominated the psychology of learning from the turn of the century. Unlike behaviorists, whose research focused upon the connections between a physical stimulus and observable behavior, cognitive psychologists attended to perception, thinking, and the higher mental processes; they accepted differentiated states of consciousness as significant data; and they employed hypothetical constructs such as concepts, plans, and intentions to explain behavior. Bruner's emphasis upon intrinsic motivation instead of extrinsic rewards stood in contrast to behaviorist conceptions of the learner as a passive organism controlled by changes in the environment. Recalling the functionalism of Dewey, cognitive psychologists tended to view learners as active agents whose behaviors are directed by their own ideas and purposes.

The major focus of Bruner's book was on science and mathematics. But if literature was discussed only incidentally as a part of the humanities, and if music and art were mentioned only in passing,[20] a number of influential curriculum theorists during this period did assign a fundamental role to the arts within the curriculum of the public school. Sharing the same cognitive orientation as Bruner, such philosophers as Philip Phenix, Paul Hirst, and Harry S. Broudy, B. Othanel Smith, and Joe R. Burnett[21] formulated synoptic curriculum theories that would be common in the sense that they would apply to all students, and general in the sense that they would focus on fundamental learnings within each curriculum area. Each of their theories stressed the existence of a number of discrete domains of learning cutting across traditional subject-matter lines. For Phenix, the arts constituted one of six independent "realms of meaning," which he argued must be developed in all persons if they were to function well within the civilized community. For Hirst, the arts constituted one of seven logically distinct "forms of knowledge" needed by students if they were to have a liberal education. For Broudy and his associates, the arts constituted one of six "categories of instruction" that were required if students were to develop the "cognitive and evaluative maps" needed to function in a modern mass society. All these theorists agreed that the aesthetic constituted a unique domain of knowledge, and that some mastery of this domain should be required of all students. Their views thus contrasted sharply with much of the rhetoric about the arts that had developed during the Progressive period, in which the arts tended to be viewed as instruments for learning other subjects, rather than as areas of knowledge in their own right.

In different ways, these three curriculum theories also presented for consideration an even more radical thesis: that the arts, themselves, were sources of knowledge.[22] In one form or another, such a thesis has been periodically asserted throughout history. During the twentieth century, it was taken up and defended by a number of eminent philosophers. Phenix and Hirst drew upon the work of Ernst Cassirer and Susanne Langer.[23] In the former's influential theory of culture, the arts were considered to be one of a number of discrete areas of human symbolic functioning, all of which shared a fundamental purpose in articulating man's consciousness and making human existence comprehensible. In amplifying Cassirer's ideas, Langer drew a distinction between discursive symbols (the symbolization of language) and presentational symbols (the symbols of art). For her, the cognitive power of the arts was located in their unique ability to express ideas that defied conventional linguistic formulation.

By way of contrast, the cognitive function of the arts for Broudy and his associates lay in their potential as models for the introjection of attitudes and values, another idea with a long lineage in the history of aesthetics. But this was only the first of a two-part rationale for the arts in education. They also concurred with John Dewey that the arts were sources of valuable experience in their own right.[24] Because the cognitive and experiential values of the arts are now both routinely used as rationales in justifying the arts in education, it is worth pointing out in passing that Dewey also viewed the arts as sources of knowledge and insight.[25] A significant affinity thus exists between the theories of Dewey, Cassirer, and Langer.

Although all three curriculum theories assigned the arts a central role in education, the comprehensiveness of each theory precluded any detailed prescription for arts education in the schools. Of all the curriculum theorists, Broudy and his associates came closest to delineating an actual plan for implementing the arts in public education. In a series of articles extending back to the early 1950s, Broudy argued for a required program of study in music, art, and literature from the seventh to the twelfth grades.[26] Instruction in such a program would utilize concepts drawn from the discipline of aesthetics, and would be aimed at developing an understanding and appreciation of music, art, and literature. In contrast to existing appreciation courses or survey courses in the history of the arts, Broudy proposed that students study a small number of works, but works of acknowledged excellence (which he referred to as classics or aesthetic exemplars). Except for the pronounced emphasis upon the classics, this recommendation was similar to what routinely transpired in most literature classes. Broudy's proposal, however, departed significantly from programs of instruction in music and art which were based almost entirely upon artistic performance and production. The idea of an "aesthetic education," nevertheless, proved to be a compelling one for arts educators. Ralph Smith and Bennett Reimer,[27] the editors of this volume, were instrumental in developing and articulating this idea for educators in their respective disciplines. Many other influential educators in music, art, and literature contributed to its development as well.

One of the most significant outcomes of the academic reform movement was the convening of a number of conferences on curriculum development in the arts. Before the Woods Hole meeting, English educators had met with college professors of English in a series of "Basic Issues Conferences" to discuss the teaching of English as a "fundamental liberal discipline." Following Woods Hole, conferences were organized in all the arts along the same lines. Educators met with representatives from the subject disciplines and representatives from such allied disciplines as psychology and philosophy to discuss fundamental issues in the teaching of the arts as disciplines, that is, as bodies of specific knowledge to be transmitted to students. Conferees addressed such questions as: What constitutes knowledge in music, art, and literature? How should that knowledge be organized? How and when should it be taught? How should learning be evaluated?

One outcome of these meetings was the funding of a number of curriculum development projects in music, art, and literature by the federal government and by some large private foundations. A few of these projects, such as the Aesthetic Education Program of the Central Midwestern Regional Educational Laboratory, embraced several of the arts. Others, such as the Manhattanville Music Curriculum Program, the Kettering Project in art, and the many projects funded under the aegis of Project English were devoted to a single art form.

These projects did much to energize thinking and inquiry in arts education. As a result, arts educators today have changed perceptions of their subjects. In music and art, for example, there is a general recognition that such disciplines as aesthetics, history, and criticism have a bearing upon education in each subject, and that response to works of art has a place in the school curriculum. These projects were also instrumental in bringing about changes in class texts and textbooks for teachers. Yet, granted these changes, an overall assessment would have to conclude that these projects had only a modest impact upon the schools.

In retrospect, one can point to numerous reasons for the difficulties curriculum developers had in effecting change. There was difficulty in securing agreement about the structure of the disciplines. Unlike mathematics and science, it has been argued that knowledge in the arts does not consist of a logical hierarchy with general concepts subsuming more specific ones.[28] Programs of instruction, therefore, can be organized and structured in different ways. There was also the problem of effecting change itself, which turned out to be vastly more difficult than curriculum developers envisaged. Many of the projects lacked the financial resources to implement the curricula that were developed and there was an inadequate appreciation of the role of the teacher in providing instruction. Many of the curricula that were developed never made their way into the schools, and of those that did some were more effective with the academically able than they were with average or below-average students.[29] Finally, overshadowing all the efforts at reform, was a changing social climate. School desegregation, the Vietnam War, the financial exigencies of the early 1970s, all had an impact in changing educational priorities.

Cognition and the Arts: From the 1960s to the Present

More than one commentator has noted that the trends which dominated education during the late 1960s and 1970s had their counterparts in the Progressive era. There was a movement to refocus attention on the concerns and needs of students, a form of child-centered education; educational reformers sought to use the schools for redressing the problems of minorities, a form of social reconstructionism; and there was a widespread movement toward making the schools more "accountable" through an emphasis upon the "basics" and testing, a revival of social efficiency.

The arts were affected by all of these trends. Perhaps the most noticeable impact of the first was upon the teaching of English. The study of literature shifted from a focus upon the text to an emphasis upon student response to the text. Composition classes began to place more emphasis upon personal feeling and the need to communicate rather than upon rules of grammar. The second trend served to sensitize educators in music, art, and literature to cultural differences among student groups, and to the political implications involved in choosing works of art for study in the classroom. All the arts suffered to a greater or lesser degree from the narrowed educational goals and the misplaced behaviorism of the "back to basics" and the "account-ability" movements.[30]

If all these trends hearkened back to the Progressive era, the current interest in cognition and the arts recalls the concerns that dominated education during the period of academic reform. There is a renewed call for academic excellence, but one in which recognition is given to the legitimacy of the arts and humanities in education. A key figure in generating an interest in cognition and the arts was the philosopher Nelson Goodman. In his *Languages of Art*, published in 1968, he returned to ideas about the symbolic nature of the arts and their cognitive import that had been treated earlier by Cassirer and Langer. Although their work continues to influence thinking in aesthetics, it was regarded by many as more suggestive than convincing. Goodman's contribution was a theory of notationality that served to explain how symbol systems function and the principles underlying their construction. Utilizing this theory, he was able to precisely characterize different art forms on the basis of how well they satisfied the requirements of an ideal notational system, and to distinguish symbol systems in the arts from those in other domains.

In establishing that the arts constituted distinct kinds of symbol systems, Goodman argued that they had an essentially cognitive function in human life. Aesthetic experience, for Goodman, was "cognitive experience distinguished by the dominance of certain symbol characteristics and judged by standards of cognitive efficacy."[31] A primary motive for human engagement with works of art is curiosity, and its reward is insight and understanding. A persistent critic of the epistemological tradition inherited from Descartes and Locke, Goodman argued that experience of works of art is not a matter of passive reception, but rather one of active inquiry. Unlike epistemologists who distinguished between science and art on the basis of a difference between cognition and emotion, Goodman argued that perception, cognition, and the emotions are involved in both domains, and that emotion, itself, has a cognitive component. The symbol systems of art, like those of science, are used in constructing different versions of the world, and none of these systems can be reduced to another.

The influence of Goodman's book would in and of itself have brought it to the attention of educators in the arts, for it has been a major force in redirecting contemporary aesthetics. But Goodman's ideas have also been influential because of his interest in arts education.

As the founder and director of Harvard University's Project Zero, he has been instrumental in bringing together psychologists, philosophers, and educators interested in basic issues of arts education. Since its inception in 1967, Project Zero members have conducted investigations into such areas as the artistic and aesthetic development of children, aesthetic perception of works of art, problem solving and creation in the arts, and practical problems of curriculum construction and evaluation, often using Goodman's theory as a conceptual basis. Research undertaken under the auspices of the project, such as that into children's aesthetic development, has been of interest to many in arts education.[32] Co-director Howard Gardner's theory of multiple intelligences has generated considerable attention for its recognition of a wide range of human intellectual potential. His theory posits seven major realms of intelligent human functioning: linguistic, musical, logical-mathematical, spatial, bodily kinesthetic, interpersonal, and intrapersonal. Gardner's theory raises important questions about the kinds of educational intervention needed to foster these abilities and the optimal timing for their development, and it suggests that the schools have greater responsibilities in developing human intellectual potential than they have assumed.[33]

All this has encouraged educators to reconsider the nature of the arts and their role in education. Some have been motivated to conduct research along the lines established by Project Zero members.[34] Others have reevaluated the rationales which underlie education in the arts.[35] Still others have presented critiques of the current state of education in the schools.[36] The joining of philosophical, psychological, and educational concerns has been a fruitful one. In directing educational attention to the cognitive processes involved in making and responding to works of art, and to the intellectual abilities which these activities call forth, educators have challenged common prejudices and stereotypes about the arts that have their origin in a now thoroughly discredited view of knowledge and the mind. In taking their principal mission to be the fostering of knowledge and development of intellect, the schools have often viewed the arts as peripheral to their main concern. A growing number of educators are coming to realize that this is a distorted and dehumanizing view of both education and the arts.

NOTES

1. Lawrence Cremin, *Popular Education and Its Discontents* (New York: Harper and Row, 1990).

2. A. Theodore Tellstrom, *Music in American Education: Past and Present* (New York: Holt, Rinehart, and Winston, 1971), p. 35.

3. Arthur D. Efland, *A History of Art Education* (New York: Teachers College Press, 1990), pp. 86-114.

4. Arthur N. Applebee, *Tradition and Reform in the Teaching of English: A History* (Urbana, IL: National Council of Teachers of English, 1974), pp. 28, 29.

5. For these rationales see Tellstrom, *Music in American Education*, pp. 35-100; Efland, *Art Education*, pp. 86-147; and Applebee, *Tradition and Reform*, pp. 28, 29.

6. Herbert Spencer, *Essays on Education and Kindred Subjects* (London: J. M. Dent and Sons Ltd., 1963), p. 32.

7. Even today art and music instruction together account for less than 6 percent of instructional time at the elementary school level; only 50 percent of American students are enrolled in art and music in the middle schools; and approximately 10-20 percent are enrolled in art and music in the high school. See National Endowment for the Arts, *Toward Civilization: A Report on Arts Education* (Washington, DC: National Endowment for the Arts, 1988). The picture is more complicated with regard to instruction in literature and creative writing. As components of language arts and English, they account for 24 percent of instructional time in grades kindergarten to twelve. But much of this is devoted to developing basic reading and language skills. See the report of the Committee on National Interest, National Council of Teachers of English, *The National Interest and the Teaching of English: A Report on the Status of the Profession* (Champaign, IL: National Council of Teachers of English, 1961). Many today are even concerned about the erosion of literature in the English curriculum, the most secure of the arts. See Maxine Greene, "Literature in Aesthetic Education," the *Journal of Aesthetic Education* 10 (July-October 1976): 61-76.

8. As Applebee notes, the teaching of language skills has provided the defensive screen behind which the study of literature has flourished. See Applebee, *Tradition and Reform*, p. 249.

9. Lawrence Cremin, *The Transformation of the School* (New York: Vintage Books, 1961), p. ix.

10. Ibid.

11. For Parker, such art activities were some of the "nine modes of expression" spontaneously exhibited by children. These required exercise and training to realize the "highest possibilities of manhood and character." See Francis W. Parker, *Talks on Pedagogics* (New York and Chicago: A. S. Barnes and Co., 1894). According to Dewey, the curriculum was to be organized around four chief impulses: the social impulse, the constructive impulse, the impulse towards inquiry, and the expressive or art impulse. See John Dewey, *The School and Society* (Chicago: University of Chicago Press, 1899), pp. 55-60.

12. Jacob Kwalwasser, "The Composition of Musical Ability," in *Music Education*, ed. Guy M. Whipple, Thirty-fifth Yearbook of the National Society for the Study of Education, Part II (Bloomington, IL: Public School Publishing Co., 1936), pp. 35-42; Norman C. Meier, "Recent Research in the Psychology of Art," in *Art in American Life and Education*, ed. Guy M. Whipple, Fortieth Yearbook of the National Society for the Study of Education (Bloomington, IL: Public School Publishing Co., 1941), pp. 379-400; Earl Hudelson, *English Composition: Its Aims, Methods, and Measurement*, Twenty-second Yearbook of the National Society for the Study of Education, Part I (Bloomington, IL: Public School Publishing Co., 1923).

13. Some of John Dewey's sharpest criticisms were directed at extreme proponents of child-centered education. See his comment on the views of the Viennese art educator, Franz Cizek, an early proponent of self-expression in the classroom. John Dewey,

"Individuality and Experience," in John Dewey, et al., *Art and Education* (Rahway, New Jersey: Barnes Foundation Press, 1929), p. 180.

14. Much of this criticism reflected concerns that had been earlier expressed by educational leaders during the Progressive movement. For a discussion of this see Herbert M. Kliebard, "What Happened to American Schooling in the First Part of the Twentieth Century?" in *Learning and Teaching the Ways of Knowing*, ed. Elliot Eisner, Eighty-fourth Yearbook of the National Society for the Study of Education, Part II (Chicago: University of Chicago Press, 1985), pp. 18-21; and also Cremin, *The Transformation of the School.*

15. Nelson B. Henry, ed., *Basic Concepts in Music Education*, Fifty-seventh Yearbook of the National Society for the Study of Education, Part I (Chicago: University of Chicago Press, 1958); W. Reid Hastie, ed., *Art Education*, Sixty-fourth Yearbook of the National Society for the Study of Education, Part II (Chicago: University of Chicago Press, 1965). The yearbook on music more consistently represented these concerns as well as a growing cognitive orientation in the arts. In the yearbook on art, these concerns were reflected in chapters written by Ronald Silverman and Vincent Lanier, Stanley G. Wold and W. Reid Hastie, and Elliot Eisner.

16. Roderic Botts, "Writing and Rhetoric in American Secondary Schools: 1918-1930," *English Journal* 68 (April 1979): 57.

17. See Applebee, *Tradition and Reform*, pp. 199, 200.

18. Jerome Bruner, *The Process of Education* (New York: Vintage Books, 1963).

19. Ibid., p. 33.

20. Bruner's comments urged that the arts not be bypassed in the push for excellence in science education. Ibid., pp. 78, 79.

21. Philip R. Phenix, *Realms of Meaning* (New York: McGraw-Hill, 1964); Paul H. Hirst, *Knowledge and the Curriculum* (London and Boston: Routledge and Kegan Paul, 1974); Harry S. Broudy, B. Othanel Smith, and Joe R. Burnett, *Democracy and Excellence in American Secondary Education* (Chicago: Rand McNally, 1964).

22. In Hirst, this thesis is entertained as a possibility rather than as one conclusively established.

23. Ernst Cassirer, *The Philosophy of Symbolic Forms*, 3 vols. (New Haven: Yale University Press, 1953-59 [original German publication, 1923-29]); Ernst Cassirer, *An Essay on Man* (New Haven: Yale University Press, 1944); Susanne K. Langer, *Philosophy in a New Key* (Cambridge, Massachusetts: Harvard University Press, 1942); *Feeling and Form* (New York: Charles Scribner's Sons, 1953).

24. John Dewey, *Art as Experience* (New York: G. P. Putnam's Sons, 1934).

25. See John Dewey, "Experience, Nature and Art" in John Dewey et al., *Art and Education*, p. 8.

26. Broudy's ideas have been presented in several NSSE yearbooks. See Harry S. Broudy, "A Realistic Philosophy of Music Education," in *Basic Concepts in Music Education*, ed. Henry, pp. 62-87; and Harry S. Broudy, "A Common Curriculum in Aesthetics and Fine Arts," in *Individual Differences and the Common Curriculum*, ed. Gary D Fenstermacher and John I. Goodlad, Eighty-second Yearbook of the National Society for the Study of Education, Part I (Chicago: University of Chicago Press, 1983), pp. 219-247.

27. In addition to numerous articles, Ralph Smith has edited a number of volumes on aesthetic education including *Aesthetics and Criticism in Art Education* (Chicago: Rand McNally, 1966); *Aesthetic Concepts and Education* (Urbana, IL: University of Illinois Press, 1970), and *Aesthetic Problems and Education* (Urbana, IL: University of Illinois Press, 1971). The *Journal of Aesthetic Education*, which Smith edits, has been a major forum for discussion and debate on this topic. A foundational work in music

education, Bennett Reimer, *A Philosophy of Music Education* (Englewood Cliffs, NJ: Prentice-Hall, 1970), is now in its second edition (1989).

28. Broudy, "A Realistic Philosophy."

29. For a discussion of the difficulties encountered in implementing the new curricula, see Elliot W. Eisner, ed., *Confronting Curriculum Reform* (Boston: Little, Brown, and Co., 1971).

30. Discussions of these trends as they pertain to English can be found in the following NSSE yearbooks: James R. Squire, ed., *The Teaching of English*, Seventy-sixth Yearbook of the National Society for the Study of Education, Part I (Chicago: University of Chicago Press, 1977); Alan C. Purves and Olive Niles, eds., *Becoming Readers in a Complex Society*, Eighty-third Yearbook of The National Society for the Study of Education, Part I (Chicago: University of Chicago Press, 1984); and Anthony R. Petrosky and David Bartholomae, eds., *The Teaching of Writing*, Eighty-fifth Yearbook of the National Society for the Study of Education, Part II (Chicago: University of Chicago Press, 1986).

31. Nelson Goodman, *Languages of Art* (Indianapolis: Bobbs-Merrill Co., 1968), p. 262.

32. For accounts of Project Zero research see Nelson Goodman et al., *Basic Abilities Required for Understanding and Creation in the Arts, Final Report, Project No. 9-0283* (Washington, D.C.: Office of Education, U.S. Department of Health, Education, and Welfare, 1972). Howard Gardner, Vernon Howard, and David Perkins, "Symbol Systems: A Philosophical, Psychological, and Educational Investigation," in *Media and Symbols: The Forms of Expression, Communication, and Education*, ed. David R. Olson, Seventy-third Yearbook of the National Society for the Study of Education, Part I (Chicago: University of Chicago Press, 1974), pp. 27-55. See also the special issue of the *Journal of Aesthetic Education* 22 (Spring 1988). For an introductory volume presenting Project Zero research, see David Perkins and Barbara Leondar, eds., *The Arts and Cognition* (Baltimore: Johns Hopkins University Press, 1977).

33. Howard Gardner, *Frames of Mind: The Theory of Multiple Intelligences* (New York: Basic Books, 1983).

34. See for example, Michael Parsons, *How We Understand Art* (Cambridge: Cambridge University Press, 1987).

35. Reimer, *A Philosophy of Music Education*; Ralph A. Smith, *Excellence in Art Education: Ideas and Initiatives* (Reston, VA: National Art Education Association, 1986).

36. Elliot W. Eisner, *Cognition and Curriculum* (New York and London: Longman, 1982).

Section Two
EDUCATION AND AESTHETIC KNOWING

CHAPTER II

What Knowledge Is of Most Worth in the Arts?

BENNETT REIMER

The Spencerian View

The title of this chapter asks the central curriculum question as it applies to the arts. It is intended to start my attempt to deal with this question on an ironic note.

Herbert Spencer wrote his famous essay "What Knowledge Is of Most Worth?" (first published in 1859 and then in 1860 as the first chapter of *Education: Intellectual, Moral, and Physical*)[1] as a critique of the prevailing values of liberal arts study, which focused on the great artistic and intellectual achievements of Western culture. He effectively achieved his aim of starting a revolution in how education should be conceived. On the basis of his application of Darwin's theory of evolution to education, Spencer argued that the values then current needed to be reversed, so that the arts and humanities were no longer to be regarded as the finest fruits of civilization but should be relegated to leisure-time pursuits. "*As they occupy the leisure part of life, so should they occupy the leisure part of education.*"[2] What should occupy the primary position? That which is of most functional value in ministering to self-preservation directly and indirectly, followed by those activities related to child-rearing, followed still further behind by concerns for maintaining proper social and political relations, and finally, in the basement, "those miscellaneous activities which make up the leisure part of life, devoted to the gratification of tastes and feelings."[3] And what, specifically, best ministers to self-preservation and therefore should be regarded as of the highest value?

Bennett Reimer is the John W. Beattie Professor of Music, Northwestern University.

What knowledge is of most worth?—the uniform reply is—Science. This is the verdict on all the counts. For direct self-preservation, or the maintenance of life and health, the all-important knowledge is—Science. For that indirect self-preservation which we call gaining a livelihood, the knowledge of greatest value is—Science. For the due discharge of parental functions, the proper guidance is to be found only in—Science. For that interpretation of national life, past and present, without which the citizen cannot rightly regulate his conduct, the indispensable key is—Science. Alike for the most perfect production and highest enjoyment of art in all its forms, the needful preparation is still—Science. And for the purposes of discipline—intellectual, moral, religious—the most efficient study is, once more—Science. The question which at first seemed so perplexed, has become, in the course of our inquiry, comparatively simple.[4]

The shift from an older notion of liberal education conceived as appropriate for a small elite to a functional, utilitarian view of education as necessary when the masses are to be schooled reflected historical changes occurring not only in intellectual paradigms but in social-political life as well. When education was conceived as being for all rather than for a privileged few, it could no longer afford the luxuries of the leisured class—"the gratification of tastes and feelings." Science, representing those subjects dealing with the hard realities of survival and success, would have to become basic. The cultivation of intrinsically qualitative and therefore nonutilitarian dimensions of individual experience would have to be given up (at least, of course, for the masses) in exchange for social and political democracy.

Spencer's view of what is real and what is valuable, historically determined as it was, has had continuing influence because it is persuasive at a certain level of analysis, and the Spencerian argument continues to be made to this day. So it is remarkable that in the face of its strong influence over the past century of education in Western culture, a counterargument continues to be offered and is by some people passionately advanced (and to some degree heeded). That argument is that the primary reality and value of human life remains its inherent quality as immediately experienced. "Science"—the utilitarian dimension of life and education—is, in this view, valuable not only or even primarily for its functionality (necessary as this is) but as a mode of understanding by which humans know and therefore incorporate into experience an important dimension of their reality. Yet there are other domains of knowing which constitute the multidimensional reality of human experience, including, out of the basement, the persistent and often insistent domain of the arts.

Justifying the Arts

In the United States, the major burden of justifying the arts in education in the face of the dominant Spencerian value system has fallen to the professional fields devoted to the arts in education—music education and visual arts education primarily and in recent years also the slowly growing fields of dance education and theater education. Of course, an active community of professional philosophers and aestheticians has produced a wide-ranging literature on all aspects of art and its role in culture. That literature remains a significant dimension of Western intellectual life. And a fair number of these professional intellectuals have offered ideas and guidelines for education in the arts, ranging from broad general principles to moderately detailed prescriptions for how the arts should be taught in schools. Yet despite such ongoing work at the level of professional scholarship the arts education professions tended, until about three decades ago, to go their own ways little influenced by that literature, to fight their own battles for survival and recognition, and to manufacture their own justifications for why they should be included in schooling (if only in the basement). And they did so with little if any cross-fertilization among art fields, each of which tended to be a self-contained unit not only operationally but intellectually as well. That situation continues to the present.

It will be instructive to look briefly at the ways the professional art education fields went about the task of justifying their existence in a period of history dominated by utilitarian values because the question of what knowledge is of most worth, while having the most practical consequences for curriculum building, is essentially a philosophical question. A good school curriculum is likely to be conceived as one that is in consonance with a dominant belief and value system. What philosophical stances have been devised not only to justify the presence of the arts in education but also to answer the practical question of what about them is most worth knowing?

A good many attempts have been made to answer that question because it is itself rather complex and can be approached in a variety of ways.[5] I focus here on three influential arguments.

THE CLAIM FOR FUNCTIONALITY

The first argument adopted a Spencerian value structure. What is most valuable is that which best functions to secure the most important needs for humans—self-preservation, productive work, parenting, and so forth. While science (broadly conceived) may fulfill such functions most effectively, anything else contributing in some way to fulfilling them might be perceived as also useful to some degree and worthy, therefore, of being included in schooling.

A host of functional claims have been made for the arts in education over the century and a half that they have been included as part of school programs. The specifics of such claims have reflected the general value system that good education is utilitarian in the broad sense, but they have also focused on particular values that crop up from time to time. If "discipline" is a matter of great concern at a particular time (as it seems to be in fifteen- to twenty-year cycles), then it must be shown that involving students in art activities provides them with it, and instruction in art should therefore emphasize its demands for regularized, concentrated accomplishment of tasks. If social skills are highly valued at particular times, the contribution of art study to developing such skills can be pointed out. Programs then shift to an emphasis on socially interactive aspects of art involvement. If "the basics" are being touted as primary, the arts need to be shown to contribute to better learning of them. Instruction accordingly emphasizes the conceptual, numerical, symbol-system dimensions of arts study. Needs for security, moral development, self-esteem, self-expression, mental growth, emotional catharsis, knowledge of history and cultural mores, identification with a particular culture, ability to solve problems, leisure-time activities, and on and on, can all be met by art instruction catering to them. The more of such functions the arts can be shown to serve, and the more pertinent they can be shown to be to favored values, the more important they might become as an integral part of education.

Given the general acceptance of functionality as a major value basis for education as a whole, a certain degree of effectiveness has been achieved by utilitarian approaches in justifying the arts in education and building programs based on them. But a good many problems have also arisen on both sides of the justification-application coin. A deep scratch on the surface of the argument is hardly necessary to uncover the disconcerting fact that no such functional claim can establish the arts as necessary to achieve it. In all cases the value can be realized by a great many other and often far more direct means. In addition, it is hard to establish persuasively that the study of any art actually does contribute to the value in question, except as a result of instructional style rather than any inherent characteristic of art itself.

Therefore, instructional style in any other subject would contribute to the value as effectively.

While the arts can then be conceived as more or less useful as one means to foster important values, they cannot themselves be conceived as important or valuable in any essential sense, nor as requiring instruction endemic to their own nature. The many attempts to secure a place for the arts in education based on the argument for functionality have left them both poorly justified and without a valid curriculum basis, however much they may have won the day in this or that particular advocacy skirmish.

THE CLAIM FOR TALENT DEVELOPMENT

The second way an attempt has been made to secure a place for the arts in American schools has also had a utilitarian cast but in a different sense from the first. This has been the argument that a society to be and remain viable requires a system for identifying and fostering the varieties of competencies needed to fulfill all its specialized roles. In our society the need for professional artists is generally recognized as both legitimate and important. It is also recognized that individuals who are blessed with what seems like a mysterious talent for creating art deserve to have their talent noticed and developed, to have their personal potentials fulfilled, and to be enabled to contribute as professionals to the communal artistic life. As our major institution for enculturation, the public school would seem to be the logical place to provide opportunities for nurturing artistic talent. Supplementary experiences can then be offered outside the school, but to rely entirely on nonschool arts involvements would be to deprive all children of an equal opportunity to have their talent incubated.

When conceived in this way, art instruction logically consists of apprenticeship training in that its purpose is to develop artistic talent. This might seem to be at odds with the claims that art study is instrumental to procuring a variety of other values. In fact, statements of purpose for school arts programs often propose both rationales with little if any awareness that they may be contradictory in their implications for how the arts should be studied. Usually, if thought about at all, the dichotomy is glossed over; after all, if students are learning how to be artists perhaps those other values will also be achieved. What is not brought to consciousness (and not mentioned by art teachers or other advocates for education in the arts) is that many people in our culture do not hold an image of artists as paragons of social virtue. The behavior of artists is often regarded as divergent if not deviant, a degree of leeway being tolerated for them (especially when they happen to be successful). Generally, however, it may be assumed that most parents do not expect that school art instruction will make their children either social deviants or professional artists. They are likely to view such instruction as generally beneficial for a variety of ancillary reasons, and as a way to develop their children's artistic creative talent to some modest degree. Some few children, of course, will take hold in an art and give promise of a professional career.

When Spencer said that the best preparation to both enjoy and produce art is "science," he meant that the essentials of the arts curriculum are (a) training in the techniques, craft, and processes required to be a functioning artist, and (b) a supportive knowledge about what science has to say about human behavior, human biology, human physiology, and so forth, as they are related to producing art.[6] Given his influence, given the high value many people place on creativity and the widely shared belief that the arts are the paradigm of creativity, and given the variety of other individual and social values ascribed to the activity of creating art, the model of education in art as training to be an artist has been dominant in American schools. This model accounts for the most common historical answer to the question of what is most worth knowing about the arts—knowing how to create them.

THE CLAIMS OF AESTHETIC EDUCATION

The third argument has been more philosophically as well as experientially grounded than the previous two.

Some three decades ago a shift in thinking about education in the arts began to take place in both music and visual arts education. An extensive literature detailing the changes in both theory and practice of music and visual art education during the 1960s and afterward testifies to the magnitude of what occurred.[7] Under the influence of the curriculum reform movement, several educational thinkers began to argue that the qualities of experience mediated by the arts, the meanings they make available through their various modes of representation, and the ways those qualities and meanings are generated and shared, are peculiar to the arts. Thus the aesthetic dimension of human experience is seen as a distinctive cognitive domain requiring to be understood and valued on its own terms and taught in ways relevant to those terms. In addition, creating art, although valuable and necessary as one aspect of experiencing and knowing aesthetically, is not sufficient to gain the breadth and depth and variety of meanings available from the arts. To be literate in the aesthetic domain requires a broad-ranging array of responses to the arts. Such responses depend on refined capacities and dispositions (a) to perceive, discriminate, feel, and evaluate works of art; (b) to understand them as objects and events with distinctive cognitive characteristics; (c) to be aware of the historical, social, cultural, political, and religious contexts in which they reside; and (d) to be cognizant of the many issues and controversies surrounding them. Education in the arts, if it is to influence the development of such learnings, would have to be essentially different from an instrumentality for achieving a variety of aesthetically ancillary values or from professional training to be an artist. Both may be included and provided for, but the broader goal or aim of education in the arts would have to be the development of aesthetic literacy in a sense neither of the previous rationales was able to define. And the question of what is most worth knowing about the arts would have to be addressed by including for consideration a far more comprehensive selection of subject matters than had previously been identified.

The striking movement in the school arts fields over the past three decades toward an image of arts education as focused on the aesthetic nature of the arts, and as responsible for cultivating aesthetic sensitivity/awareness/literacy as its primary mission, soon began to be known by the term "aesthetic education." (The *Journal of Aesthetic Education* began publishing in 1966.) For some this was a confusing phrase in that it seemed to signify an interest in teaching conceptual material from or about the branch of philosophy called aesthetics, which lies outside the training of most arts teachers. But as curricula claiming to be instances of aesthetic education appeared and more books and articles on it were published, the term became ubiquitous and a general sense of its nature became more pervasive. This is not to say that the meaning of the term "aesthetic education" is entirely clear to its theoreticians or to arts teachers in the schools.[8] It is also not to say that its applications in school arts programs have been consistent or unanimous. Many teachers continue to follow models of arts education based on a variety of assumptions including that its purpose is to assist in the promotion of extra-aesthetic values or to train incipient artists (neither of which purposes is necessarily ruled out by many conceptions of aesthetic education). And, of course, some theoreticians simply did not and do not find this point of view attractive.

Several characteristics associated with the term "aesthetic education" became extremely influential in the school arts education fields over the past thirty or so years. Recent important influences have reinforced the belief that education in the arts requires tuition in a broad range of disciplines relevant to the cultivation of the characteristic mode of cognition the arts represent.[9]

The Arts as Cognitive

What knowledge, then, is of most worth in the arts according to the general point of view often called aesthetic education? Another important intellectual movement in recent years bears on how this question might be answered. This is the growing recognition that traditional conceptions of cognition, equating it with verbal and symbolic conceptualization, are inadequate to describe or explain the varieties of modes in which human knowing occurs and by which human knowing may be represented. We can trace to Plato the history of the idea that cognition, to be considered authentic, must be as abstract—that is, free from the vagaries and errors of the senses and the intuitions—as it is possible for rationality to make it. The most dependable, most genuine knowledge therefore is achieved through a movement away from the concrete toward the abstract. "Basic" subjects are those fulfilling the assumption that cognition is essentially a function of abstract thinking achieved through higher and higher levels of verbal and symbolic conceptualization.

In education, the equation of cognition with rational conceptualization is most dramatically apparent in the influential *Taxonomy of Educational Objectives*,[10] in which the "Cognitive Domain" consists of progressively higher levels of conceptual functioning, ranging from knowledge (of specifics; of ways and means of dealing with specifics; of the universals and abstractions in a field), to intellectual abilities and skills (comprehension; application; analysis) to synthesis, and finally to evaluation. The "Affective Domain" (construed in the Taxonomy to include primarily attitudes and values) and the "Psychomotor Domain" are not, ipso facto, cognitive. The assumption, then, that cognition exists only when the mind is processing conceptual materials in the ways the "Cognitive Domain" handbook outlines them is so widespread that few recognize that this is but one way to conceive of cognition. It has, in short, become a dominant myth of our times.

That myth has begun to unravel. Ironically, a major tear in its fabric occurred with the dramatic rise during the 1950s of skepticism about the epistemological foundation of the basic sciences. As D. C. Phillips summarizes it,[11] John Dewey had much earlier raised the issue of whether the warranted knowledge claims of science were more authentic than other types. But the middle of the century brought together several lines of thought inimical to the previous belief system. Popper argued that scientific knowledge claims cannot be proved or fully justified but only refuted. The credibility of logical positivism, which provided a foundation for the traditional scientific epistemology, was eroded. Thomas Kuhn explained how contextual factors determine what qualifies as scientific truth. Lakatos, Feyerabend, and others severely criticized the notion of scientific objectivity. All these constitute a significant literature that questions the myth of rationalistic scientific truth. As W. H. Newton-Smith suggested,

The scientific community sees itself as the very paradigm of institutionalized rationality. It is taken to be in possession of something, the scientific method, which generates a "logic of justification." . . . For Feyerabend, Kuhn, and others, not only does scientific practice not live up to the image the community projects, it could not do so. For that image, it is said, embodies untenable assumptions concerning the objectivity of truth, the role of evidence, and the invariance of meanings.[12]

The atmosphere created by challenges to the concept that truth is unitary and peculiar to "objective science" has led to a more relativistic stance toward what can be known, how knowing is generated, and what are appropriate representations for what is known. A striking example is found in the "Editor's Preface" to the Eighty-fourth NSSE Yearbook, *Learning and Teaching the Ways of Knowing*: "The roads to knowledge are many. Knowledge is not defined by any single system of thought, but is diverse."[13] The contributors to this volume described numerous modes of cognition: aesthetic, scientific, interpersonal, intuitive, narrative and paradigmatic, formal, practical, and spiritual. Is it possible that a conception of knowing different from the prevailing one is being born?

The notion of aesthetic cognition as one among several bona fide cognitive modes holds great promise, and one is led to ask once more the persistent, contentious, puzzling question, "What is aesthetic cognition?" Stretching back at least to Plato, the history of the issue of aesthetic cognition has been a tortuous one. I have no intention of tracing that history here.[14] I will, however, offer some selective reflections about it in light of possible educational implications. I will concentrate on one dimension of aesthetic cognition, often called "knowing of" or "knowing within." A second dimension, frequently termed "knowing how" (about which I will remark only briefly), is intimately related to "knowing of." The two together, I shall argue, constitute the nature of cognition in the aesthetic domain. Supplementary to these ways of knowing are two further dimensions of cognition relevant to improving the quality of knowing of and knowing how—"knowing about" or "knowing that," and what I will term "knowing why." These must also be treated briefly. I will then offer some suggestions about effective curricula in aesthetic education based on these four dimensions of cognition.

KNOWING OF OR WITHIN: THE ROLE OF FORM

"Knowing of" or "knowing within" consists of a particular combination of involvements of the self with particular qualities of an encountered object or event. Any object or event may be encountered in an aesthetic way; my discussion will emphasize encounters with works of art.[15] A work of art in some cultural settings is generally conceived to be a product while in others it is more widely construed to be a process. Both meanings are included in my explanation.

One necessary (but not sufficient) aspect of aesthetic involvements is the directionality of attention or discrimination required. To perceive an object or event in the aesthetic mode, one's focus must include, to some degree, attention to its intrinsically interesting qualities. This kind of focus requires an awareness of such qualities as being not entirely "about" something for which they act as signs, but as yielding a set of meanings contained *within* the qualities.

The term most often used to refer to the "within-ness" of intrinsically related events (colors, sounds, actions, and so forth) is "form." The form of a work of art is in this sense its sum total of interrelated events. The qualities that constitute the interrelationships may be described at several levels. One may speak of repetitions, contrasts, variations, developments, tensions, resolutions, unities, disjunctions, expectations, deviations, uncertainties, symmetries, distortions, energies, and so forth. Such terms call attention to the dynamic nature of aesthetic form—the sense it gives that forces are at work (across the broadest range from tremendous activation to stillness and quietude)—and to their effects on us when we internalize them. "Repetition" is an identifiable, objective quality of an object or event, while "expectation" is an internal, qualitative state of a person. But since expectation (of sounds, of actions, of movements, and so forth) is generated by conditions within the work, we tend to ascribe it to the perceptual qualities we are noticing as well as to its effects on us. Careful distinctions between the two can indeed be made, as in phenomenological analysis: in common language the distinctions are often conflated because cause and effect are so closely tied to each other in experiences of art.

At another level of description of the intrinsic qualities to which one attends when one is attending aesthetically, one may enumerate the characteristic means by which each art achieves the interrelations constituting its forms. In music, for example, relations among pitches heard successively are called "melody," while relations of pitches heard simultaneously are called "harmony." In poetry, relations are established by the use of rhyme, meter, alliteration, imagery, and so forth. Each art has a comparable list of elements by which it establishes its forms. At this level of description of the qualities one has an experience "of" when perceiving aesthetically, the terms include the relational dynamics they capture and display but refer to the means by which they are so captured and displayed.

Some works of art or types of art present to the percipient nothing more than formed qualities (a Mozart symphony, a late Mondrian painting, a Merce Cunningham dance, a John Coltrane improvisation). In such cases our perception can be of form as such—of sets of relations which have meaning when meaning is conceived as a function of purposeful structure. The purpose of the structure of a work of art is to embody, through the use of perceptual qualities, implications, connotations, intentions, suggestions, possibilities. When we perceive such relationships they function as meaningful with no need for meaning in its more limited and more common sense as requiring conventional denotative signs or symbols. The fullness of meaning in an aesthetic structure is often referred to as its significance or import or expressiveness. Precisely because such meanings are not literal, or are not limited to the literal, aesthetic cognition is *sui generis*.

For example, when a theme from the exposition section of the first movement of a Mozart symphony is treated in a variety of ways in the subsequent section, we recognize that it is being "developed": that is its meaningful effect. Upon hearing it in the recapitulation section we encounter it in light of its revealed potentials as Mozart chose to develop them. Its "meaning" has changed from its initial statement, and we find this change—this "hearing as" or "knowing as"—to be meaningful. The theme is "heard as" imbued with the structural associations that were at first only implicit but were then made explicit. It is now "known as" it has been revealed—as richer with implications than it would first have seemed. We do this analogously with the Coltrane improvisation as he develops musical ideas, with the Mondrian painting as the shapes, colors, and lines structurally define balances, imbalances, implications of bounded with unbounded spaces, and tensions of ambiguities against resolutions of symmetries, and with the Cunningham dance as it unfolds through more and less determinate events.

It is important to recognize that the perceptible structure presented by these and all other works of art includes every interaction among every detail, and that hierarchical patterns of interactions emerge out of particular interactions. In a highly successful work of art *nothing* exists unrelated to and unessential to its total structure of interconnecting events at different levels of complexity and inclusiveness. That is why the perceptual processing of a work of art is not likely to occur once and for all with any one, particular interaction with it. Important works of art, no matter their style, type, genre, are those with the maximum richness and integration of interrelationships possible within that style, type, genre. Perception of such works requires an ongoing program of engagements in which the potential meanings in a work—its sum total of meaningful interactions—are revealed more fully to and experienced more subtly by the percipient. The active contribution to the process by the percipient is also an essential factor in aesthetic engagements. A competent percipient does not simply recognize structured events but also determines what will be perceived, in what degrees, and at what levels of discriminative precision. Aesthetic experiencing requires a reconstruction by the imagination of the percipient of the imagined interplay of occurrences built into the form by the artist.

I will discuss later the kinds of knowing that assist us in performing these cognitive operations with form. The point here is that the scope, detail, perspicacity, and ingenuity of one's perceptual structuring of formal qualities are essential determinants of what one knows within an aesthetic interaction. Such knowing, I suggest, is an essential component of aesthetic cognition, and is an essential component of aesthetic intelligence construed as a capacity to gain such cognition. Such knowing is amenable to improvement through learning.

KNOWING OF OR WITHIN:
THE ROLE OF CONTENT AND FUNCTION

In addition to form-making qualities such as those discussed above, most works of art contain some manner and degree of reference to people, things, ideas, issues, places, and events. Whether called figurative or representational or programmatic, they are often said to contain "content" or "subject" in addition to "form."

According to one view in aesthetics, called "formalism," such material is entirely or at least largely irrelevant to the kind of knowing appropriate to works of art. One must ignore or bypass content because the only aesthetically valid way to perceive a work is to perceive its form-causing qualities devoid of referential associations. As Roger Fry, an archetypal formalist, put it:

No one who has a real understanding of the art of painting attaches any importance to what we call the subject of a picture—what is represented . . . all depends on *how* it is presented, *nothing* on what. Rembrandt expressed his profoundest feelings just as well when he painted a carcass hanging up in a butcher's shop as when he painted the Crucifixion or his mistress.[16]

An opposite view focuses on content as the essential ingredient of knowing in an aesthetic interaction. Often called "referentialism," this position argues that form is merely a way to point up or enhance the associations a work of art presents, and the goodness or effectiveness of a work is a function of the desirability of its explicit message and how well (clearly, powerfully) a work transmits that message. Socialist Realism is a clear, if extreme, referentialist doctrine.

Content, I suggest, is an important ingredient in the knowing of art because content is an important determinant of the form of the work in which it is contained. That is, when one interacts aesthetically with a work of art, the form of the work as perceived is the determining factor of the knowing one gains from it, but the knowing now includes the role of content as one ingredient of the form.

In a crucifixion scene, for example, the shape of the cross is seen not as an abstract set of two lines intersecting at right angles but as a cross, its intersecting lines being a function of the object we recognize. But in a painting, unlike an actual event (except when the event is being perceived aesthetically), the size of the cross, its placement in the composition, its width, color, texture, and relation to other shapes in the painting are all essential aspects of the form of the painting and of our aesthetic perception of the painting. If any change is made in any of them the aesthetic meaning is changed concomitantly.[17] We see the intersecting lines as an object, but as an object which is part of a "composition"—a form "composed" to be meaningful as form. We judge the painting good or mediocre or bad, not on the basis that it contains a cross, as thousands of others equally do, but on the basis of how the cross has been incorporated as an element of meaningful structure. A great painting of a crucifixion is considered great—that is, to yield meaning of a profound, enduring nature—not because it has an object called a cross in it but because the object, while recognized to be one, has been "trans-formed" by its contributing role within the larger structure of interrelationships of which it is a part. The cross as an object is "seen as" or "known as" aesthetically meaningful in light of its structural associations within the complex of visual events with which it interacts. Art transcends content through form.

⸳   But in addition to the recognition of the cross as a particular object, it is also recognized, if one has been so acculturated, as an object with particular symbolic significance. Because of its association with an important religious event (and for other reasons of interest to archetypal psychologists) the cross is an object so saturated with symbolic meanings as to resist being seen neutrally. The values and affects we attach to it, whatever they may be, are inevitably called into play when we recognize the object in the work of art, adding their impact to our experience of the work. Such impact is also transformed by structure, while at the same time contributing to the impact of the structure.

This holds for all the other layers of associations, values, attitudes, beliefs, symbolic meanings in the crucifixion scene, including the body of Christ, his crown of thorns, the spear piercing his side, the grieving figures at the foot of the cross, and so forth. Each contributes to the total aesthetic cognition available from the painting as meaningful ingredients which have been metamorphosed, that is, changed in and by form to have meanings generally called aesthetic. A different painting containing identical content—even by the same painter—will yield different aesthetic meanings by virtue of differences in its form. That is why every crucifixion painting is unique in aesthetic meaning despite identical or similar contents. It is such meanings that painters—all artists—pursue. As Francis Sparshott explains in his discussion of programmatic music:

Perhaps we should say that (as in painting) the most approved uses of the [extramusical] devices are those in which what is recognized and relished as referential is at the same time experienced as musical—that is, in which we feel that what we hear would be formally justified even if nothing were being referred to. . . . The characteristic musical delight in all such devices, for composers as much as for audiences, lies in the way *music is being made of them:* the exact way in which, having been what they were, they have now become completely music.[18]

The principle raised by this example applies to all the arts (given the necessary adaptations each would require), and to all manners and types and levels of content in the arts.[19] Aesthetic cognition, then, requires knowing about content, given the contributory role content plays, but also, and most importantly, requires the ability to go beyond such knowing to the knowing of or within yielded by meaningful structure. I will discuss later the kinds of learnings that would be useful in order to help students gain the aesthetic knowings available from art, including the knowings about content which contribute to them.

Another factor implicated in aesthetic perception is the variety of uses to which works of art are often put and the various functions they are expected to perform. It is a convention of modern Western culture that works of art, usually as products but also often as processes, are often regarded primarily or solely as a source of the kind of experience called aesthetic (one aspect of which I am here attempting to clarify). Symphonies being performed in concert halls; jazz improvisations listened to in clubs; paintings displayed in museums, galleries, homes; theater productions and dances and movies performed for audiences, and so forth, are understood as being occasions for aesthetic experiencing (however many other motives people may have for engaging in them). But throughout Western history and in many other world cultures, art has been associated with other activities.

For an example let us return to the crucifixion painting. Displayed in a cathedral the painting clearly serves a function emphasizing its content, calling the attention of worshippers to the religious meanings depicted in that important event. In this case the form of the painting—its intrinsically meaningful structure of interrelated visual events—is contributory rather than focal, reversing the relationship between form and content as it obtains in aesthetic experiencing. Because that relationship is usually a matter of *degree* of focus, rather than an exclusive focus on form or content devoid of influence from the other, it may be envisioned as occurring on a continuum. At one far extreme, a devout worshipper, glancing briefly at the painting in the cathedral to which she has come to pray, is reminded of the event depicted by the painting and thinks of and is affected by its religious significance, the form of the painting being minimally influential in or perhaps entirely absent from the experience. The painting has in this case served a largely religious function. At the other extreme, a museum curator of Renaissance art, on closely examining the painting displayed in a museum she is visiting, is struck by the power of the artist's use of color as an aspect of structure in relation to other such paintings by this and other Renaissance artists. The religious content is likely to be minimally influential if not entirely absent in her experience, which would seem to be entirely or largely of intrinsic formal relations. And, of course, every possible degree of balance between focus on function and form exists along the continuum.

Just as content is likely to influence form to at least some degree, function is also likely to play a role in how form is perceived. And while I am suggesting the principle that aesthetic meaning requires going beyond content and function to that which form adds to them, I am unable to stipulate the degree to which that must occur in order for an experience to qualify as aesthetic. Nor am I suggesting that there is some optimal balance, or that an experience is "aesthetically better" if it is 100 percent of form, as formalists would say. It is possible that different works, with different contents (or none) and different functions (including entirely aesthetic ones), can be experienced across a broad range of foci on various aspects of perceptual processing and be understood to be aesthetic in experience when form plays a significant role. Aesthetic cognition requires involvement in form to some degree, and with meanings from content and function as they have been modified by form.[20]

Aesthetic education, I would propose, is the systematic attempt to influence the degree to which students can incorporate aesthetic meanings in their experience of works of art and other phenomena.

KNOWING OF OR WITHIN: THE ROLE OF FEELING

A second necessary aspect of aesthetic engagements has to do with the role of affect or feeling in the knowing of or knowing within yielded by such engagements. The treatment of aesthetic reaction here must be selective, especially given the vast and venerable literature on it. That literature has existed as long as the concept of art has existed[21] because it seems to be an essential characteristic of art that we care about it in a way involving ourselves as creatures who feel. So from the writings of Plato to the latest issues of the various scholarly journals devoted to the arts, the relation of the arts to feeling remains an ongoing point of contention. It is a particularly recalcitrant one because of the difficulties entailed in conceptualizing about awarenesses that are essentially internal, unobservable, unquantifiable, and ineffable. The point I want to focus on here has to do with ineffability.

Feelings, or affects, as I use the terms, are experiences at the level of internal awarenesses of subjectivities.[22] Although we are aware that we are undergoing subjective events we are not able to express or describe them in words (they are ineffable) for a variety of reasons. First, words, by their nature (I am referring here to words as discursive symbols in common language) are unsuitable to express the dynamically evanescent and fleeting character of feelings. Further, feelings are complex amalgams of a variety of felt qualities undergone simultaneously, and the mixtures of qualities are also transitory in that they shift among their combinations and interrelations from moment to moment. Language syntax is not constituted to represent this kaleidoscopic quality of feeling. And feelings are in constant motion in their intensity, each change of degree of intensity changing the nature and quality of what is being experienced. In depth as well there is a constant movement, as feelings are experienced as more or less significant or portentous from moment to moment. All such characteristics of feeling and their sum account for the gap between the richness and density of our inner subjective reality of felt awareness and the limited capacity of ordinary language to mediate or represent it.[23]

What language *can* do is represent those broad classes of feeling clusters which share sufficient common characteristics to constitute inclusive feeling categories. Words such as *love, joy, fear, anger, sadness, happiness* name "the emotions." These are broad, classificatory concepts each of which subsumes the infinite numbers, qualities, gradations, and combinations of what is actually experienced as "feeling" or "affect." The emotion category symbols (the names of emotions) bear the same relation to feelings as experienced as names of diseases bear to the actualities of what is experienced by someone undergoing them. Experience is "of" or "within" feeling. Words are "about" feeling.

With Dewey, Susanne K. Langer, and many others, I agree that the structures or forms of works of art are the most apt, cogent representations of the reality of human experience as being subjective—as being feelingful. The qualities constituting the meaningful, purposive interrelationships of aesthetic form are able to capture the

inherent dynamics of feeling (not "emotion") with a level of precision, fidelity, complexity, and subtlety unavailable in any other mode
of mentation. In experiences of meaningful form the "knowing of,"
then, includes, as an inseparable aspect, an internalized awareness of
expressiveness—that is, feeling constituting an essential component of
what is being experienced and known. Interrelations among qualities
are not just noticed. They are felt, and do not reach the fullness of
meaning of which they are capable unless and until they are felt. But
because of the widespread confusion of *feeling* as I am using the term
with *emotion* as that term is ordinarily used, and because of the
association of art with emotion that we have inherited from nineteenth
century Romanticism, it is important to reiterate that art is not
"emotional." The distinction is essential. Emotions are classificatory
concepts while experiences of feeling are undergone subjectivities, no
one of which, as such, is classifiable conceptually.

This distinction is particularly pertinent in cases when the
expressive gestalt of a work of art seems to be aptly categorized by an
emotion term. Many works of art are simply not amenable to such
categorization: no emotion term applies comfortably to a Brahms
symphony or to a Cézanne still life or to a Balanchine dance. But one
can so categorize them if one chooses. Little disagreement would arise
if one characterized the second movement of the Beethoven Third
Symphony ("Marcia funebre") as sad, or if one called the entire
symphony, as Beethoven did, "heroic" (Eroica). It would seem as
easy and obvious to call Picasso's *Guernica* "anguished," and
Hemingway's *The Old Man and the Sea* "tragic."

I suggest that emotions serve the same purpose in works of art as
content does, and in fact may be conceived as another type of content.
Just as the symbolic meanings of the crucifix influence its aesthetic
meanings, the emotion "sadness" in the "Marcia funebre" influences
the ineffable feeling caused by the form of that movement.

This is not to say that the aesthetic meanings of these works are
limited to or equatable with or in any way contained within or to be
understood as essentially *caused* by the object (the cross) or the
emotion (sadness). Aesthetic cognition transcends any content—
including emotional content—through form. The "Marcia funebre"
is, as Beethoven designates it, also "Adagio assai," and this "quite
slow" is where aesthetic feeling as "knowing of" begins to exist. It
exists as well in the contour of the first theme and its minor modality,
in the contrasting contour of the subsequent theme of the trio (in
major), in the tone colors of oboe against strings as contrasted with

violins against the other strings, in the ritards at ends of sections, in the recurring dotted-note figure and its suggestions and implications in other rhythmic motives and on and on with all the infinite, subtle, expressive, and meaningful details that constitute the purposive structure of this movement. Further, a different *performance* of the movement will inevitably alter its aesthetic meanings, because the slightest change in, say, how the dotted-note figure beginning the first theme is articulated, will change significantly what is perceived and felt.

To explore within all the meanings of form as perceptually and subjectively processed, including the general quality of sadness as one dimension influencing that which is perceived and undergone, is to gain the aesthetic cognitions available from this music. It is not enough to hear the music "as sad," which is like seeing the object in the painting "as a cross." The "knowing as" required in aesthetic engagements must transcend, through form, the designations, including objects and emotions, which may be present in particular works. When commentators on art dwell on the emotions art designates (and argue endlessly about how art manages to designate emotions),[24] they are fixated at the not yet expressive level of how art functions aesthetically. The notorious difficulties in explaining how perceived qualities can be identified as emotions arise, I suggest, from the inherent differences between form as expressive and language as denotative. Emotions exist at the level of concepts; feelings exist at the level of experiences which by their very nature are ineffable. Attending *in the direction of* meaningful, expressive form allows one to be influenced by but to *pass through* designations of whatever sort, including designated emotion categories, and reach their aesthetic conclusions in cognitions form has substantiated. In such conclusions emotion terms give way to qualitative subjective states ineffable in essence.

Aesthetic education, I propose, is the systematic attempt to influence the degree to which students can incorporate yet transcend any kind or type of content (including emotional content) employed by works of art as one aspect of their ineffable meanings, and thus approach closer to meanings perceptually and affectively experienced as qualities of purposeful structure. Mikel Dufrenne described feeling as a "capacity of receptivity, a sensibility to a certain world, and an aptitude for perceiving that world."[25] I would argue that this capacity, sensibility, and aptitude are amenable to improvement by effective education, which focuses on the distinctive cognitions art exists to provide and the distinctive way art provides them, through perceptual/affective processing of formed qualities and contents. *Feeling as proactive.* Such processing engages feeling as more than reactive to perceived interrelations in formed events. Feeling also serves a proactive role in aesthetic involvements, a role not given sufficient attention in the literature. For if it is an act of cognition to feel, through absorbed perception, the implied subjectivities an artist has imagined within a perceptual structure, it is cognitive as well to employ attentive feeling as a major means for discovering those implied subjectivities. Feeling, here, is not just the effect of a cause (the work's structure including its content as an aspect of its structure) but is the cause of experienced effects.

The proactive role of feeling as an inherent dimension of cognition in aesthetic involvements is likely to be multidimensional. Feeling is probably implicated in processes of making discriminations among events, classifying event-clusters, abstracting parts from wholes, integrating levels of hierarchical interrelations, comprehending relations, anticipating incipient events, synthesizing wholes out of parts and forming gestalts at higher levels, and so forth.[26] The point is that opportunities to employ feeling in these cognitive operations, and the experience of the expansion of the self such engagements afford, are at the core of the value of the arts and of aesthetic education. The central function of education in the arts is to help all students develop their capacities to gain such cognition, which is likely to be what is of most worth from the arts.

KNOWING HOW

People who bring meaningful forms into existence are generally called artists and anyone so engaged is, at the time of engagement, being an artist. Given that art cannot exist without people being artists, and given that what artists essentially produce are works (whether construed as products or processes) which are a source of aesthetic meanings, an understanding of the nature of artistry as a cognitive endeavor would seem to be important for any viable concept of aesthetic education. Other chapters in this volume deal with this matter; so I will limit my remarks here to a few concerning the knowings entailed in knowing how to create art.

I suggest that to be an artist is to know of or within through the act of causing such knowing to come into being as a work, whether as a product or a process. In this discussion I follow common practice in using the terms "artistic knowing" or "artistic cognition" or "artistic experience" to refer to interactions with art while creating it. The terms "aesthetic knowing" or "aesthetic cognition" or "aesthetic experience" refer to those interactions occurring when experiencing a work that someone else has created.[27] Other terms generally used to make this distinction are "expression/impression" or "production/ appreciation." What does one need to know how to do in order to cause the coming into being of meanings as a product of formed interrelations among qualities and contents?

First, one needs to know how to imagine such interrelations. "Imagine" implies the ability to form a mental image of potential or actual relations among some sets of qualities. That image requires two interdependent ingredients—having "in mind" the materials out of which the relations are to be made (sounds, shapes, movements of the body, people acting, verbal images, etc.) and having "in mind" the feeling of the ensuing relation. Relations do not exist as abstract: they are brought into existence by some interplay of one thing with another, and the relation is imaged as how one thing interacts with another, the "interaction" being the "feeling." Artists, then, know how to imagine relationships among qualities of the materials they have "in mind," and how to imagine the affect of those related qualities.

But for artists, "in mind" is not in the ideal mind Plato envisioned. It is a mind in which the body and its actions, the feeling of the body in action, and the critical, discerning response to the images and feelings caused by the involvement of the body in action are all essential dimensions of knowing. In dance, the "body in action" can be taken literally, as it can be in any other artistic involvement in which skillful use of the body is an essential aspect of engagement with material being formed (playing an instrument, singing, painting, sculpting, acting, shaping clay). But even in less obviously physical artistic acts (writing a poem, composing, designing a building) the inward "embodiment" or "sensuosity" of the experience of the relations being formed is an essential ingredient in what is known and how it is known—the knowing Dufrenne terms "presence."[28]

Inasmuch as artists think in terms of meaningful relations among qualities, including how any content may be cast in terms of such relations, the effectiveness of such thinking depends in large part on how well the artist can envision potential relations, and respond opportunely to discovered relations, in the materials out of which the work is being formed. At base, after any considerations of content influence, of functionality or practicality, of any other related factors impinging on the creative act, artists think directly in terms of materials being organized so as to be meaningful. The ability to think this way is tied intimately to the grasp, control, and mastery of the materials *in terms of which* the artist is thinking. The quality of artistic thinking depends on the richness of an artist's "vocabulary" of available gestures in the materials being formed, control over the subtleties and complexities of the form the material is taking, and ability to take the material in whatever direction the unfolding meaning requires. The term denoting such artistic mastery of material is "craftsmanship."

Craftsmanship includes skill but transcends it: craft is the ability to think in terms of meaningful material—material which has taken on and is taking on meaning as a function of its created structure. To know how to create art is to know how to think in this mode. This accounts for the centrality of developing craftsmanship in any attempt to teach people how to be artists; one's ability to "think art" is tied directly to one's ability to control the material within which one is thinking. To the degree that aesthetic education is concerned with helping students become artists and understand how artists think, it must engage them in the development of their craftsmanship with one set or several sets of materials the arts generally employ.

Two other "knowings how" to be an artist should be mentioned; knowing how to be sensitive and knowing how to be authentic.

Since the exercise of artistic imagination requires thinking in terms of and through control over the materials in which thinking is taking place, the sensitivity of an artist to the possibilities of meaning emerging from this thinking is a crucial factor in what the artistic result will be. Sensitivity is the level of discernment of rightness or convincingness or meaningfulness of each decision an artist makes as a purposive structure unfolds. Each decision has its consequences in what the form is becoming and what it cannot therefore become. A sensitive artist is guided to decisions leading in fruitful directions— directions productive of the meaningful gestalt being brought into life. Sensitivity to such meaning, perceptually and affectively and sensuously, is, I suggest, cognitive—a way of knowing the significance coming into being in the creative act as one is causing that significance to occur. Imagination, craft, and sensitivity are interdependent dimensions of knowing in artistic creation; each contributes its essential character yet each is dependent on the others for its existence.

Finally, all this must take place in a context of devotion to the inner integrity of the form coming into being, a form which is uniquely meaningful and which therefore makes its demands on the artist bringing it into existence. Knowing how to submit oneself to the requirements of the emerging form as they become apparent through one's sensitivity to what is occurring is knowing how to be an artist authentically. Authenticity, here, is the capacity to serve the needs of artistic meanings in their demands to be created honestly, that is, to be realized not only by the needs of the artist but also by the needs of the form to be whole and meaningful and genuine. In the maelstrom of complex decision making constituting the artistically creative act, it is so easy to make false moves—to do what is convenient or adventitious or unchallenging to one's imagination and sensitivity and craftsmanship, forcing or allowing the result to be less than it has demanded one to make it be. Knowing how to be authentic is, in artistic creation, knowing how to be artistically moral. Artists who act "in the service of their art" are, in this sense, acting morally, and this moral posture in turn pervades the quality of the imagination, sensitivity, and craftsmanship they exercise as they create.

Artistic knowing, or "artistry," is the sum of these four knowings how. Such knowing is a component of cognition dependent on but additional to knowing of or within and is amenable to improvement through learning. Such learning requires the exercise of this cognition through engagements of the four dimensions of knowing how in the actual creation of meaningful forms. One can, of course, "know about" these dimensions just by reading about them. But that is not artistic cognition, just as "knowing about" the qualities of aesthetic experiencing does not constitute aesthetic knowing. Yet conceptualizing about the ingredients of aesthetic experience and creation can be a powerful aid in developing people's capacities to know of and to know how. This leads to the final two knowings aesthetic education should impart.

KNOWING ABOUT OR THAT

Knowing of or within and knowing how are ends of aesthetic education. Knowing about or knowing that (and knowing why, discussed next) are means. This distinction between ends and means is crucial. It is a common error to think that people are aesthetically educated to the degree they have a great deal of conceptual knowledge about art, so that education *about* art in the sense of verbal learnings about art replaces the education *in* art I am insisting must take place in order for education to influence the cognitions available from art. A major and well-deserved anxiety in the arts education community about the Getty Discipline-based Art Education project is that verbal knowing might be emphasized over aesthetic/artistic knowing, thereby undermining the very reason for the existence of education in the arts.[29]

By "knowing about" or "knowing that" I refer to the conceptual understandings most germane to the enhancement of one's ability to know of or know how. These understandings about art exist at several levels but all focus on the actual interaction of a person with a work. Since this interaction requires perceptual, affective, and sensuous discernment, knowings about what to discern and how to discern are implicated directly in what can be discerned and at what levels of complexity discernment can take place. Aesthetic education consists, in important part, of bringing students' conceptual attention to that which can be known aesthetically and artistically in works of art.

The activity of calling attention to various aspects and levels of meaningful forms may be called "analysis." As I use this term it applies to widening concentric rings of examination, description, and integration of aesthetic and artistic materials and processes.

Closest to the work itself is the scrutiny of the components of its form, in as much detail as is possible for the age and experience of particular students. Such scrutiny, when supportive of the inward knowing of the form of a work as immediately experienced, can clarify what is presented in a completed work and what is becoming in a work being created. As a means toward heightened awareness, such analysis is essential. But it fulfills its role in heightening both aesthetic cognition and artistic cognition when the knowings *about* form become submerged in consciousness within the knowings *of* form. That is, *thinking about* meaningful details of form must lead to *thinking with* what has been brought to conceptual awareness in order for the experience to yield the kinds of cognition available from engagements with art, which are always "knowings within" and, additionally, "knowings how." I cannot here discuss the ways to teach art to best insure that thinking about what is going on in a work will become transformed into the thinking with or within which constitutes cognition in art. Such matters fall into the domain of method. I want to make the general point here, applicable to the rest of this section, that all knowings about or knowings that (and knowings why), at any level of generality, must become, through processes of internalization, integrated within aesthetic and artistic cognition as I have tried to explain them, operating as tacit or subsidiary elements of such cognition.[30]

Connected with and widening out from analysis of significant formal details at increasingly higher hierarchichal levels of complexity are all the matters relating to the role of content in particular works. Given the important influences of content on form, those influences must be clarified as to how content impinges on what a particular form could be and the corresponding impact of content on what an experience of a particular work might include.

Expanding further, analysis will include the particularities of historical and cultural contexts surrounding this or that work or body of work, influencing or determining its artistic choices and aesthetic contents. For example, to experience more deeply what is available to know from a particular performance of jazz, one needs to understand what was happening in jazz at the time of, say, John Coltrane's performance of "One Down, One Up." One needs to understand where Coltrane was in his own development as an artist and where that was to lead, and how jazz was reflecting in this work in particular and in Coltrane's style as a whole a changing sense of musical possibilities rhythmically and harmonically and tonally.

An aesthetically astute experience of "One Down, One Up" is a cognitive achievement, just as it is a cognitive achievement to create it. Aesthetic education is obligated to influence positively the capacities of mind that make possible both aesthetic cognition and artistic cognition.

KNOWING WHY

What I have termed "knowing why" adds a broader dimension to knowledge about the contexts in which particular aesthetic and artistic processes occur. This dimension has to do with general understandings about art as a cultural-psychological phenomenon. Here one conceptualizes matters such as these: why art exists; why all cultures have developed arts in some ways like and in some ways different from arts of all other cultures; why standards for judging art might be both general and also dependent on particularities of this and that art, style, genre; why the experience of art and why creating art seem to be so important for people; why different groups of people have different beliefs about art, what it is good for, and how it should be used; why philosophers of art have debated for centuries every conceivable issue related to art, its nature, its value; why some people think education in the arts is essential for all; why some students choose to engage themselves in special efforts to develop creative capacities in an art.

While the experience of a specific work is determined in large part by its specificities of form and content as they are structured by a percipient who brings to it particular habituations, capacities, and knowledge, the beliefs and understandings that person possesses about what art is all about in the first place will color all that happens in the interaction. Art, after all, is a human construct. Its meaning is a function of what one believes it to mean as one's culture has led one to adopt and adapt such beliefs. Aesthetic education, as a culture's mechanism for sharing an important cultural value, must include examinations of that value in its many complex dimensions. Knowing why provides a value structure—a logically consistent system of examined beliefs—within which the other knowings can be experienced as meaningful.

General and Special Curricula in the Arts

Given the preceding discussions (about knowing within, knowing how, knowing about, and knowing why), a curriculum in the arts would be the playing out of their implications in the myriad details to be attended to in building a coherent program of instruction. In the context of this chapter only one issue relating to curriculum development can be addressed—the issue of general learnings essential for all students and special learnings for particular students who choose them.

By general education in the arts I mean programs of instruction required of all students in schools, or electives providing the same learnings. By special education in the arts I mean arts electives that concentrate on a particular aspect or related set of aspects of the general arts curriculum and that are conceived to be appropriate only for those students interested in developing particular competencies or understandings.

General education in the arts should be as comprehensive and as extensive as possible. The four basic dimensions of cognition should all be included and should stress the development of each student's capacities to know of and know how. The contexts for such learnings can be single art classes as have traditionally been available or (as I would prefer) comprehensive arts classes in which interdisciplinary learning episodes would be used as (occasional) unifiers for the learnings about particular arts. These classes should concentrate on the unique ways each art functions cognitively, and also call attention at strategic points to the general characteristics of cognition all the arts share.[31]

Whatever the context, learnings related to knowing of or within will provide the unifying core. The experience of many works (from one art if a single art is being taught or from several arts if a comprehensive context exists), repesenting various historical periods, regions of the world, styles, genres, types, including folk, popular, "classical," ethnic, and so forth, will be the central activity, supported by the knowings about or that and knowings why essential to make aesthetic sense of them. In my view, emphasis should be placed on works of high quality (works demonstrating high levels of imagination, craftsmanship, sensitivity, authenticity) within each type or genre. Comparisons of the relative value of differing types of art should be avoided. Works of lesser quality can be used to heighten the sense that higher and lower levels of aesthetic value exist in particular examples of art.

Knowing how—creating art—serves both as an end and as a means in general education. As an end it engages all students in the mode of cognition called upon to be an artist—a way of thinking and knowing unavailable except by being (or acting as) an artist. All students need to share this cognition for the sake of knowing what it uniquely allows one to know.

In addition, attempts to create art by using qualities one is experiencing in already created works (for example, attempting to paint distorted figures as related to distorted figures one is perceiving in a painting) can illuminate powerfully the meaningful form(s) created by an artist who chose to use distortion as one element. So it is important that creating art be included in general education both as artistically meaningful in and of itself and as adding an educative dimension to aesthetic meaning.

The balances among experiencing and creating works, and of how much and what levels of conceptual learnings about and learnings why will be included, will largely be determined by developmental factors such as those discussed in other chapters in this book. The mix for second graders will be different from the mix for eleventh graders, especially because as students get older their abilities to know of, about, and why will far outstrip in depth and breadth their ability to know how (even if they have chosen to elect special study in creating art). But given that age-related and individual capacity-related factors will be an important influence on the balances among the modes of cognition, the principle for general education in the arts remains to aim for as inclusive a program of studies as is possible.

The special learnings segment of the arts curriculum is, on the other hand, essentially selective and intensive. From the several dimensions of aesthetic and artistic cognition, particular ones are chosen as foci for study. The selective nature of such study allows it to be intensive, with more thorough study of one or a few aspects of art than is possible in the general education segment. What is lost in breadth is gained in depth, but the necessary restrictions on how much and what can be studied in depth makes such study appropriate as electives for particularly interested individuals or groups.

The most popular selection from among the various knowings in art has been and is likely to continue to be knowing how. In special programs devoted to creating art, learnings how will appropriately dominate instruction. Experiences of already created works serve here primarily as a means for heightening growth in the understanding of creating, rather than as an end as they do in the general program. Similarly, knowings about and knowings why are selectively focused toward those relating to and helpful for developing creative abilities. A much more restricted range of styles or types of art will be studied than those encountered in the general program—a chorus, after all, deals with choral music, a ceramics class with shaped clay, a play production with acting and staging, and so on, and each of these with only those instances capable of being handled within the constraints of the students' creative skills and the time available.

All these factors make artistic creation appropriately an elective when conceived as the primary mode of interaction with and study of art. (Most students do not choose to devote the time and energy necessary to achieve even modest levels of success in creating art). Approaches to general education in an art that consist entirely of creating are misconceived and unfortunate. They narrow unconscionably the range of knowings that general education in the arts should provide and give the impression that arts education consists of a limited set of learnings related to one particular mode of engagement and that the study of art is a special endeavor for only those students especially interested or talented.

Other appropriate special art program electives might emphasize aspects other than creating—a high school course devoted entirely to the plays of Samuel Beckett, or to how to be a music critic, or to the arts of Africa, or to issues of avant-garde art, or to the role of technology in the arts. Such foci could be included as specific *parts* of general education, as, for example, units in a required or elective course on "All About the Arts." What separates special from general education is the difference in *degree* of extensivity, general education aiming toward one end of the whole-part continuum, special education toward the other.

Education in the arts, I suggest, required of and available to all students in schools as part of general education, and available to all those who choose to study particular aspects of art, exists to serve the needs of all to share the cognitions available only from art. Some few students will go on to become professional artists or professionals in other aspects of the arts, and such students need a broad general education in the arts as the foundation for their special study and special vocation. The rest, for whom the arts can provide a singular dimension of cognition in their lives, deserve to be helped to learn what is most worth knowing in the arts—the ways to share the vividness, clarity, significance, and depth of experience the arts provide.

ACKNOWLEDGMENT. I am grateful to Philip Alperson for his reflections, and to Forest Hansen for his detailed and perspicacious suggestions.

NOTES

1. Herbert Spencer, *Education: Intellectual, Moral, and Physical* (New York: D. Appleton, 1896). My discussion of Spencer's influence on education draws on Herbert M. Kliebard, "The Liberal Arts Curriculum and Its Enemies: The Effort to Redefine General Education," in *Cultural Literacy and the Idea of General Education*, ed. Ian Westbury and Alan C. Purves, Eighty-seventh Yearbook of the National Society for the Study of Education, Part II (Chicago: University of Chicago Press, 1988).

2. Spencer, *Education: Intellectual, Moral, and Physical*, p. 75. Emphasis his.

3. Ibid., p. 32.

4. Ibid., pp. 93-94.

5. A helpful overview of aesthetic and psychological orientations influential on concepts of art and the teaching of art is given by Arthur D. Efland, "Conceptions of Teaching in the Arts," in *The Teaching Process and Arts and Aesthetics*, ed. Gerard L. Knieter and Jane Stallings (St. Louis: CEMREL, 1979).

6. Spencer, *Education: Intellectual, Moral, and Physical*, pp. 75-81.

7. For treatments of the changes that took place in music education, see Michael L. Mark, *Contemporary Music Education* (New York: Schirmer, 1986). For a concise summary of changes in visual art education, see two articles in the *Journal of Aesthetic Education* 21, no. 1 (Summer 1987): Ralph A. Smith, "The Changing Image of Art Education: Theoretical Antecedents of Discipline-based Art Education," pp. 3-34, and Arthur D. Efland, "Curriculum Antecedents of Discipline-based Art Education," pp. 57-94. Both give useful bibliographies.

8. For a discussion of various assumptions about aesthetic education, see Harry S. Broudy, "Some Reactions to a Concept of Aesthetic Education," in *Arts and Aesthetics: An Agenda for the Future*, ed. Stanley S. Madeja (St. Louis: CEMREL, 1977), and

Bennett Reimer, "Essential and Nonessential Characteristics of Aesthetic Education," *Journal of Aesthetic Education* 25, no. 3 (1991): 193-214.

9. "Discipline-based Art Education" is a concept supported by the Getty Center for Education in the Arts, an operating entity of the J. Paul Getty Trust. It is an important attempt to expand traditional curricula in the direction of greater comprehensiveness of learnings. For an overview, see Ralph A. Smith, ed., *Discipline-based Art Education: Origins, Meaning, and Development* (Urbana: University of Illinois Press, 1989), originally published as the Summer 1987 issue of the *Journal of Aesthetic Education*.

10. Benjamin S. Bloom et al., eds., *Taxonomy of Educational Objectives, Handbook I: Cognitive Domain* (New York: David McKay, 1956); David R. Krathwohl, Benjamin S. Bloom, and Bertram B. Masia, eds., *Taxonomy of Educational Objectives, Handbook II: Affective Domain* (New York: David McKay, 1964); Anita J. Harrow, *A Taxonomy of the Psychomotor Domain* (New York: David McKay, 1972).

11. D. C. Phillips, "On What Scientists Know, and How They Know It," in *Learning and Teaching the Ways of Knowing*, ed. Elliot W. Eisner, Eighty-fourth Yearbook of the National Society for the Study of Education, Part I (Chicago: University of Chicago Press, 1985), pp. 38-39.

12. Ibid., p. 39.

13. Elliot Eisner, "Editor's Preface," in *Learning and Teaching the Ways of Knowing*, ed. Eisner, p. xi.

14. For an overview of concepts of aesthetic cognition until the early 1960s, see the index listings under "Knowledge and art" and "Truth and art" in Monroe C. Beardsley, *Aesthetics from Classical Greece to the Present* (New York: Macmillan, 1966). For discussions of concepts of aesthetic cognition held by a variety of important contemporary thinkers, see Ralph A. Smith, *The Sense of Art: A Study in Aesthetic Education* (New York: Routledge, 1989).

15. The distinctions between art and other phenomena are important (and complex) but cannot be explored here. It should be mentioned that works of art are generally conceived to be human creations in which their aesthetic meaning is their major or sole reason for being. Anything else—a mathematical formula, a sunset—when regarded for aesthetic meaning is being regarded "as if" it were art, that is, for meaning as a function of its perceived significant structure rather than as a function of its mathematical proof or its indication of the pollution content of the air. Aesthetic education should clarify this distinction and sensitize students to aesthetic meanings in works of art. Yet it should not neglect other things not conceived primarily to exist for aesthetic meaning but able to offer it as one aspect of their nature.

For an influential discussion of the role of social tradition and authority in determining what counts as art, see Arthur Danto, "The Artistic Enfranchisement of Real Objects: The Artworld," in *Aesthetics: A Critical Anthology*, 2d ed., ed. George Dickie, Richard Sclafani, and Ronald Roblin (New York: St. Martin's Press, 1989). In this same volume see also George Dickie, "The New Institutional Theory of Art" for another view of the role of institutional sanctions in defining art.

16. Roger Fry, *The Artist and Psycho-Analysis* (London: Hogarth Press, 1924), p. 308.

17. Several characteristics or "symptoms" of art described by Nelson Goodman, *Languages of Art* (Indianapolis: Bobbs Merrill, 1969), pp. 252-255, are included in my description—"syntactic density," "semantic density," "relative repleteness," "multiple and complex reference." The characteristic of "exemplification" also figures in my view when construed as responses to aesthetic events reaching to a "knowing as."

18. Francis Sparshott, "Aesthetics of Music: Limits and Grounds," in *What Is Music?*, ed. Philip Alperson (New York: Haven, n.d.), pp. 66-67.

19. As with any claim applied generally to art, there will be exceptions, such as the attempt by "conceptual art" to achieve aesthetic meaning through content alone or by emphasizing content. We can understand what this attempt entails, and admire its aspiration, only on the basis of a generality to which it aspires to be an exception. Generalities should be construed, then, to apply "in most cases" or "in practically all cases," given the historical propensity (or compulsion) of artists to challenge any generality about art. Aestheticians, driven to generalize, attempt to fend off artists' attacks on generalizations by settling for concepts such as "art enough," or "when" rather than "what" art is, or "symptoms" rather than "preconditions" of art. When generalizations are understood to be "generally applicable" they allow us to make general sense of phenomena—including those phenomena which challenge the generalizations.

20. Compare the treatment in Ralph A. Smith, *The Sense of Art*, chapter 2, in which the views of Beardsley, Osborne, Goodman, and Kaelin are brought to bear on the issues I am discussing here.

21. Chapter 1 of Beardsley's *Aesthetics from Classical Greece to the Present* speculates on the origin of the concept of art.

22. For a detailed and exhaustive treatment of the many meanings of "feeling," "affect," "emotion," and their relevance to the experience of art, see W. Ann Stokes, "Intelligence and Feeling" (Ph.D. diss., Department of Music Education, Northwestern University, 1990).

23. For an early yet trenchant discussion of the gap between experienced feeling and conceptual language, see Otto Baensch, "Art and Feeling," in *Reflections on Art*, ed. Susanne K. Langer (New York: Oxford University Press, 1961).

24. The literature on this issue is so extensive that one hesitates to select examples. For a historical overview, see Beardsley, *Aesthetics from Classical Greece to the Present* under the index listings "Expression" and "Emotion." See also, Marcia M. Eaton, *Basic Issues in Aesthetics* (Belmont, CA: Wadsworth, 1988), under the index listings "emotion," "feeling," "expression," "formalism," "formal properties," "intrinsic properties," "regional qualities," "representation," "resemblance," "subject matter."

25. Mikel Dufrenne, *The Phenomenology of Aesthetic Experience* (Evanston, IL: Northwestern University Press, 1973), pp. 379-386.

26. Stokes, "Intelligence and Feeling," chapter 8.

27. Compare Dewey's discussion of this point in *Art as Experience* (New York: Capricorn Books, 1958), p. 46, in which he deplores the fact that there is no word in English which includes both aspects of involvements with art.

28. See Dufrenne, *The Phenomenology of Aesthetic Experience*, pp. 335-344, in which he richly describes the role of the body in aesthetic knowing.

29. One need only browse in *Art Education*, the journal of the National Art Education Association, over the past half dozen years, to find article after article devoted to accusations and defenses on this issue.

30. For a helpful explanation of how these processes occur, see Harry S. Broudy, "Tacit Knowing and Aesthetic Education," in *Aesthetic Concepts and Education*, ed. Ralph A. Smith (Urbana, IL: University of Illinois Press, 1970), pp. 77-106.

31. My arguments for why a comprehensive arts curriculum would be desirable, and suggestions for how it might be carried out, are given in Bennett Reimer, "A Comprehensive Arts Curriculum Model," *Design for Arts in Education* 90, no. 6 (July/ August 1989), pp. 2-16.

CHAPTER III

Toward Percipience: A Humanities Curriculum for Arts Education

RALPH A. SMITH

When we perceive the arts as "humanities" it is crucial that we interpret them as a demand that we pause, and in their light, reexamine our own realities, values, and dedications, for the arts not only present life concretely, stimulate the imagination, and integrate the different cultural elements of a society or of an epoch, they also present models for our imitation or rejection, visions and aspirations which mutely solicit our critical response.

—Albert William Levi

The major theme of this volume, cognition and arts education, is predicated on the belief that art is a basic form of human understanding. Although it may share features with other forms of knowing, artistic expression is distinctive enough to be appreciated for its own characteristic values. This view of art achieved prominence in the modern era with the writings of the German philosopher Ernst Cassirer (1874-1945). His *An Essay on Man* popularized a conception of knowledge that features six symbolic forms of human culture: myth, language, religion, history, science, and art. These forms of human culture constituted the characteristic work of man and defined what Cassirer called the circle of humanity. "A 'philosophy of man' would therefore be a philosophy which would give us insight into the fundamental structure of each of these human activities, and which at the same time would enable us to understand them as an organic whole."[1]

The idea that there are varieties of knowing is now commonplace in conceptions of human understanding and learning. The theoretical

Ralph A. Smith is Professor of Cultural and Educational Policy, College of Education, University of Illinois at Urbana-Champaign, and editor of the *Journal of Aesthetic Education*.

assumptions and terminology of writers may vary, but the root idea remains the same: there are realms of meaning, ways of knowing, types of intelligence.[2] What is particularly significant about such theorizing so far as this volume is concerned is that art is increasingly accepted as a basic form of understanding. It seems only reasonable, then, to say that one of the principal functions of schooling should be the provision of instruction in aesthetic knowing. Such insight into the fundamental structure of art as we possess would provide the basic content or subject matter for teaching while the psychology of human development would yield suggestions for scheduling appropriate learning activities. Since other contributors to this volume discuss arts education from the point of view of human development, I will concentrate on the substantive dimensions of aesthetic understanding.

First, however, it will be helpful to indicate the basic situation around which we should organize teaching and learning in the arts. This situation is one in which persons confront works of art for the sake of realizing the worthwhile benefits such works are capable of providing. Typically we find works of art in a cultural institution called the art world; hence we may understand arts education as preparation for traversing the world of art with intelligence and sensitivity, which in turn presupposes capacities and inclinations I shall call "percipience." It follows that the goal of arts education is percipience in matters of art and culture.[3] The learner, in turn, is appropriately viewed as a potentially reflective observer and art-world sojourner. I think a perceptive stance is appropriate because it is the one most persons take toward works of art in our type of society. To be sure, a number of theorists and practitioners continue to stress competence in creative and performing activities as the cornerstone of arts education. I, too, think such competence is important, but I view it as but one of several components of aesthetic learning that contribute to the development of aesthetic percipience.

One might think it a relatively straightforward matter to organize the components of aesthetic learning. But given contemporary cultural circumstances it is not. Pluralism reigns, and a multiplicity of objectives is accepted by many as a professional fact of life. How then does one develop a context for responding to art under such conditions? I believe a humanities interpretation of arts education can not only address certain cultural and educational needs of contemporary society but also feature what is necessary for sensitive and tactful encounters with works of art. Accordingly, this chapter describes two types of objectives for arts education: the more general objectives of the humanities and the more specific objectives of arts education. The former are a response to the cultural crisis of our times that requires a restatement of the role of the humanities in the human career. The latter concern the more practical matters of teaching, curriculum design, and assessment.

The Humanities Today

Albert W. Levi, whose epigraph appears at the opening of this chapter, emphasizes that the humanities cannot be dismissed. They are eternally relevant because they are the liberal arts of communication, continuity, and criticism. He associates communication with languages and literatures, continuity with history, and criticism with philosophy in its ordinary sense of critical reasoning. This is Levi's redefinition of the traditional humanities for today's world. How did he arrive at it and why did he feel the need for reconceptualization?

Levi's writings on the topic are a response to many of the problems besetting contemporary society: the need to restore historical memory and to recall the ideal of human excellence; the need of a democratic, egalitarian society to come to terms with an essentially aristocratic tradition of learning; the need to articulate a plausible relation between the taught and the lived humanities; and the need to defend the humanities against their newest rival, the social sciences. In responding to these challenges, Levi, a strong believer in historical continuity, recalls two ways of interpreting the humanities and, in Hegelian fashion, suggests a third option that combines both.[4]

From the tradition of the Renaissance, Levi recalls a substantive definition of the humanities as subject matters. This definition is consistent with the tendency of Renaissance thinkers to recover and transmit the literary texts of antiquity. From the earlier tradition of the Middle Ages, he recalls a procedural or functional definition of the humanities that construed them as skills or ways of organizing and understanding human experience. These skills ultimately became known as the liberal arts. Levi's third option consists of a synthesis of these two traditions—the Renaissance and the Medieval—in which he defines the humanities procedurally as the liberal arts of communication, continuity and criticism, and substantively as languages and literatures, history, and philosophy. Thus almost two decades ago Levi foresaw, and steered to avoid, the trap of educational formalism into which E. D. Hirsch, Jr., thinks American schooling has fallen:

that is, the tendency to separate the teaching of skills from specific content or background knowledge.[5]

Now, if we subsume the creative and fine arts under languages and literatures, which is surely permissible inasmuch as we commonly speak of artistic expression as aesthetic communication, then we will have assimilated another "c"—the arts of creation (in which I include performance)—to Levi's redefinition. This emendation enables us to say that the humanities are indispensable and eternally relevant because they are the arts of creation, communication, continuity, and criticism. Teaching the arts as humanities would mean bringing to bear at appropriate times and junctures the ideas and procedures of these arts. Works of art would be understood as artistic statements created in the stream of time whose meanings and significance are disclosed through historical and art criticism. The basic problem for a humanities interpretation of arts education would be the orchestration of these arts of thought and action for purposes of aesthetic learning and curriculum design.

Ultimately, pedagogical considerations center on what is involved in understanding and appreciating works of art. And of any work of art we may ask the following questions:

1. Who made it?
2. How was it made?
3. When was it made?
4. For whom was it made?
5. What is its message or meaning, if any?
6. What is its style?
7. What is the quality of experience it affords?
8. What was its place in the culture in which it was made?
9. What is its place in the culture or society of today?
10. What peculiar problems does it present to understanding and appreciation?[6]

An awareness of these questions and a degree of competency in answering them are important in building a well-developed sense of art in the young. A good sense of art is, in turn, prerequisite to engaging works of art with intelligence and sensitivity and to traversing the world of art in a way that makes students less dependent on the judgments and value preferences of others. Armed with the perspectives required to address these questions, young people can venture into the art world with a measure of autonomy. What kind of a curriculum would be congruent with cultivating such percipience?

A Humanities Curriculum for Arts Education

In the following discussion "percipience curriculum" and "humanities curriculum" are used interchangeably. A percipience curriculum extends from kindergarten through twelfth grade and is part of a program of required general studies for all students. If, with Cassirer, we believe that art is a basic symbolic form of human culture, then all members of a democratic society deserve the opportunity to reap its benefits. This belief gives meaning to the idea of becoming human through art.[7] I further assume that efforts to cultivate aesthetic percipience will have different accents at various points along the curriculum path. Aesthetic learning should also be cumulative in the sense that early learning should be foundational for what comes later. I am not recommending a lockstep series of highly specific behavioral objectives, but I am saying that it pays to know the lay of the land before exploring it in greater detail. Assessment of aesthetic learning will thus estimate the extent to which a learner's framework for understanding and experiencing art is expanding and developing in appropriate ways. Once more, I take for granted that the setting of learning tasks should be congruent with what we know about human learning and development.

I've said that arts education is concerned with whatever is necessary to get persons to confront a work of visual, auditory, or verbal art with a well-developed sense of art for the sake of realizing the benefits that works of art are capable of providing. Let us further supplement this image of a reflective percipient with that of the curriculum as itinerary and the aesthetic learner as potential art-world sojourner. Art-world sojourners should know, of course, not only where to seek aesthetic value but also how to realize it. True, when in the privacy of one's home we view a painting, listen to music, or read a poem, we don't ordinarily imagine ourselves as participating in the art world, which has a public, institutional connotation. Yet many of the same conditions and problems obtain whether we attend to a work in a private or in a more social setting. However, before we can prepare art-world sojourners we must know what it is that works of art do best. We must be clear about the special role they play in the human career. After all, why traverse the art world in the first place? Without coherent ideas about such matters, arts education will suffer from lack of purpose and the question of justification will go begging.

The Values of Art

Works of art are valuable for their capacity to bring about a high degree of aesthetic experience in a well-prepared beholder. Aesthetic experience is important for its twofold function of shaping the self in positive ways and providing humanistic insight. This is a way of saying that works of art have both constitutive and revelatory powers; they integrate the self and provide aesthetic wisdom.[8]

CONSTITUTIVE VALUES OF ART

Regarding the constitutive values of works of art—their capacity to shape personality in beneficent ways—we can trace a line of thought from Plato in antiquity to Friedrich von Schiller in the eighteenth century to Herbert Read and John Dewey and other theorists in the twentieth. In this literature, Schiller's *On the Aesthetic Education of Man in a Series of Letters* (1795) stands out as a work that celebrates art's constitutive powers.[9] Writing during the political century of the great democratic revolutions, Schiller, a poet and playwright as well as a philosopher, believed that true civil and political freedom could be achieved only through the formation of an ennobled character, and that before citizens could be given a constitution one must see to it that they themselves are soundly constituted. How was this to be achieved? Schiller's response was through aesthetic education, which in his idea of it placed great importance on the study of the immortal works of the masters. The aesthetic, that is, was the key to the problem of political and individual freedom. Aesthetic education, which consisted of a middle state between the realm of brute force and the rule of law, was where character building was to occur. What was it about masterworks that released what Schiller called the living springs of human experience? Schiller's answer was their form, which meant not merely a work's shape but also its structure, balance, symmetry, harmony, and integrity. These qualities were at once the essence of the work of art and of the "properly constituted" self. In short, aesthetic education for Schiller did not exist in contrast to moral education; it had itself an important moral function.[10]

Aesthetic education performs a similar function in Herbert Read's thinking in which moral education essentially consists of education through aesthetic discipline. Where Schiller spoke of aesthetic education's contribution to an ennobled character, Read, in *The Redemption of the Robot*, designates grace as the end result. "We must," says Read, "give priority in our education to all forms of aesthetic activity, for in the course of making beautiful things there will take place a crystallization of the emotions into patterns that are the moulds of virtue."[11]

John Dewey likewise recognized the role of organic unification that art plays in both the perception of the external world and in the integration of human consciousness. In his *Art as Experience* art not only breaks through conventional distinctions and stereotyped thinking, which is in part a moral as well as an aesthetic function; it also composes psychological strains, conflicts, and oppositions into a greater, richer, and more harmonious personality structure.[12]

REVELATORY POWERS OF ART

Art has shaping or constitutive powers; it also is a source of humanistic insight. In revelatory theories, works of art are understood in connection with an artist's cognition of reality and criticism of life. Coming to prominence in the modern Romantic period, revelatory theories underline the exaltation of self, energized spirit, and self-discovery that we experience in encounters with great works of art. What is revealed through such experience is not scientific knowledge of verifiable fact couched in propositions or warranted assertions but rather the human truth of things expressed in aesthetic or dramatic form, a truth more like aesthetic wisdom. We avail ourselves of such wisdom whenever we contemplate artists' visions of man's relations to the external world, to others, and to himself. Giotto, Fra Angelico, Giovanni Bellini, and Raphael on religious commemoration, adoration, and inspiration; van Ruisdael, Poussin, Constable, and van Gogh on the transcendental values of landscape; Holbein, Rembrandt, Velázquez, and Ingres on human character in portraiture all testify to the revelatory powers of artistic expression.

Both constitutive and revelatory theories of art are inherently cognitive in the sense that they presuppose the exercise of significant mental functions—perception, memory, discrimination, analysis, judgment, and so forth—in the making and experiencing of works of art. Revelatory theories, however, contain a cognitive bonus inasmuch as they highlight a work's meaning as well as its potential shaping power. This does not imply that feelings or emotions play no strategic role in either group of theories. Simply to be told what a work means or that it has potential for shaping the self is of little help unless one feels or realizes for oneself in a personal sense a work's theme or thesis or actually experiences a sense of integration or wholeness. This point—that knowing is suffused with feeling, that we know with our emotions—is featured in the cognitive theory of Nelson Goodman.[13] If the contributors to this volume stress knowing in the arts it is not because they undervalue feelings and emotions. Rather, their intention is to counteract a narrow conception of the nature and role of cognition. The aim is not to overintellectualize the experience of art but to highlight the important role that intelligence and knowledge do play in it.

We may now consider a third option that combines the essence of both constitutive and revelatory theories. For this purpose I turn to the later writings on aesthetic experience by Monroe C. Beardsley. In these writings Beardsley specifically takes into account the cognitive character of aesthetic response, largely, he says, as the result of the influence on his thinking of E. H. Gombrich, Rudolf Arnheim, and Nelson Goodman.[14]

Aesthetic experience, writes Beardsley, is both compound and disjunctive. By "compound" Beardsley means that aesthetic experience cannot be reduced to a single feature, say, a pure aesthetic emotion or attitude of disinterestedness; rather it consists of a number of characteristics that tend to cluster. By "disjunctive" he means that experiences with aesthetic character separate themselves quite readily from ordinary experiences, even though the latter may partake of some aesthetic features. Accordingly, Beardsley suggests five criteria of the aesthetic, although he is prepared to admit the possibility of there being more or fewer features. These criteria are object directedness, felt freedom, detached affect, active discovery, and personal integration or wholeness. The following is a condensed account of Beardsley's analysis.

The feeling of object directedness involves a realization that things in one's phenomenally objective field of awareness—for example, works of visual, auditory, and verbal art—are working or have worked themselves out in fitting and appropriate ways. Presupposed is some presence or object to which attention is directed and which in turn guides perception. We regard intensely and seriously what is happening in a painting, a musical composition, a work of sculpture, a poem, a film, and if we feel the rightness of what is unfolding then the first criterion of the aesthetic is satisfied. Felt freedom is a feeling of having suddenly put aside or pushed into the back of one's mind troubling or obtrusive thoughts in favor of freely giving oneself to phenomena. It is a sense, says Beardsley, "of being on top of things, of having one's real way, even though not actually having chosen it or won it" (p. 290). One has willingly acceded to a change of attitude because of the pleasure or gratification garnered in doing so.

The feeling of detached affect implies the act of experiencing something at a certain emotional distance, which is necessary in order to avoid two undesirable outcomes. The first is losing ourselves in the object, in which case we would give up contact with its intricate and demanding form and content and thus with its peculiar richness. The second is fooling ourselves into thinking that we are perceiving real rather than imaginary or fictional objects. Implicit in the notion of detached affect is the tendency of works "to lend some degree of detachment to the effects they produce." They give "an air of artifice, of fictionality, of autonomy and reflexiveness, of separation from other things, and so on" (p. 291). Not always, but often enough to suggest that detached affect is an important feature of many aesthetic experiences.

It should be clear that cognitive powers and knowledge are important ingredients of aesthetic experience. We freely give our attention to an object because we discern or feel something special that invites further scrutiny. Scrutiny in turn is unrewarded unless animated by perceptual skills and background knowledge. But it is in the feeling of active discovery, Beardsley's fourth feature of aesthetic experience, that its cognitive character becomes most evident. Beardsley came to realize that one of the central components in our experience of art "must be the experience of discovery, of insight into connections and organizations—the elation that comes from the apparent opening up of intelligibility." This opening up draws attention "to the excitement of meeting a cognitive challenge, of flexing one's powers to make *intelligible*—where this combines *making sense of something* with *making something make sense*" (p. 292). This sense making is what aesthetic experiences have in common with other kinds of experiences. A feeling of discovery is not limited to our encounters with artworks; the scholar and the scientist know the same kind of exhilaration. When there is little to discover there can, of course, be little to make sense of, and aesthetic experience will be thin. This obvious fact is why masterworks rank high on the list of things that have the capacity to stimulate aesthetic experience.

If Beardsley's notion of active discovery highlights the cognitive character of aesthetic awareness, his fifth feature, wholeness, draws attention to art's constitutive powers. In discussing the ways in which the experience of an artwork can generate a feeling of wholeness, Beardsley concentrates on the coherence of aesthetic experience. By coherence he means both "the coherence of the elements of the experience itself, of the diverse mental acts and events going on in one mind over a stretch of time" and "the coherence of the self, the mind's healing sense . . . of being all together and able to encompass its perceptions, feelings, emotions, ideas, in a single integrated personhood" (p. 293).

What I have done in this section is to use Beardsley's theory of aesthetic experience to suggest an alternative to theories that stress either the constitutive or revelatory power of art. Just as Levi in his redefinition of the humanities combined the Medieval and Renaissance traditions of the humanities into a third option that features the liberal arts of communication, continuity, and criticism, to which I have added the arts of creation and performance, so I have combined elements of classic and romantic theories of art in describing art's peculiar values. Having now offered an answer to the question why the art world is worth traversing, I return to the more concrete question of curriculum design.

Phases of Aesthetic Learning (K-12)

At their best, works of art require years of study and half a lifetime of experience and growing familiarity may be necessary for their full appreciation. So opined Harold Osborne in his *The Art of Appreciation*.[15] Aesthetic learning in the schools is likewise a long journey. It begins early and gradually extends into the middle and secondary years. Its overall purpose is the cultivation of percipience, which implies the possession of a well-developed sense of art. This goal is reached through a number of learning phases that culminate in a rich apperceptive mass. Such learning recognizes the demands of the current society and the subject of art as well as the requirements of the learner. These latter requirements are articulated in cognitive studies which assume that learning occurs most efficaciously when new information is related to a young person's conceptual framework. Concepts, organized in a hierarchy, undergo change as new information is assimilated. This view of learning means that teachers must have a good grasp of the conceptual character of art and an understanding of how to relate new information to the learner's existing schemes of knowledge.[16]

Learning in the arts will proceed from simple exposure and familiarization as well as making and perceiving in the elementary grades to more demanding historical, appreciative, and critical studies during the secondary years. As particular objectives change, so will teaching and learning methods. Assessment will center on the progress that learners make in expanding their conceptual frameworks. The entire scheme is built on the assumption that phases of aesthetic learning are instrumental to the goal of greater percipience. It should not be thought, however, that this assumption implies aesthetic learning will lack moments of immediate enjoyment. Still, aesthetic satisfaction usually stems from the development and strengthening of new mental powers, which by definition are instrumental. I now briefly discuss five phases of aesthetic learning (see figure 1).[17]

PHASE ONE: PERCEIVING AESTHETIC QUALITIES (K-3)

Although very young children are hardly prepared to engage works of art in all their formal complexity and dramatic intensity, to say nothing about their thematic and symbolic import, they are sensitive to the simple sensory and expressive qualities of things, and the years from kindergarten through third grade are thus the time to exploit and expand this capacity. This can be done through exposure to the aesthetic qualities of all sorts of things, whether in nature or in ordinary objects or in works of the children's own making. During this phase it might be said that the general goal is an appreciation of the qualitative immediacy of life. The young learn to enjoy things for their freshness and vividness. They cultivate a delight in the looks, sounds, tastes, and smells of things around them. But since visual, auditory, and verbal works of art are the principal loci of such qualities, it is important that young students' attention also be directed toward artworks. Learners in the early grades should be encouraged not only to note their aesthetic qualities but also to understand that artworks are special objects found in special places that society maintains at considerable effort. Thus do young learners begin to develop an elementary sense of art and the art world. At the same time they intuitively acquire a sense of object directedness, a fundamental feature of aesthetic experience.

In short, formal aesthetic learning begins during phase one. The understanding the young bring to school undergoes modification and expansion. The job of building dispositions gets underway. An initiation occurs into the mysteries of art and into a cultural institution known as an art world. In making their own works of art, young learners also gain insight into the nature of the artistic creative process. They come to realize that a work of art is a product of an artist's having composed the special qualities of materials into an aesthetic

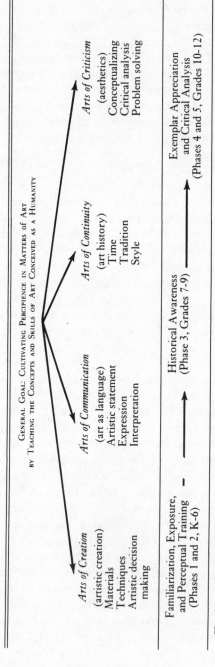

General Goal: Cultivating Percipience in Matters of Art
by Teaching the Concepts and Skills of Art Conceived as a Humanity

Arts of Creation
(artistic creation)
Materials
Techniques
Artistic decision
making

Arts of Communication
(art as language)
Artistic statement
Expression
Interpretation

Arts of Continuity
(art history)
Time
Tradition
Style

Arts of Criticism
(aesthetics)
Conceptualizing
Critical analysis
Problem solving

Familiarization, Exposure,
and Perceptual Training
(Phases 1 and 2, K-6)

Historical Awareness
(Phase 3, Grades 7-9)

Exemplar Appreciation
and Critical Analysis
(Phases 4 and 5, Grades 10-12)

Teaching and learning proceed along a continuum from exposure, familiarization, and perceptual training to historical awareness, exemplar appreciation, and critical analysis, stressing discovery and reception learning, didactic coaching, and dialogic teaching methods. Evaluation of aesthetic learning concentrates on the development of aesthetic conceptual maps and the conditions conducive for doing so. Reprinted with permission from A. W. Levi and R. A. Smith, *Art Education: A Critical Necessity* (Urbana: University of Illinois Press, 1991. Slightly edited.)

Fig. 1. A percipience curriculum (K-12)

object that features medium, form, and content. They learn, in other words, the way of aesthetic communication. In terms of the humanities interpretation presented in this chapter, this is, in effect, to bring the arts of creation and communication to bear on the study of art. Learning during phase one should not be inordinately formal, and a child's propensities should constantly be kept in mind. And although all phases of aesthetic learning are instrumental to the achievement of a certain level of percipience, there will, once more, be numerous moments of intrinsic satisfaction when ulterior objectives recede or are forgotten.

Much of what now goes on in the early years of school can suffice for achieving the objectives of phase one. However, if teachers plan these activities and lessons with the long-term goal of aesthetic percipience in mind, they might go about their teaching in slightly different ways. The important consideration is that all learning should have point and lead in a certain direction, most immediately toward greater perceptual finesse in phase two of aesthetic learning.

PHASE TWO: DEVELOPING PERCEPTUAL FINESSE (GRADES 4-6)

A precise dividing line between learning phases cannot, of course, be drawn, but by the upper elementary years the young are capable of concentrating their energies and powers. They can perceive greater complexity in works of art, their own as well as those of more mature artists. Gradually, however, attention shifts more and more to the latter, for it is only by perceiving works of some complexity that perceptual skills can be honed and developed.

In addition to the immediate qualities of artworks, their complex webs of relations and meanings are now also brought more fully and clearly into view. It is time for looking at artworks more closely while simultaneously learning about the art world in which works of art find a home and caretakers. Still not inordinately formal, phase-two learning is more structured than that of phase one. Beside making, seeing, and listening, students during this period also begin to acquire a vocabulary or language for talking about art and its various components.

Although it is possible to teach even the very young a methodical way to do something, it is during phase two especially that some system can be introduced. Harry S. Broudy recommends paying close attention to a work's sensory, formal, expressive, and technical aspects. Scanning such aspects is a way to make initial contact with artworks, and it can be effective provided excessive claims are not made for it and the method is not oversimplified.[18] To guard against the latter outcome, it might be helpful to see scanning within a larger pattern of response. Kenneth Clark, the distinguished art historian, once described his own perceptual habits this way. First, there is the initial impact a work of art makes, then a period of close scrutiny and examination during which one attempts to find what is actually in a work to be perceived and enjoyed. The phase of scrutiny is followed by one of recollection. Relevant kinds of information—biographical and historical, for example— are summoned in order to render a work intelligible. Additional periods of scrutiny and recollection then renew and revitalize initial aesthetic responses. The point is that aesthetic experience is difficult to sustain for very long, and the senses need time to regroup. What is more, although one's initial impressions of a work are fresh and spontaneous, they are often not a reliable key to a work's real character or import.[19]

At the end of phase two, far more than at the end of phase one, students should be able not only to convey to others the character of their first impressions (impact), but also to engage in formal analysis (scrutiny) and apply what knowledge they have acquired (recollection) in sustaining their interest in a work (renewal). When they practice the skills of aesthetic perception during what may be called the complete act of informed aesthetic response, learners experience, though not necessarily self-consciously, those additional features of aesthetic experience that Beardsley termed felt freedom, detached affect, and active discovery, that is, feelings of freely taking up a special point of view toward something for the sake of what can be discovered in doing so. During phases one and two it is, of course, appropriate to show and discuss works created by members of different groups and from other cultures and civilizations. A humanities curriculum, in other words, should have a multicultural dimension. However, I understand multiculturalism not as an ideological attack on the values of Western civilization but simply as a recognition that the study of alternatives is a revered humanistic objective, a way to avoid a narrow ethnocentrism.[20] Indeed, a well-developed sense of art implies an awareness of a broad range of artworks.

PHASE THREE: DEVELOPING A SENSE OF ART HISTORY
(GRADES 7-9)

Having learned how to perceive the qualitative immediacy, relational properties, and meanings of works of art, students are now ready to examine works under the aspects of time, tradition, and style. In what should be a well-designed survey course, students discover how artists have both celebrated and criticized a society's beliefs and values. Learning still serves the same general goal of a percipience curriculum, but now the development of historical awareness deepens the learners' cognitive stock and helps them to expand their sense of art. Not only that; discovering something new about what is important and valuable and interesting to perception is intrinsically satisfying.

Phase three also contributes to an appreciation of the ways works of art reflect the growth of civilization. They do so by providing records of extraordinary efforts to impose form and style on raw, unshaped material.[21] This is to say that works of art are preeminent symbols of man's struggle to free human existence from a life of necessity in order to enjoy one of freedom and leisure in which human powers can be cultivated for their own sakes. The study of such works further serves to emphasize that just as works of art have survived their severance from religion, magic, and myth,[22] so also, we may say, do they transcend gender, class, and race. Finally, the study of art history leads to an appreciation of the idea of a tradition.

In contrast to the pedagogy of the first two phases of aesthetic learning, phase three by necessity is more formal and requires systematic instruction. Although there won't be time in a survey course to linger long over any particular work, students will develop important insights into the processes of historical continuity and change and will come to realize that continuity is by far the greater part of the story.

An appreciation of tradition and of continuity and change can, of course, be attained through the study of practically any culture or civilization. But it is only natural that American youth should be initiated first into the major cultural heritage of their own society. Even Richard Rorty, the philosophical revisionist, acknowledges this as common wisdom.[23] The "war against Eurocentrism" currently being waged by certain advocates of multiculturalism is thus ill-advised and counterproductive. It generates cultural particularism instead of promoting the nobler goal of cultural pluralism.[24] The latter, as I have pointed out, will be taken into consideration during the first two phases of the percipience curriculum.

PHASE FOUR: EXEMPLAR APPRECIATION (GRADES 10-11)

The purpose of phase four is neither skill training nor historical study so much as appreciation in the best sense of the term. This is also the time to study works of art in some depth, without which any talk about excellence in arts education is mere rhetoric. During phase four, students pause simply to admire some of the finest achievements of humankind—great works of art resplendent in their beauty, form, significance, and mystery as nothing else is. It matters not, moreover, the ethnic origin or gender of the artist; we are talking about human excellence.

As I conceive of it, exemplar study also provides an opportunity to understand the role of contextual factors in appreciating art. One can appreciate a work of art on its own terms without much regard for the historical factors that helped to shape it, but we fail to give the arts their due as humanities unless, as Levi remarked, we pause to understand the ways they integrate the different cultural elements of a society or of an epoch. We may call this the figure-ground relationship of exemplar appreciation, with the artworks being the figure. But this relationship should not be reversed; contextual information is primarily an aid to appreciation. Most of all, a work of art should not be dissolved into its context.[25]

Given the aim of cultivating an appreciation of artistic excellence during the fourth phase of aesthetic learning, it follows that examples of artistic excellence from different cultures are also candidates for appreciation. Although one would expect masterworks from the Western cultural heritage to be featured, efforts should be made to appreciate exemplars of artistic quality of non-Western cultures.

PHASE FIVE: CRITICAL ANALYSIS (GRADE 12)

Beyond exemplar appreciation the percipience curriculum offers critical reflection on the role of art in human life and society and on the innumerable conundrums such relations generate.[26] But the principal purpose of the last phase of aesthetic learning is to provide opportunities for young adults to fashion something of their own philosophies of art, to formulate beliefs and to stake out positions, at least tentatively, on such questions as the relations of art and morality, art and the mass media, art and the environment, art and politics, and so forth. Certainly not least among the questions that should be considered are those about artistic value and worth. When students address these questions the rich apperceptive mass they have built up through previous phases of learning will now be put to good uses. Given the public controversy that has attended a number of recent artistic events, there should be no difficulty stimulating the interest of twelfth-graders. In truth, older students are curious about artistic controversies and their teachers' views on them. In senior seminars a start can be made in asking the right questions and sorting out the relevant issues.

Toward Needed Reform

The humanities justification of arts education presented in this chapter is grounded in a redefinition of the traditional humanities in procedural and substantive terms. Under this redefinition the teaching of the arts involves bringing to bear in appropriate ways and at relevant times the arts of creation, communication, continuity, and criticism. The mastery of these arts at levels suitable for the ages of learners eventually yields percipience in matters of art and culture, the ultimate goal of arts education. Aesthetically percipient, the well-educated nonspecialist can be expected to traverse the art world with intelligence, tact, and a measure of autonomy. A student achieves this level of percipience through a series of learning phases: exposure and familiarization, perceptual training, historical study, exemplar appreciation, and critical analysis.

Obviously, before a percipience curriculum could be implemented in the schools, major progress would have to be made in the reform of teacher education.[27] Prospective teachers of art, for example, would need considerably more work in the humanities. And there would have to be a greater commitment on the part of society to the importance of realizing a fundamental human right—the right to realize as fully as possible significant human capacities, including aesthetic capacities. Such capacities have been understood in this chapter in connection with the constitutive and revelatory powers of art that can shape the human personality in positive ways and provide humanistic understanding. These benefits have value not only for the individual but also for the society. A society is more likely to enjoy cultural health when inhabited by persons with aesthetic intelligence. Arts education is thus a critical necessity.

NOTES

1. Ernst Cassirer, *An Essay on Man* (New Haven: Yale University Press, 1944), p. 68.

2. For representative works, see Philip H. Phenix, *Realms of Meaning* (New York: McGraw-Hill, 1964), P. H. Hirst, *Knowledge and the Curriculum* (Boston: Routledge & Kegan Paul, 1974), L. A. Reid, *Ways of Understanding and Education* (London: Heinemann, 1986), and Howard Gardner, *Frames of Mind* (New York: Basic Books, 1983).

68   TOWARD   PERCIPIENCE   IN   THE   ARTS

3. I borrow the notion of percipience from Harold Osborne's *The Art of Appreciation* (New York: Oxford University Press, 1970), chap. 2, "Appreciation as Percipience." The term "art world" is intended in the sense that Arthur Danto uses it in his *The Transfiguration of the Commonplace* (Cambridge: Harvard University Press, 1981). Commenting on the role of theory in constituting an art world, Danto writes: "To see something as art at all demands nothing less than this, an atmosphere of artistic theory, a knowledge of the history of art" (p. 135). By "percipience" I imply the ability to generate such an atmosphere with some skill and finesse.

4. Albert William Levi, *The Humanities Today* (Bloomington: Indiana University Press, 1970), chap. 1; idem, "Literature as a Humanity," *Journal of Aesthetic Education* 10, nos. 3-4 (July-October 1976): 45-60; idem, "Teaching Literature as a Humanity," *Journal of General Education* 28, no. 4 (Winter 1977): 283-289.

5. E. D. Hirsch, Jr., *Cultural Literacy* (New York: Vintage Books, 1988), chap. 5, "Cultural Literacy and the Schools." Cf. Ian Westbury and Alan C. Purves, eds., *Cultural Literacy and General Education*, Eighty-seventh Yearbook of the National Society for the Study of Education, Part II (Chicago: University of Chicago Press, 1988); and Ralph A. Smith, ed., *Cultural Literacy and Arts Education* (Urbana: University of Illinois Press, 1991).

6. Levi, "Literature as a Humanity," p. 60. Levi's questions are slightly amended for purposes of this discussion.

7. I refer here to Edmund B. Feldman's *Becoming Human through Art* (Englewood Cliffs, NJ: Prentice-Hall, 1970), one of the more substantive art education textbooks of the 1970s.

8. The following discussion is condensed from A. W. Levi and R. A. Smith, *Art Education: A Critical Necessity* (Urbana: University of Illinois Press, 1991), chap. 2, "The Arts and the Human Person."

9. Friedrich von Schiller, *On the Aesthetic Education of Man in a Series of Letters*, trans. Elizabeth W. Wilkinson and L. A. Willoughby (New York: Oxford University Press, 1976).

10. Ibid., especially pp. 7, 9, 55, 215.

11. Herbert Read, *The Redemption of the Robot: My Encounters with Education through Art* (New York: Simon and Schuster, 1969), p. 143.

12. John Dewey, *Art as Experience* (Carbondale and Edwardsville: Southern Illinois University Press, 1987), pp. 252-53.

13. Nelson Goodman, *Languages of Art*, 2d ed. (Indianapolis: Hackett, 1976), pp. 245-52.

14. Monroe C. Beardsley, "Aesthetic Experience," in *The Aesthetic Point of View: Selected Essays*, ed. Michael J. Wreen and Donald M. Callen (Ithaca: Cornell University Press, 1982), pp. 285-97. All quotations are from this essay.

15. Harold Osborne, *The Art of Appreciation*, p. 36.

16. For a discussion of such principles, I have found the writings of Joseph D. Novak quite helpful. See his *A Theory of Education* (Ithaca: Cornell University Press, 1986), and David P. Ausubel, Joseph D. Novak, and Helen Hanesian, *Educational Psychology: A Cognitive View*, 2d ed. (New York: Holt, Rinehart and Winston, 1978).

17. The following discussion is a condensed version of the accounts given in Ralph A. Smith, *The Sense of Art: A Study in Aesthetic Education* (New York: Routledge, 1989), chap. 6, and in Levi and Smith, *Art Education: A Critical Necessity*, chap. 8.

18. Harry S. Broudy, *The Role of Imagery in Learning* (Los Angeles: Getty Center for Education in the Arts, 1987), pp. 52-53.

19. Kenneth Clark, *Looking at Pictures* (New York: Holt, Rinehart and Winston, 1960), pp. 16-17.

20. For example, in his *The Future of the Humanities* (New York: Thomas Y. Crowell, 1977), Walter Kaufmann writes that the objectives of the humanities are four: the conservation and cultivation of the greatest works of humanity, the teaching of vision, the fostering of a critical spirit, and thoughtful reflection on alternatives (pp. xvii-xxi).

21. This is the theme of Kenneth Clark's *Civilisation* (New York: Harper and Row, 1969) and *Toward Civilization: A Report on Arts Education* (Washington, D.C.: National Endowment for the Arts, 1988).

22. Hannah Arendt, *The Human Condition* (Chicago: University of Chicago Press, 1958), p. 167.

23. Richard Rorty, "The Dangers of Over-Philosophication—Reply to Arcilla and Nicholson," *Educational Theory* 40, no. 1 (Winter 1990): 41-44.

24. Diane Ravitch, "Multiculturalism: E Pluribus Plures," *American Scholar* 59, no. 3 (Summer 1990): 337-354. See also, idem, "Multiculturalism: An Exchange," *American Scholar* 60, no. 2 (Spring 1991): 272-276 for the author's response to a critique of "Multiculturalism: E Pluribus Plures" by Molefi Keti Asante that also appeared in the Spring 1991 issue of *American Scholar*. See also my "Forms of Multicultural Education in the Arts," *Journal of Multi-cultural and Cross-cultural Research in Art Education* 1, no. 1 (Fall 1983): 23-32; and Rachel Mason, *Art Education and Multiculturalism* (London: Croom Helm, 1988), esp. pp. 1-2, "Four Types of Multiculturalism."

25. What one must avoid is what Hilton Kramer (*The New Criterion* 9, no. 4 [December 1990]) calls the postmodernist mode of analysis termed deconstruction, whose aim is "to deconstruct every 'text'—which is to say, every art object—into an inventory of its context and thus remove the object from the realm of aesthetic experience and make it instead a coefficient of its sources and social environment" (p. 7).

26. For a number of such conundrums, see Margaret P. Battin, John Fisher, Ronald Moore, and Anita Silvers, *Puzzles about Art: An Aesthetics Casebook* (New York: St. Martin's, 1989), and the chapter in this volume by Marcia Eaton.

27. I have discussed some initiatives toward such reform in my *Excellence in Art Education: Ideas and Initiatives*, updated version (Reston, Va., National Art Education Association, 1987), chap. 5.

CHAPTER IV

Cognition as Interpretation in Art Education

MICHAEL J. PARSONS

Perhaps the main story in art education in the last quarter century is the influence of the cognitive approach, the ways it has been understood, digested, and resisted. This approach has given us our dominant paradigm for thinking about the arts and about issues of teaching, learning, and curriculum. It has appeared in two distinguishable but interacting streams. One has its origin in the psychology of art and has been most concerned with investigating the abilities of children. The other comes from philosophers and art educators and has addressed itself more to the goals and curriculum of art education.

Other chapters in this volume chronicle the several versions and past history of this paradigm. In this chapter I am more interested in its future possibilities. I identify changes occurring in the environment of art education and discuss the changes they call for in our thinking. I suggest that we can no longer take for granted much about children's abilities and the goals of art education that the cognitive movement did take for granted. I suggest that the idea of cognition in the arts should be understood more radically as interpretation, and I discuss, with examples, what that would mean. In particular, it would mean a different understanding of the mutual relation of studio work and the discussion of art—of thinking in an art medium and thinking in a natural language.

The Cognitive Movement: Psychological Aspects

The cognitive movement in the psychology of art was a part of a more comprehensive movement in psychology in general, and that larger movement has affected our thinking about children's abilities in

---

Michael J. Parsons is Head of the Department of Art Education, The Ohio State University, Columbus, Ohio.

all the subjects in the school curriculum. Perhaps it has caused most change in the arts. If so, the reason is not hard to find. In the late 1950s and early 1960s, when the new cognitivism began to replace the old behaviorism, a categorical change in how we understand the arts was required. Behaviorism, and the positivist philosophy that lay behind it, divided the human mind into the cognitive and the affective, two categories defined by opposition. The arts were the only traditional school subjects that fell clearly into the "affective" category. Most of science, mathematics, language, and the social studies fell into the cognitive category. There were exceptions, since morality and religion, defined as personal "values," were also deemed noncognitive; this affected particularly the social studies.

In the new cognitivism, of course, all our mental activities were considered cognitive. The cognitivists investigated the hidden mental processes whose existence the behaviorists had either denied or ignored on the principle that one can be scientific only about what can be publicly observed and quantified. This was change enough. But with respect to science, mathematics, and most of the other school subjects, it did not involve a change in how they were categorized. These subjects were cognitive before the change and cognitive afterwards. What changed was the idea of the cognitive, which now included the processes and contents of unobservable thinking. In the case of the arts, it *was* a change of category. They had been affective, which meant noncognitive. Now they were cognitive, which included the intuitive, the creative, and the emotional.

This was a change that at least appeared to be greater for the arts than for other subjects, and it was certainly more confusing. For many people, to call the arts cognitive appeared to deny that they have something important to do with emotion, with intuition, or with creativity. It would have meant this for behaviorists but it did not for the new cognitivists. The new cognitivist view was that emotions, intuition, creativity were just as cognitive as anything else. *All* mental activities were cognitive. There was no more "affect," empty of thinking; there was now emotion, which could be more and less thoughtful. "Affective" and "emotional" are not equivalent notions, and whereas affect had been incompatible with the old view of cognition, emotion was not incompatible with the new view.

The change proved hard to sell to many art teachers, who for several reasons had become rather attached to the "affective" label. It had become a symbol of their difference and gave them freedoms. It allowed them, for instance, to resist the kind of narrow objective testing that was forced on teachers of other subjects. The price paid for this freedom, of course, has been the relative isolation of art from the rest of the curriculum.

The most successful adaptation of the new psychology to the arts focused on thinking in the art medium. It looked for mental representations of aspects of the medium, operations conducted on these representations, the knowledges and awarenesses required for dealing with the stuff of which an art object is made. Little use was made of other major variants of the cognitive approach in psychology. For example, the influence of Piaget has been slight in the arts. So has that of Vygotsky and other Neo-Piagetians. Nor has much use been made of the information-processing model, whether or not computer-based. Instead, the psychology of art has looked at how we solve problems in a medium, for example, how we draw diagonals on a two-dimensional surface,[1] how we make figures with clay,[2] or how we construct maps.[3] There has also been interesting work on the cognitive aspects of craftsmanship[4] and of creativity.[5] Project Zero has been a leader in this work.[6] Much of its research has been based on Nelson Goodman's notion[7] that we can treat an art medium as a symbol system, as being in some ways analogous to a natural language.[8] This approach has provided a systematic research agenda and also the clearest and most comprehensive rationale of the medium-based approach to education in the arts. Each art medium is regarded as a symbol system in which meanings can be shaped and presented. One can categorize the various elements and rules of such a symbol system and then investigate the ways and sequences in which children learn those elements and rules. This has proved to be a powerful model of cognition in the arts. Creativity and artistry consist of thinking in terms of a medium, which is after all the very essence of the art form, the stuff that artworks are made of: paint, in the case of paintings; sound, in the case of music. Thinking consists of the discrimination and manipulation of the elements of that stuff, the response to their meaningful variations and nuances and to the constructions, combinations, and qualities they make possible. Aesthetic response is very similar: it consists of reading the medium. This view makes thinking intrinsic to the art-form, clearly a matter of intelligence, and different for each medium. It is an intuitive view for many people involved with the arts. It has the great strength of clarifying what is cognitive about the arts without giving up the sense that they are different in a fundamental way from language study, science, and so forth.

It is important to notice that the kinds of educational goals that flow naturally from this model are closely related to perception. They include such things as the discrimination of significant elements, the perception of qualities, the detection of styles, the awareness of similarities and differences, the solving of problems, all of these couched in terms of a specific medium. Perception and cognition are closely related. Cognition is almost recognition.

An example has to do with children's abilities to perceive artistic styles in paintings, a topic much investigated at Project Zero. In a number of studies[9] Gardner and his associates looked at children's abilities to detect the style of paintings and to group together works that are in the same style. They used a number of variations on a basic sorting task used by a number of other researchers.[10] This task requires subjects to look at a number of reproductions and to pick out those that are in the same style. It is a task requiring the discrimination of similarities and differences in the use of the medium and their recognition across various examples. Gardner showed that children of age twelve and younger normally do not attend to style in paintings and are usually more interested in subject matter.[11] He also showed that ten-year-old children and many seven-year-olds can be trained to sort works by style, by a combination of practice and feedback, but with no discussion.[12] In addition, Gardner also talked with the children about how they selected works. He concluded that young children do have the ability to "detect" style and can discriminate aspects of texture, composition, and color, even though they cannot articulate the cues they use. In a different study, Dennie Wolf showed that older children, given a half-finished drawing of a man in a distinctive style, can finish it in much the same style. Younger children, however, seem unable to do this.[13]

One logical outcome of this identification of cognition with perception and of thinking with the manipulation of the medium is the notion of multiple intelligences recently advanced by Gardner.[14] According to this notion, intelligence is basically the ability to work within a medium, and it follows that a different intelligence is called on to work within each different medium, or symbol system. This also is a powerful conception, one that goes beyond the arts and will free up our sense of educational goals in general. A major purpose of schooling will be the nurturing of the different types of intelligences. This is a good case of an increasingly plausible phenomenon: that ideas originating in the arts can affect thinking about other aspects of the curriculum.

The Cognitive Movement: Philosophical Aspects

The other cognitivist stream of influence in art education has led to similar, though not identical, conceptions of goals. This stream is less affected by developments in psychology than by those in philosophy. It is associated with the work of a varied number of philosophers and educators, prominent among whom are Harry S. Broudy, Manuel Barkan, Elliot W. Eisner, and Ralph A. Smith.[15] A primary influence has been the work of modernist aestheticians, particularly Monroe C. Beardsley and Harold Osborne. The emphasis is on aesthetic experience, understood as the perception of the qualities of the artwork. The artwork is autonomously meaningful, its significance deriving largely from the internal relations of its elements with each other and with the whole. Beardsley in particular stressed the importance of the regional qualities that are properties of complex formal arrangements of parts. The grasp of such qualities, and of the formal relations on which they depend, is for him the hallmark of aesthetic experience and the condition of the gratification it affords. This grasp is clearly cognitive in character and is closely related to perception. It requires the discrimination, perception, apprehension, and savoring of the visual elements, formal properties, and resulting qualities that constitute artworks. It may be intuitive or analytic, but in either case it is cognitive. Smith, following Harold Osborne, has used the notion of "percipience" to summarize the goals of this approach. Percipience is a disciplined and highly attentive kind of perception in which the properties of objects

are brought into focus according to their own inherent intensities, their similarities and contrasts, and their peculiar groupings. Perception of this kind is unusually full and complete and avoids the narrow focus on practical purposes that is characteristically maintained during our nonaesthetic pursuits.[16]

Smith stresses that percipience is more than just perception. It has an element of interpretation to it and requires skills and background understandings. These, however, consist largely of knowing what to attend to and how to organize the response. He continues:

Aesthetic experience calls for direct and synoptic vision. To illustrate this contrast [with nonaesthetic experience]: the activities of discussing the antecedents of Picasso's *Guernica* or assigning it a position in Picasso's oeuvre, although they focus on an artwork, are not the same as the direct apprehension of the work's fusion of subject and form; only the latter counts as an act of expressive perception. Yet it should be pointed out that by "direct perception" Osborne does not mean unmediated perception; being cognitive, perception and percipience are not equivalent to instantaneous emotional reaction. Osborne talks about the *way* the viewer orders and interprets the elements of the aesthetic object being contemplated, about what directs an act of percipience and what is being omitted from it.[17]

Percipience, then, is interpretive in character—a grasp of *meaningful* qualities. But, as the first quotation suggests, meanings are constructed mostly in light of the *internal* relationships of elements of the work—their own inherent intensities, similarities, and contrasts. If this were all, then percipience would remain a matter of thinking within the art medium. But increasingly there has been interest in the way in which meanings also derive from the connections of the work with aspects of the culture of its origin. Smith probably takes this tendency further than others.[18] Much of his recent work has shown an increasing interest in the importance of context for interpretation. It is a tendency that I expand on and advocate later in this paper. In general, writers in this stream, when they do talk about connections external to the work, tend to emphasize connections within the art world rather than with more general aspects of a culture. Hence they advocate teaching a knowledge of the art world as the background needed to respond to art intelligently.

In practice this has meant an appeal to the notion of art-related disciplines. The notion of discipline is notoriously difficult to clarify and it has a checkered history in art education, one that runs from Bruner through Barkan and Broudy down to the present idea of discipline-based art education.[19] But appealing to disciplines suggests that thinking in art occurs in words as well as in an art medium. For example, a discipline has at times been identified with the way the experts in a discipline think. Certainly the expert artist's way of thinking can be imagined to be wholly in terms of an art medium. But what about the thinking of the art historian or the art critic? It seems plausible to say that these experts think at least partly in linguistic terms when they think about such things as historical periods, styles, social context, the connections of a work with other works, or the nature of art in general. All of these topics are part of an art discipline and their discussion seems to require the use of language and the networks of connections that language enables. For this reason an appeal to disciplines in art education suggests that students should be taught to think *both* in the terms of an art medium and in more general linguistic terms. Later I will claim that, though this may appear to advocate cultivating two types of intelligence, we can actually reach one achievement this way more fully than with either alone.

I conclude that, insofar as we define our goals in terms of disciplines, it is hard to construe cognition as thinking only within a medium. In general, the philosophical stream has been more flexible in this way than the psychological stream. Nevertheless, its emphasis is on the perception of elements and qualities of the medium, informed to varying degrees by a knowledge of the art world.

The Role of Interpretation

My purpose so far has been to identify the way in which the idea of the cognitive has been interpreted in art education. Now I will speak of the idea of interpretation, understood not as an alternative to cognition but as an elaboration of it. Interpretation, I believe, plays a fundamental role in cognition, one that has generally been taken for granted. I would like to make more visible the intelligent meaning-making activities that have gone unnoticed, occurring underneath, as it were, the sorts of activities that we have thought to be cognitive in the arts. I do not question that discriminative intelligence, percipience, and disciplined understanding are worthwhile goals in art education. But I believe those goals require us to pay more attention to children's interpretive abilities. My argument for this view consists mostly of pointing to changes in the context of art education that have occurred since the cognitive movement took hold and suggesting that they raise issues that could previously be ignored.

First, what is meant by "interpretation"? Interpretation is mental activity that results in understanding. It may be conscious or unconscious activity. It may be laborious and self-aware, or intuitive and taken for granted. It is essentially cognitive. The activity of interpretation becomes obvious only when there is some initial difficulty in understanding. We can say that, for our purposes, interpretation is what we do when we try to understand something, to grasp its significance. Charles Taylor says something like that in an article written in 1971 and since reprinted a number of times.[20] He writes:

Interpretation, in the sense relevant to hermeneutics, is an attempt to make clear, to make sense of an object. This object must, therefore, be a text, or a text-analogue, which in some way is confused, incomplete, cloudy, seemingly contradictory—in one way or another unclear. The interpretation aims to bring to light an underlying coherence or sense.[21]

I believe that the art object—a prime "text-analogue"—is less clear today than it was at the beginning of the cognitive movement. What we then saw clearly and took for granted has become unclear. Perhaps it was never so clear and we were mistaken at the time. Certainly, thirty years ago we assumed much about art that we can no longer assume. It seemed clear enough then which objects were artworks and which were not, what media they were constituted in, where to draw their boundaries, which works were worth studying, and which aspects of them were to be studied. It was this relative clarity that allowed us to define the task of art education in terms of recognition, perception, discrimination, percipience. Now, however, the art object, in Taylor's words, is more "confused, incomplete, cloudy, seemingly contradictory—in one way or another unclear." The consequence is that we must identify and interpret before we can perceive and recognize. Underneath perception lies interpretation. We can no longer attend to perception and take interpretation for granted. The need for interpretation becomes greater when the object becomes unclear.

Why is the art object less clear than it was? One could cite many reasons. I will refer briefly to two general classes of reasons, those that originate within the world of art and those that come from outside it. The shorthand phrase for the first kind is the "postmodern condition." There is the rise in acceptance within the art world of a multitude of movements and traditions that have less and less in common and yet manage to coexist. Where the art world used to allow only one movement to be "mainstream," we now have a welter of alternatives. We also have experiments with new media and combinations of media, the rise in esteem of folk and regional art traditions, greater acceptance of the art of various ethnic groups and cultures, and more appreciation of the art traditions of cultures across the world. Where there was a sense that art was a stream moving in a direction determined by history, there is now the sense of a mosaic, or perhaps a jigsaw puzzle, colorful, multitudinous, moving in all directions, difficult to understand as a whole.

Many of the newer parts of the mosaic rest on assumptions different from those of the old "modern" art. So we are urged to modify or abandon our old assumptions and traditional ways of thinking about the arts. The old criteria, canons, and hierarchies are challenged and no successors to them are widely accepted. In aesthetics, there is less emphasis on the artwork and its autonomy. Instead, there is more interest in the relations of the artwork with the culture of its origin, an elaboration of the connections of culture and artwork that threatens our old belief that we could recognize where one ended and the other began. There is also more interest in what the viewer does with the artwork. In short, the question of interpretation is predominant in philosophy.

I am describing, not advocating, a state of affairs. Of course, "the postmodern condition" is accompanied by "postmodernisms," theories about the condition that in different ways depend on it. Such theories often go further than is helpful here. Some, for instance, elaborate the connections of art with culture in such a way that an artwork becomes just another cultural object with no distinctively aesthetic qualities, no independent meaning of its own. Others stress its dependence on the viewer to the point where the artwork has no public existence, no existence at all other than in the readings of individuals. Such views, taken seriously, would mark a break with the cognitive movement, which has always supposed that the artwork is objectively there to be seen. But even if we avoid the wilder reaches of continental hermeneutic philosophy and deconstructionism, and remain within the staid confines of the Anglo-American tradition, Arthur Danto is a more representative figure today than Goodman, Beardsley, or Osborne. And one of Danto's major themes is interpretation. He insists that interpretation is required to turn an object into an artwork. He says:

Indiscernibly different objects may become quite different and distinct works of art by dint of different and distinct interpretations. . . . Interpretations [are] functions which transform material objects into works of art. Interpretation is . . . the lever by which an object is lifted out of the real world and into the art world, where it becomes vested in often unexpected raiment. Only in relation to an interpretation is an object an artwork.[22]

The second kind of change affecting art education comes from outside the artworld (although the sense of what is inside and outside the artworld has itself become unclear). The shorthand for this kind of change is "cultural pluralism." I do not need to describe in detail the increasingly diverse cultural backgrounds of our students in school, nor the demand for educational programs that are responsive to those backgrounds. This diversity includes both the traditional minority groups in the United States and newer immigrant groups from across the world. The important fact is that we are further along the path to a genuinely pluralist society, where different cultures are publicly respected and where membership in a particular cultural group is a matter of pride. Our society regards cultural diversity as desirable because it is a fulfillment of democracy, a national strength, and a stimulus to greater understanding. We expect our schools to help students understand their own cultural background. We also expect them to teach understanding across cultural differences, so that students will learn from each other. And the same thing is increasingly taken as desirable across national boundaries; students should understand something of the cultures of other continents.

These two kinds of changes greatly affect art education. The art of our own culture has become unclear; the art of other cultures has always been unclear to us but is now more important than it used to be. Both developments raise issues of interpretation more radically than before. We will have to pay more attention to issues of interpretation and understanding even though our goals remain the same: to help students perceive the complex qualities and meanings of artworks. If we respond well, art education could become a model within the school curriculum as a whole, because the issues of interpretation and understanding across cultures are central everywhere, though most obvious in art.

Language and Interpretation

What does it mean to pay more attention to issues of interpretation? One issue has to do with the role of language in cognition. I have already referred to the view that thinking in the arts has little to do with language because it is essentially thinking in the terms of the medium. The painter, at his or her essential best, wrestles with images of paint, its colors, shapes, textures, struggling to capture some half-grasped complexity of visual form. Similarly with the viewer, since viewing is a kind of re-creating. On this view, there is no real need to use language when we think artistically or aesthetically. If in practice we often do use language, it is because it is helpful as a shortcut or a crutch for learners. But it is not essential. Talking is not what really counts and the best artistic thinking is not in words. As for disciplines having to do with art, they are not artistic or aesthetic in themselves. They are *about* art, but they are not art. They are part of the humanities. Thinking *about* art is not the same as thinking *in* art.

This is an attractive doctrine and many artists respond to it. As I have suggested, it has been adopted by many psychological and philosophical cognitivists. It fits especially well with the symbol-systems view in which intelligence is identified with thinking in the terms of a medium. It is a coherent and attractive view, and no one could deny much truth to it. But it is a partial view because it allows no significant role for language.

To argue the case, I could point to what contemporary artists actually do. In fact, they do not always seem to work in terms of a medium. They often mix or cross media in strange ways. Computer graphics, to mention one case, are produced with the use of algorithms, which are at some distance from the visual media in which the final product is usually displayed, and there is considerable discussion of whether or not the computer is itself a new medium—in which case the notion of "medium" itself becomes unclear. Another example comes from "ready-mades," which have always been provocative. Duchamp displayed a snowshovel in an art gallery. What is the medium there? And there are conceptual artists and photographers who add words to old photos. And so on.

A more important point is that many works cannot even be identified without considerable information and discussion. Danto's writing is full of examples. In one famous imaginary case, he discusses six solid red square panels that look exactly alike and yet are six quite different paintings. The six paintings are:

The Red Sea Having Been Crossed by the Israelites;

Kierkegaard's Mood, a work that expresses his inner state;

Red Square, a Moscow landscape;

Red Square, a minimalist painting;

Nirvana, a Buddhist image;

Red Table Cloth, a still life by a pupil of Matisse.[23]

Danto's point is that no one of these works could be identified, let alone understood, without a grasp of some background ideas. Some of these ideas are from the art world, as with the minimalist painting, which requires some understanding of New York art theories of the 1960s. Other ideas are more general. For *The Red Sea Having Been Crossed by the Israelites*, one would need to know at least the Biblical story; for *Nirvana*, something of Buddhist thought; and for *Kierkegaard's Mood*, something of human emotions and of Kierkegaard. One might add also that to understand Danto's aesthetics one has to know something both of the buzzing prolixity of the artworld and of philosophy in general.

Commonplace examples of the point are easy to find. There is plenty of evidence, for example, that most people can make no sense of abstract expressionist paintings (De Kooning, for example) without education, and that what they see when they look at such works is scribble, unintelligible visual marks. I will quote from the actual case of Jennie, a twelve-year-old student, who was asked about the style of Picasso's *Weeping Woman*, one of many studies for the *Guernica*.[24] Jennie was a perceptive student and could see that the work was done with a particular kind of line and a consistent kind of distortion. She identified the style quite well and would surely have passed the test for "detecting" styles if she were asked to group this work with other studies for the *Guernica*. But she could make no sense of the style. She thought it was the result of a mistake, an accidental departure from a more realistic approach.

Jennie: I think she's (the Weeping Woman) got the hand backwards. It can't go like this and be showing these knuckles right here.

Interviewer: That's right. Then why is it done that way?

J: Cause it's mixed up.

I: Would it be better if the knuckles were on the right side?

J: No, because if everything were perfect in the picture, it wouldn't be—it wouldn't have the same style as it does.

I: It's a style that's meant not to be perfect?

J: Yeah.

I: Why would the artist do it that way?

J: Maybe the artist knew—found out that he did it wrong, and then made the whole picture the same.

There would be no sense asking Jennie to look harder at the *Weeping Woman*. She could *recognize* the style well enough but could make no sense of it. This was confirmed when she was asked a little later about another nonrealistic painting that she could describe quite well:

I: Why do you suppose he painted it like this?

J: Because he's done so many realistic paintings he's sick of them.

I recently saw, in a museum, a small carved wooden figure from Africa. It was of strange proportions, had an odd gesture, hair was attached to it in places, small strings of beads and bones were wound round it, and parts of it were covered with old nails. Because it was in a museum I studied its visual appearance, but I could see it only as grotesque, that is, some combination of interesting and unintelligible. In fact, it is a powerful charm from Songye, Zaire, a votive figure of a god with certain powers, an image of connection with particular aspects of the universe. Each addition of natural or man-made materials to it is a sign of its power, and *it has the look* of this power for those who understand the structure of ideas from which it came and so can directly apprehend its qualities.

The general point of these examples is this: the view that thinking in the arts can be language-independent is plausible only when the art object is already clear. If we already know how to identify the art object, what aspects of it are significant, what ideas inform it, then we can think in terms of its medium alone and perceive its qualities directly. But when the object is unclear, we need access to ideas that can be developed only within language. We need to talk about artworks as well as to look at them because we need to connect them with aspects of both the art world and the world in general. It appears that, at the birth of the cognitivist movement, it was possible, in normal cases, to take those ideas and connections for granted, by virtue of the hierarchical structure and relative coherence of the art world and the culture. The reasonableness of this assumption has since been eroded.

On the interpretive view, then, language becomes an essential part of cognition in the arts. If an object is unclear, we try to express our sense of it in words. In practice, this means we must try to say it as well as see it. More accurately, since only part of the sense will be more clear in the interpretation than in the object itself, and vice versa, we must be able to discuss what is hard to see and to see what is hard to say. And then the two kinds of thinking—that is, thinking in the two different media—will be interactive and combine to form one understanding. We clarify in words relations of the object so we can see those relations in the object. It follows that the words are not just a crutch. They are as important as the looking. Not more important but equally so, because both the talking and the looking are constitutive of the artwork, of the qualities it has and the meanings it carries. In Danto's words: "Only in relation to an interpretation is an object an artwork." If we stayed with thinking in one medium, interpretation would be impossible and the object would remain obscure.

I do not mean, of course, that in talking about an artwork we put into words exactly what we see. For one thing, that is impossible. No translation is ever exactly equivalent. Every interpretation omits something and adds something. And, for another thing, if exact synonymy were possible, it would not be worthwhile because there would be no increment in insight. It is just because interpretation can give only a partial account of an object that it can enrich the object.

Culture and Interpretation

It might be asked why one should emphasize language as the medium for interpretation. What is the importance of language? Why not some other medium? Why not translate visual art into dance, or music? Or two-dimensional art into three-dimensional art? The answer is that, while these translations might be worthwhile, language is not just another medium to think with. It is unique because it is indissolubly merged with our understandings of the world in general. It embodies and represents our whole lifeworld, the horizon of meanings against which we live our life, the water in which we meaning-making humans swim. The lifeworld consists of our attitudes, assumptions, emotions, institutions, relationships, behaviors, all of these being meaningfully connected into what we call a culture. What connects these together, however loosely, is our language. All our cultural objects, including artworks, are related within a loose network of ideas and assumptions that are embodied in language and accessible only through language. Language cannot be separated from them, nor they from language. Objects and language acquire their meanings and connections from each other. It follows that when we discuss something in language we relate it, explicitly or implicitly, to other aspects of culture. This includes artworks, which, though they may be autonomously meaningful, are not unconnectedly so. These connections become more important when they are with more general elements of the culture rather than with the art world only.

Consider the case of the *Guernica*, which seems to be a favorite case of art educators. What ideas does one need to interpret the *Guernica* intelligently? It is, among other things, a powerful expression of outrage at the cruelty and destruction of war. To see this expression of outrage, one would need a general idea of war, which is basic to our culture but not to all cultures. One would need a sense that the cruelty and destruction of war is morally deplorable, which is even less universally had. And one would need an empathetic grasp of the suffering depicted, which cannot be taken for granted at all. All these must be learned through language, or, the same thing, by living in a culture. Consider what Scott, eighteen years old, said about the *Guernica*:

Scott: It's almost demonstrating cruelty of one man to another, or a picture of war in the real sense, instead of what we get through magazines: what it's really like.

Interviewer: What do you mean by "real"?

S: Well, from what I've seen of war—I've read Remarque's *All Quiet on the Western Front*—it tends to be almost glorified to the people back home—when they go out there, what it's really like to be in the action, being attacked . . .

I: Is this a beautiful work?

S: I don't think that art necessarily has to be beautiful—well, beautiful in a way, that it can express something that nothing else can—but not necessarily beautiful as in pretty. And I don't think that this is beautiful in that way; I think it's gross in that way, physically. So it isn't beautiful. But perhaps war isn't beautiful, violence isn't beautiful.

I: Does that add to the value of the painting?

S: Yes. How can you portray violence when everything is neat and clean and orderly, instead of knocked over and twisted?

It seems from this that Scott has, as Smith put it, "a direct apprehension of the work's content and form." Notice what it takes for him to do this. It requires him to get past the idea that art should be beautiful and pleasing, which he does with a kind of reasoning about expression and beauty that is philosophical in character. He also relates the *Guernica* to *All Quiet on the Western Front*, which he happens to have read. This relation is significant because it helps him construct the sense of suffering and of moral outrage that he sees in the work. Imagine a student from a culture where war is always glorified, as it once was in ours. That student would not see what Scott sees, because the relevant idea of outrage would not be available. Scott's understanding of the cruelty of war has been shaped by the ideas of our present culture, which require language and are not specifically of the artworld.

This example is a case of relatively successful understanding. But Scott is a good student (how many have read Remarque?) and even he struggles with the question of beauty. Scott's remarks are clear enough to show what resources he has to draw on. I could easily cite the reaction of other students who cannot understand this same work and who call it, in various ways, stupid or ugly. They cannot call on

at least one of the two resources Scott reveals: the idea that a work
need not be pleasant or the empathy for suffering structured (in his
case) by Remarque.

Another example comes from a recent paper by Koroscik.[25] She
recounts how, when a student in junior high school, she was taken to
see Seurat's *La Grande Jatte* in the Chicago Art Institute. She was
impressed by the dots with which it is painted and she stared hard at
them. She was impressed by how many dots there are and what care
it took to paint them. But she did not see them as meaningful. She
quotes Nochlin as saying about the style:

[The] historical presence of the painting is above all embodied in the notorious
dotted brushstroke—the petit point—which is and was the first thing
everyone noticed about the work—and which in fact constitutes the
irreducible atomic particle of the new vision. For Seurat, with the dot,
resolutely and consciously removed himself as a unique being projected by a
personal handwriting. He himself is absent from his stroke. . . . The paint
application is matter-of-fact, a near- or would-be mechanical reiteration of the
functional "dot" of pigment. . . . In these machine-turned profiles, defined by
regularized dots, we may discover coded references to modern science, to
modern industry with its mass production, to the department store with its
cheap and multiple copies, to the mass press with its endless pictorial
reproductions.[26]

Nochlin, in short, interprets the work as an ironic comment on the
industrial revolution (as well as on the puritan joylessness of a Parisian
bourgeois Sunday afternoon in the park at the turn of the century).
Meantime Koroscik and her peers knew no better than to stare at the
dots and, knowing that they did not understand them, to stare still
harder. She says that

students might fail to see that the dots in Seurat's painting contribute to its
expressive meanings. Their knowing that the artist used Pointillism does not
reveal whether they see the connection between the artist's technique and the
expressive meanings. In my own case, I knew that Seurat used Pointillism, but
I did not understand the concept of Pointillism nor did I grasp any meaningful
relation between Pointillism and the "dot painting" made in my junior high
art class.[27]

Notice the wealth of ideas referred to by Nochlin in her
interpretation. These ideas are culturally and historically specific and
cannot be taken for granted among our students, or even among art
teachers. They are required to see the work meaningfully and are
available only through language. It is no use staring harder at the dots.

A second issue may be mentioned more briefly. It is that, while perception may be thought of as an individual achievement, understanding is necessarily social. Perception can easily be conceived of as the interaction of a lone subject with a lone artwork. But when one introduces the notion of interpretation, one makes reference, if only implicitly, to a social group and its culture. This is a corollary of the fact that interpretation requires the use of language. Language is transparently a social creation. No lone individual could create or sustain a language by herself. For language is related to the life-world, which is the group's way of life, and its changes reflect changes in that way of life. To revert to the previous example, ideas like war, cruelty, and outrage are social and not individual creations, even though individuals must grasp them.

Our psychological models have notoriously been based on individualist models of cognition, with a very few exceptions, such as the work of Vygotsky. But art is obviously interpretive and social in character, and that again gives it the opportunity to assume a larger role within the school. Art can dramatize what is true of the whole school curriculum: the curriculum is a matter of interpretation and is made possible only by an active social group that has a common culture. Since this is obvious in the case of art, art education could be a leader in terms of changes in curriculum and instruction. Whereas the cognitive model was more difficult for the arts to digest than for other subjects, the adaptation to an interpretive model is less difficult.

Interpretive Aspects of Cognition in Other Subjects

Interest in students' interpretive abilities shows up in research on teaching other subjects. It occurs with the growing support for teaching for understanding in the various subjects, itself a reaction against the reductivist tests that come from our behaviorist legacy. In my view, teaching for understanding, if it survives, will inevitably become teaching for interpretive ability, though this may take a while.

The most plausibly parallel case is the whole language approach to teaching language. I will mention it briefly just because it is so plausible. The idea is that one learns language best by focusing on the meanings it carries, rather than on the symbol system itself—the letters, words, sentences. The approach focuses students' attention on content, expecting that they will learn the symbol system as they wrestle with the meanings it embodies, and they will do it with a more complex understanding. It also requires students to translate meanings between different situations and modalities of use. If students read a story, they are asked to talk about it; if they tell a story, they are asked to write it. They may be asked to create, alter, critique, or compare stories. They may also be asked to discuss a visual illustration, or to make one. Each of these transformations requires students to put meanings in the context of a different network of ideas and skills, to think them through again both in the terms of the medium and in the terms of more general assumptions and understandings of the world, and with these two sets of terms interacting. In short, students must each time make an interpretation.

But the example that is perhaps more interesting comes from the teaching of mathematics. Mathematics and art appear to many people to be at opposite ends of a number of continua, including the continuum of vulnerability to talk about postmodernism and hermeneutics. So it is of interest that there is a movement toward the teaching of mathematics for understanding, much of which touches on interpretation. A recent study of the efforts of the State of California to reform the teaching of mathematics summarizes current criticisms of the way mathematics is often taught:

Mathematics teaching in most elementary classrooms emphasizes rules, procedures, memorization, and right answers. . . . Mathematics is presented as calculation. . . . "Problem solving" most often means symbolizing and calculating routine word problems. . . . While many students are able to perform basic arithmetic calculations, few are able to reason about mathematical questions or to solve even moderately complex problems.[28]

The authors go on to describe what they would prefer teachers to do:

Instead of asking them to memorize algorithms for solving time-speed-distance problems, for example, teachers should help students to figure out how to turn a story about traveling from New York to Chicago into a mathematically solvable problem. Instead of helping students translate "how many more miles" into minus signs or to convert hours methodically into minutes, teachers should help students make and interpret their calculations in the meaningful context of the travelogue itself. . . . Rather than relying exclusively on symbolic representations, teachers and students would use blocks, fractions bars, beans and pictures and diagrams of many different sorts to represent their mathematical ideas. Students would talk much more in mathematics classes. . . . They would be working together, filling the air with ideas about how to solve problems, about what made sense, and why it made sense.[29]

Although there are important differences, this is intriguingly analogous to the situation in art. The educational paradigm is certainly cognitivist. But an emphasis on the medium of calculation has resulted more in the mastery of skills than in understanding. Students too often wind up knowing how to work problems but not how to understand them. The reforming advice is to get students to relate problems to what they commonsensically know about the world, to put them into language, to talk them through with their peers. The point is that students will think better in the symbol systems of mathematics if they think in more than those symbol systems, if they translate back and forth from ordinary language, and if they learn through social interaction.

Implications for Curriculum and Assessment

In summary, I have argued that our cognitive paradigm has served us well in the arts. It has encouraged us to teach our students to think well in a medium and to perceive the qualities of artworks. It has given us a useful way of understanding the value of studio work and of aesthetic experience.

However, it has not given us a good way to understand the value of thinking about art with language. Yet changes in both the artworld and the culture increasingly require artistic and aesthetic work to be linguistically based if it is to be intelligent. Artworks increasingly present difficulty for perception alone, even for perception informed by a knowledge of art history. The cognitive movement appears to have taken for granted things about art that we no longer can: an established ability to connect artworks with multiple cultural, political, religious, and personal threads of meaning deriving from both an artworld in particular and a lifeworld in general. This ability can only be secured through an interpretive interplay between language and the art medium. Therefore we have to find a model of cognition that allows a legitimate place for thinking in language as well as for thinking in the art medium. This model is the model of interpretation.

What would this mean in practice? It would be pointless for me to speak in any but the most general terms. With respect to curriculum, we would be careful to relate studio work to critical and thematic discussions. We would relate it also to the study of artwork from around the world. We would build into the curriculum a good deal of background material from both the artworld and the lifeworld. Much of this would be of a cultural and cross-cultural kind, with an emphasis on the ideas that connect culture with art as well as on the ways art can transcend culture.

Instructionally, there would be emphasis on making sense of artworks, including students' works. There would be more situations where students discuss and debate with peers their interpretations of works and the contextual connections that are important to them. Studio work would be focused on solving problems identified during class discussions. As in mathematics classes, "students would talk much more in [art] classes. . . . They would be working together, filling the air with ideas about how to solve problems, about what made sense, and why it made sense." There would also be cultivation of a reflective awareness of the kinds of thinking and talking involved, of problems of interpretation, of the connections of art with culture, and so forth.

Assessment of student learning would become more common and more useful. This is a crucial matter for art education. Obviously, an interpretive approach would focus on the assessment of students' understandings. We would try to assess both the particular understandings of artworks that students acquire through instruction and also how their interpretive abilities in general develop. This would require a multiplicity of kinds of data—about students' backgrounds, about artworks and art traditions, about instructional approaches, about kinds and levels of understandings—collected over a period of time. In other words, assessment itself would have to be heavily interpretive, and for this reason would probably be used as much for diagnostic as for summative purposes. It might best be locally devised and administered in order to respond to local circumstances affecting curriculum. At the same time, we need some concrete examples of assessment and some abstract models, and some notion of the important dimensions and kinds of understandings we should be assessing. This is something one might have expected the cognitive paradigm to be good at, but it has so far failed to make much difference with regard to assessment.

In terms of research, we would be more interested in students' interpretive abilities, in what they understand and say about art as well as what they can do in the terms of the medium. We would be especially interested in the relationships between their abilities in an art medium and in language. We would not think of these as two separate abilities but as two ways in which one understanding can be manifested. And we would be interested in the way students understand different art traditions and how their own cultural background affects their understandings. Cross-cultural variations of understanding would be an important topic for research, being, among other things, an obvious site for the study of the social character of learning. As important as anything else would be an acceptance of the fact that what we do, as psychologists and researchers, is also interpretive in character. If what we are finally interested in is the meanings children grasp, then we must ourselves interpret them, as we study their artworks, choices, explanations. We must not continue to allow the dream of scientific objectivity to blind us to the fact that we as researchers are also making interpretations.

Looking backwards from the 1990s, the changes brought about by the cognitive approach appear as much evolutionary in character as revolutionary. In the same way, I believe a more interpretive approach implies only modest further changes in the cognitive paradigm: an uncovering of some of the assumptions on which it stands and an expansion of the modalities within which it works. Adaptation is the way paradigms and other forms of life maintain their viability.

NOTES

1. David R. Olson, *Cognitive Development* (New York: Academic Press, 1970).

2. Claire Golomb, *Young Children's Sculpture and Drawing: A Study in Representational Development* (Cambridge, MA: Harvard University Press, 1974).

3. David H. Feldman, *Beyond Universals in Cognitive Development* (Norwood, NJ: Ablex, 1980).

4. Vernon A. Howard, *Artistry: The Work of Artists* (Indianapolis: Hackett, 1982).

5. David N. Perkins, *The Mind's Best Work* (Cambridge, MA: Harvard University Press, 1981).

6. The work of Project Zero has been summarized and reviewed in a number of places. One recent account is a special issue of the *Journal of Aesthetic Education* 22, no. 1 (Spring 1988).

7. Nelson Goodman, *The Languages of Art*, 2d ed. (Indianapolis: Hackett, 1976).

8. Howard Gardner, Vernon Howard, and David Perkins, "Symbol Systems: A Philosophical, Psychological, and Educational Investigation," in *Media and Symbols: The Forms of Expression, Communication, and Education*, ed. David R. Olson, Seventy-third Yearbook of the National Society for the Study of Education, Part 1 (Chicago: University of Chicago Press, 1974).

9. For a review and bibliography of Project Zero's work on style, see Jean Rush and Jessie Lovano-Kerr, "Research for the Classroom: An Ecological Impact Statement," *Art Education* 35 (March 1982): 11-15.

10. See, for example, R. Walk, "Concept Formation in Art: Basic Experiment and Controls," *Psychonomic Science* 9 (1967): 237-238.

11. Howard Gardner, "Children's Sensitivity to Painting Styles," *Child Development* 41 (1970): 813-21.

12. Howard Gardner, "The Development of Sensitivity to Figural and Stylistic Aspects of Paintings," *British Journal of Psychology* 63, no. 4 (Fall 1972): 605-615.

13. Dennie Wolf, "Child Development and Different Cognitive Styles," in *Issues in Discipline-based Art Education*, Seminar Proceedings (Los Angeles: Getty Center for Education in the Arts, 1987).

14. Howard Gardner, *Frames of Mind: The Theory of Multiple Intelligences* (New York: Basic Books, 1983).

15. A good account of the history is found in Ralph A. Smith, "The Changing Image of Art Education: Theoretical Antecedents of Discipline-based Art Education," *Journal of Aesthetic Education* 21, no. 2 (Summer 1987): 3-34.

16. Ralph A. Smith, *The Sense of Art: A Study in Aesthetic Education* (New York: Routledge, 1989), p. 36.

17. Ibid.

18. Ibid., passim.

19. Arthur Efland, "How Art Became a Discipline: Looking at Our Recent History," *Studies in Art Education* 29, no. 3 (1988): 264-274.

20. Charles Taylor, "Interpretation and the Sciences of Man," *Review of Metaphysics* 25, no. 1 (September 1971): 3-51. Reprinted in *Interpretive Social Science*, ed. Paul Rabinow and William Sullivan (Berkeley: University of California Press, 1979, 1987).

21. Taylor, "Interpretation and the Sciences of Man," in *Interpretive Social Science*, ed. Rabinow and Sullivan, p. 33.

22. Arthur C. Danto, *The Philosophical Disenfranchisement of Art* (Cambridge, MA: Harvard University Press, 1981), p. 39.

23. Arthur C. Danto, *The Transfiguration of the Commonplace* (Cambridge, MA: Harvard University Press, 1981), pp. 1-2.

24. The quotations from students' conversations about artworks are taken from Michael J. Parsons, *How We Understand Art* (New York: Cambridge University Press, 1987).

25. Judith Koroscik, "Novice-Expert Differences in Understanding and Misunderstanding Art and Their Implications for Student Assessment in Art Education" (Paper presented at the Annual Meeting of the American Educational Research Association, Boston, 1990).

26. Linda Nochlin, "Seurat's *Grande Jatte:* An Anti-Utopian Allegory," *Art Institute of Chicago Museum Studies* 14, no. 2 (1989): 133-53. Quoted in Koroscik, "Novice-Expert Differences in Understanding and Misunderstanding Art," p. 9.

27. Koroscik, "Novice-Expert Differences in Understanding and Misunderstanding Art," p. 12.

28. David K. Cohen and Deborah Ball, "Policy and Practice: An Overview," in *The Effects of State-level Reform of Elementary School Mathematics Curriculum on Classroom Practice*, ed. David K. Cohen and Penelope Peterson (E. Lansing, MI: College of Education, Michigan State University, 1990), p. 2.

29. Ibid.

Section Three
LEARNING AND TEACHING FOR AESTHETIC KNOWING

The Cognitive Revolution: Consequences for the Understanding and Education of the Child as Artist

JESSICA DAVIS AND HOWARD GARDNER

The Child as Artist: Romance or Reason

The vision of the child—indeed every child—as the prototype of the artist is not a recent concept; but a regard for children's art as having aesthetic value is primarily a twentieth-century phenomenon. With artists like Klee, Kandinsky, and Picasso emulating the simplicity and power of childlike images, psychologists, philosophers, and educators have taken heed. These scholars look to children's art not only for its honest and direct expression of children's understanding of the world, but also for its aesthetic content. Therein they find the seeds of aesthetic perception and production that flower in the work of the professional artist. When embraced by nineteenth-century commentators, the view of the child as artist may seem a romantic perspective. When children's art is taken seriously by twentieth-century scientists, the perspective assumes a different hue.

The "brute facts" about child art have not changed in the century and a half of adult looking. The drawings that aesthetician Corrado Ricci collected from the elementary schools of Bologna for his 1887 book, *L'Arte dei Bambini*, could appear in a book on children's drawing today. What has changed is scholars' and researchers'

Jessica Davis is with Harvard Project Zero, Graduate School of Education, Harvard University. Howard Gardner is Co-director of Harvard Project Zero and Professor in the Graduate School of Education, Harvard University.

thinking about these childhood products. This revision is largely the result of the far-reaching change in the way that researchers think about human action and human thought, a change epitomized by the cognitive revolution of the past forty years.

In this chapter we draw on the visual arts for examples, but the story we tell could be broadened to include various art forms. We begin with a description of some of the brute facts, that is, examples of the constant phenomena that constitute early artistic behavior and invite different interpretations. Next we consider the main tenets of the cognitive revolution that has transformed our conception and enhanced our understanding of that behavior. We review the impact of this new way of thinking on aesthetics, and on the investigation of child art, as well as upon general and aesthetic education. In conclusion, revisiting the brute facts, we reconsider the precognitivist perspective in terms of the insights these recent changes in thought have yielded.

The "Brute Facts":
Early Artistic Behavior Then and Now

In 1924, when two-year-old Everychild first began to draw, there was little space between child and drawing. Because the drawing of a train was made by the marks left by a crayon chugging and whistling as Everychild dragged it down the tracks, it was hard to separate the process of drawing from a product that could rightfully be called a "drawing." Gradually focusing attention more on the marks themselves, Everychild seemed to find his or her train in tangles of marks which appeared to others as scribbles. The scribbles soon became differentiated into separated forms which were later incorporated into narrative schemes. Everychild's interest in trains persisted as a fixed theme; certain combinations of marks persisted as fixed schemes, but their realization altered with further development.

By the time Everychild was five, the trains had faces and the drawings glowed with the sort of energy and expression that characterize genuine works of art. With the school years, however, Everychild's drawings became more constrained. The schemes employed followed conventional rules and the symbols used were shared by school-aged peers and by the more general culture. By age nine, Everychild's drawings were hard to distinguish from those of another child in the class; and by age twelve, Everychild had abandoned drawing entirely. Either Everychild proved inadequate to the mandates of the domain; or the domain proved inadequate to Everychild's mandates for expression. Whatever the reasons, the trajectory from complete immersion in the process of drawing to complete disassociation was the prevailing progression in the 1920s; and it remains the prevailing progression today.

In 1924, the pioneering developmental psychologist William Stern explained Everychild's behavior by evoking the well-worn distinction that children draw what they know, not what they see.[1] Thirty years later the gestalt psychologist of art Rudolf Arnheim would say as easily that children draw what they see.[2] Different understandings of seeing and knowing, of perception and representation, account for their different perspectives.

Along the same lines, in Stern's interpretation of children's early scribbling as an outlet for motor energy, he considered scribbling to be related to drawing as babbling was to speech—the necessary preliminary for the intelligent manifestation of the behavior. The modern student of children's drawings, Rhoda Kellogg (who in 1966 identified twenty basic categories of scribbles)[3] would agree that children's earliest drawings are more exploratory than purposeful. However, more recent considerations of the intricacies of intention inform the notion of "preliminary," and question the claim of "purposelessness."

Stern observed that by the age of four, many children name their presentations. The act of naming presentations after they have been completed is nowadays given the title of "romancing." Implicit in this nomenclature is an *as if* agreement. By assumption, children have not intended to represent anything in particular in their drawings. However, they have begun to understand that drawings are representational and are therefore willing after the fact to entertain and assert comparisons between their scribbling and objects in the physical world *as if* they had been intended. Stern saw the phenomenon as a precursor to the accomplishment of drawing with mimetic purpose. Contemporary cognitive psychologists, considering the same activity in terms of symbolic development, regard it as an accomplishment in its own right.

At the age of five, Stern's child seems to have a definite object in mind from the first mark that is placed on the page. This is, for Stern, the beginning of intelligent drawing: "actual drawing/real presentation"; and the start of the final stage of drawing that will satisfy the child: the "schematic stage." At the schematic stage, Stern's child renders "clumsy" but recognizable schemes with little regard for attractiveness or accuracy. It is later in the school years "that we find then the higher stages of development when efforts are made to reproduce what is apparent to the child's power of vision."[4] Stern cautions adults from applying an aesthetic point of view to the younger child's graphic play. It is an expression of inner experience which is soon to become available only to the few who are also able to master the aesthetic achievement of more accurate depiction of the objects represented in drawing. A different gloss of the term "aesthetic" recognizes aesthetic prowess in the same drawings Stern seeks to protect from aesthetic consideration.

The early stages have worn different titles. Art educator Viktor Lowenfeld identified them as "scribbling," "schematic," and what he called "dawning realism/the crisis of preadolescence."[5] Henry Schaefer-Simmern's stages of "visual conception" described the same progression as a natural unfolding from the first simple structures of form (as undifferentiated) to more complicated ones (differentiated).[6] Withal, it is the definition of the terms used in the dialogue between theorists of then and now which has changed; the marks young children put on paper have not.

As Stern describes it, the progression from scribble, to schema, to real presentation, to drawing as an activity reserved only for the talented, suggests forward linear development in which the behavior appears, rises, peaks, and disappears (except for the artistically talented who continue the linear progression). A cognitivist perspective can see the same trajectory as the beginning of U-shaped development in which the behavior appears, declines, apparently disappears, and reappears in adulthood (but only for the artistically persistent minority). Where realistic drawing in which one attempts to represent what one literally sees may once have been regarded as a step closer to the work of artists, contemporary cognitive psychologists can just as easily see it as a step away. The new vision perceives more similarities between the convention-free drawings of the youngest children and the work of artists than either shares with the drawings of older children, whose efforts are dictated by the conventions Stern respects.

A recognition of alternative criteria and an awareness of underlying aesthetic processes as intelligent manifestation of the behavior even for the youngest child are examples of the differences in thought that impact modern psychologists' interpretation of the very same development. Three issues of constant behavior emerge as apt for reconsideration with a cognitivist lens: (1) the scribbling of the youngest children; (2) the representational drawing of school-aged children; and (3) the overall progression from undifferentiated to differentiated form to a cessation of drawing activity for most children.

A Sketch of the Cognitive Revolution: The First Generation

During the 1920s and 30s, American psychology was dominated by the view that is usually called behaviorism. As a reaction against the fuzziness of accepting introspective accounts as scientific data and global philosophical notions like "will" as motivations for human action, behaviorism's focus on observable behavior promised psychology the starch and clarity of real science. The behaviorist lens was focused from outside in: individuals were reflectors of their environment which served as the determinant of their ability to behave and to learn. Accordingly, such "inside" activities as planning, problem solving, or constructing and operationalizing symbols were overlooked. Language was generally of little interest to such a perspective, much less anything that might be thought of as a language of art.

By the 1940s, it was becoming apparent to many observers that the behaviorist approach could not encompass some of the most important behavioral and mental phenomena. Studies of animal behavior had launched the discipline; but behaviorism would ultimately be limited to those behaviors that humans share with large portions of the animal kingdom. In contrast, it is the use of symbols in such powerful patterns as language that distinguishes human beings and determines their unique cultural heritage. Against a backdrop of behaviorist neglect of the rational problem-solving and imaginative capacities of human beings, the stage was set for the entrance of the cognitive revolution.

While it could already be discerned in the years after the second World War, the cognitive revolution was not truly launched until the mid-1950s. At that time a generation of researchers documented the limits of the behaviorist approach and proposed an alternative conception inspired by the advent of the digital computer. Indeed, it was the pioneering computer scientists Herbert Simon and Allen Newell[7] who introduced the electronic computer as both the model of what was known about the way human thought proceeded as well as a testing ground for the investigation of such intelligent functions as problem solving and logical reasoning. Where behaviorism had focused on visible response to stimuli, the cognitive revolution raised the curtain on the processing (the receipt, storage, manipulation, and issuing) of information which transpired largely out of sight, inside the individual's head or in the internal mechanism of the computer.

Psychologist George Miller's proposal that short-term memory could retain a limited number (approximately seven) of discrete entries exemplified the new approach.[8] Attention was being newly turned to perception, conceptualization, complex problem solving, and language acquisition. Disregarding the behaviorist emphasis on the environment as all powerful, linguist Noam Chomsky introduced the notion of an inborn "language acquisition device" which was destined to unfold *regardless* of specific cultural stimuli and environmental interaction.[9]

Two core assumptions and three methodological features of cognitive science serve as points of entry to the major tenets of that movement. One core assumption is that the computer serves as a relevant model of human thinking, that is, that the computer shapes our understanding of internal processes of thought. The other is that "for scientific purposes, human cognitive activity must be described in terms of symbols, schemas, images, ideas, and other forms of mental representation."[10] Representation can be understood as what cognitive psychologist Jerome Bruner has called "objective" representation. This is the mental machinery which constitutes (knowledge that— declarative knowledge) or allows (knowledge how—procedural knowledge) thought. Objective representation should be distinguished from what Bruner calls the "medium employed."[11] This is the representation of a referent or concept by a symbol, image, or action to oneself or in communication with others. The knowledge reflected in a child's drawing is an example of the first understanding of representation (objective); the drawing itself is an example of the second (medium employed).

The first methodological feature which can be attributed to cognitive science is a deemphasis of context and of affect. Regarding context, Chomsky's position on the environment represents an extreme example of deemphasis; the language acquisition device needs but a little "trigger" from the environment. But deemphasis need not imply disassociation. Although the cognitive or *knowing* function is often contrasted with the affective or *feeling* function, philosopher Israel Scheffler cautions against their disassociation which threatens to "mechanize science" while it "sentimentalizes art." Instead, Scheffler maintains that "emotion without cognition is blind and cognition without emotion is vacuous."[12] Significantly, the recognition that art can be viewed as a cognitive process—a most important result of the cognitive revolution—does not separate art from emotion. Rather it *emphasizes* the role of the intellect in making and perceiving art, perhaps even in the aesthetic achievement of expression of emotion.

Two methodological features remain. One is the interdisciplinary approach which has been demonstrated by our discussion so far. We have mentioned Bruner and Miller, who are psychologists; Scheffler, who is a philosopher; Simon and Newell, who are computer scientists; and Chomsky, who is a linguist—and all of them contributors to a cognitive perspective. The remaining methodological feature is the rootedness of cognitive science in classical philosophical issues, foremost of which is the subject of knowledge. For example, consider how Plato's claim that all knowledge is recollected resonates in Chomsky's bold assertion of an inborn language acquisition device.

The cognitive revolution was not initially framed in terms of developmental considerations, but it had a strong supporter within the developmental ranks in the genetic epistemologist, Jean Piaget. Carrying out most of his work before the advent of the computer, Piaget did not devote much attention to computer-related issues. However, he demonstrates the other prerequisites for cognitive science which we have described. Piaget's child moved from action upon objects to an abstract understanding of object (mental representation) upon which mental actions could be performed. Knowledge was hereby actively constructed by the child and organized into internal structures or versions of external reality known as schemata. Piaget's emphasis was on these internal structures rather than external context; on intellect rather than affect; and his background in biology, philosophy, and epistemology naturally spawned his interdisciplinary approach. His roots in classic philosophy were apparent in the Kantian concerns of his inquiry.[13]

Evoking distant images of Plato's philosopher king, Piaget's endstate is that of the rational logician. Children negotiate their ascent towards reason through (broadly) four major invariant hierarchical stages. They are: (1) the *sensorimotor* period in which experience is legislated through action upon objects; (2) the *symbolic* or semiotic period in which objects are represented even in their absence; (3) *concrete operations* in which reason is coordinated with physical objects; and (4) *formal operations* in which experience is mediated through abstractions upon which intellectual operations may be performed. Piaget conceived of drawing as a symbolic function en route to and in service of mental representation.[14] Accordingly, when he used drawing as a tool in his research, it was as an indicator of children's internal constructions of reality.[15]

Developmental psychology embraces the *orthogenetic* principle. According to its tenets, development proceeds from a state of "relative globality" to a state of increasing differentiation.[16] This principle is reflected in Piaget's progression. Indeed, Piaget's pre-operational child (stages 1 and 2) is unable simultaneously to maintain an awareness of a whole and a part. From this perspective, scribbling appears as manifestation of undifferentiated sensorimotor exploration of form, just as the detailed drawings of school-aged children reflect a more differentiated attention to and growing ability to negotiate the concrete physical parts that make a whole.

Another major early contributor to the cognitive developmental revolution was the Soviet psychologist Lev Vygotsky.[17] Where Piaget stressed the unfolding of mental structures with little attention to the details of the environment, Vygotsky and his colleagues highlighted the formative role played by social context. Social context provides the setting in which children learn (1) to give public form to their mental representations in service of communication with others, and (2) to internalize the cultural tools the world of others is presenting to them.

The orthogenetic principle takes a different form in the area of social context. Here, developing differentiation appears as a growing awareness of the difference between self and other and consequently of the points of view of various "others." This awareness may impact drawing as an awareness of audience—either deriving meaning from the child's effort or passing judgment upon it; and as an awareness of cultural conventions employed by others in the domain.

In this context, the cultural tool of language is regarded as the most important developmental acquisition. Language, informed by and indicative of the child's cultural history, is the primary mediator of the child's changing conceptualizations. It is a rule-governed symbol system which serves as a vehicle for the negotiation of complex and abstract meanings. For Vygotsky, drawing interacts with language as an intermediary process among thought, action, and speech. He saw the activity of naming presentations after they are drawn as an example of speech following action, that is, the child needs to observe the result of the action before identifying it. Action has guided the activity. Development ultimately allows speech to guide action (older children decide in advance what they will draw), enabling children to *plan*, a most important ingredient in problem solving.[18]

Further, drawing may be regarded as a graphic speech which interacts with verbal speech toward the development of written language. Vygotsky considered children's drawings to be "first-order symbols," or symbols which directly denote objects or actions. First-order symbols act as a bridge to an understanding of the second-order symbols of written words which stand for the spoken symbols for objects or actions. Children can learn to write by realizing that they can "draw" not only things, but also speech.[19]

A first generation of cognitive psychologists conceived the metaphor of the child, including the child as artist, as a problem solver. The notion of information processing invited an understanding of drawing and of visual perception in terms of constituent skills which can be modeled on a computer. The notion of mental representation anticipated a view of development in drawing in terms of the schemas involved, the increasing abstraction, and the dialectic between endogenous information-processing mechanisms and the constraints and opportunities of exogenous cultural tools.

A Second Generation of Thinkers

Building upon the strengths and responding to the limitations of first-generation theories, a second generation of cognitive developmentalists was spawned. Among other achievements, neo-Piagetians refined Piaget's notion of stage development into levels of micro and macro development.[20] They also dealt with the problem of Piagetian *décalage*, or the anomalous lack of synchronous development across cognitive domains. For example, décalage documents that, contrary to Piaget's expectations, a child who understood the concept of conservation in terms of liquid might not be able to apply that understanding to conservation of number. Neo-Piagetians have debated the possibility that décalage may be more rule than exception.[21]

Reflecting the refinements in computer simulation of the early 1970s, second-generation theorists also developed information-processing theories which featured more intricate descriptive detail.[22] They used the metaphor of acquisition, representation, and employment of information and posited the existence of a controlling executive function which would evaluate, revise, and constructively make use of the processed information.

A number of second-generation developmental researchers[23] have applied the information-processing approach to children's drawings.

Regarding drawing as an activity which offers the child the problem of reproducing three-dimensional vision in two-dimensional space, these theorists focus on issues of planning, sequencing, and deciding upon acceptable equivalences. An example can be found in Jacqueline Goodnow's investigation of children's drawings of slanted human figures. Goodnow had suspected that these curious presentations might be the result of an error in process, that is, the child began the drawing by accidentally tilting the axis of the initial circle. By providing children with the task of completing drawings that had been started with circles as faces and dots for eyes positioned at angles to the base of the page, she and Sarah Friedman demonstrated that the slanted torso et al. was indeed a solution to the problem presented by the researchers' initial configurations.[24]

As problem solvers facing this task, the children balanced the requirements (as perceived in the physical world) of spatial agreement within the parts of the body, and the convention (as established in the realm of drawing) of the base line of the drawing representing the ground. As can be seen in this example, an information-processing approach explores the way in which children respond and adapt to each element of their developing drawing as new information to be processed and mediated by a developing set of rules.

Another group of second-generation theorists developed an approach whose field of exploration was made up of the symbols children use in the construction and communication of meaning. A symbol-systems approach to cognition begins with a view of a symbol as any entity (material or abstract) that denotes or refers to any other entity. Numbers, words, and musical notes are all discursive symbols which *denote* reality, that is, they are in themselves arbitrary indicators for specific physical entities or concepts. Other equally important symbols, like drawings or gestures in dance, have meaning above and beyond the object or concept they denote; they are nondiscursive or presentational symbols and aspects of their own construction (e.g., the direction or shape of a line in a drawing) are integral to their containment and communication of meaning.

Symbols do more than denote or represent, that is, *refer*; they can *express* meaning as emotion as well. This expression is metaphoric. A symbol cannot literally be happy or sad; but when, for example, a drawing aptly expresses sorrow, we say metaphorically, "that is a sad drawing." Finally, symbols can function alone, or in concert with other symbols to construct a more intricate web or system of symbols. From such spidery webs are spun the products of symbolic functioning:

the drawings, the songs, the poems, the mathematical proofs, and the rituals which shape and define human culture(s)—the aesthetic form that humans strive to impose on experience.

Initial exploration in the symbol-system mode approached the various symbol systems in much the same way as Piaget had approached the Kantian categories of, for example, time and space. Indeed, early research into the impact of the media[25] and materials[26] on the construction of meaning through symbols contributed to an understanding of the various symbol systems as different "problem spaces," each offering unique challenges and potentials to the user of symbols. Accordingly, where Piaget had dismissed décalage as an anomalous aside, symbol-systems researchers became keenly interested in whether and when "knowing how" in one symbol system might predict performance in any other.

Early longitudinal studies[27] which explored the unfolding of referential and expressive competences in seven different symbolic media (narrative, symbolic play, drawing, clay, music, number, and gesture) addressed this issue. The results of this research suggested that there are indeed certain problems and solutions which are specific to particular symbol systems, for example, the problem of working out the basic relations to pitch that obtain in a musical scale. These were identified as "streams." However, certain other developing facilities, like the ability to vest symbols with analogic resemblance to their referents (analogical mapping), have implications across domains. These were designated as "waves." Addressing the difference in current between wave and stream, such research yielded an understanding of the child as artist on the one hand making untranslatable meaning out of graphic marks; and on the other, as a communicator, acquiring symbolic prowess of use across symbolic domains.

Symbol-systems research contributed to the development of the theory of multiple intelligences, which further illuminates a view of drawing as a cognitive process. This theory acknowledges that a vast range of human experience is not divorced from cognition as may have been supposed, but rather demonstrates highly distinctive cognitive forms. Seven different intelligences are posited as distinctive "frames of mind," potential cognitive resources for negotiating one's way (finding, creating, and solving problems) in different symbolic domains (problem-spaces). These intelligences constitute seven different sets of know-how: (1) linguistic; (2) musical; (3) logical-mathematical; (4) spatial; (5) bodily-kinesthetic; (6) intrapersonal;

and (7) interpersonal.[28] While other artistic activities draw on other intelligences, drawing is an activity which makes particularly heavy use of spatial and bodily intelligences. Although no intelligence is inherently aesthetic or nonaesthetic, an intelligence like linguistic intelligence emerges as aesthetic to the extent that it is used to present certain kinds of meanings (e.g., expressive ones) via certain devices (e.g., metaphor). For the most part, language used literally exhibits few aesthetic properties.

Whether through an information-processing or a symbol-systems approach, the cognitive revolution had generated a view of artistic behavior (here, drawing) as a cognitive process. Refinement of this vision required aesthetic criteria appropriate to the domain. The field of aesthetics provided these criteria by reconceptualizing the traditional dimensions of works of art through a cognitive lens.

The Effects of the Cognitive Revolution on Aesthetics Generally

In 1956, just as the cognitive revolution was getting under way, the art historian Sir Ernst Gombrich delivered the A. W. Mellon Lectures in Fine Arts at the National Gallery in Washington, D.C. Given what we know was "in the air" at that time, the title itself, *The Visible World and the Language of Art*, is evocative of cognitive science. The specification of a visible world suggests the presence of other sorts of worlds (perhaps even internal versions); just as the joining of hard-edged rule-governed language with soft-contoured free-formed art reflects the new perspective.

In these lectures, Gombrich introduced a new understanding of vision and knowledge. This understanding is embodied in the image Gombrich supplies of the museumgoer who, leaving the art gallery, suddenly takes in the landscape outside the museum "with a painter's eye, or more technically speaking, with a painter's *mental set*"[29] acquired in an afternoon of looking at paintings. Gombrich says that we apparently move in the history of art as we do in the drawing development of children: from representing what we *know* (concepts of physical items roughly symbolized in minimal pictorial schemes), to more faithful presentations of what we *see* (images as they are literally received by and recorded on the retina). He insists, however, that these later presentations are merely "modified schemes." The vision that is represented in, say, impressionistic art is no less conceptual than the early schematic drawings. What is happening is that artists—much like school-aged children—are learning from one another what is and is not acceptable encoding of three-dimensional vision (impossible to actually recreate on paper). Artists learn the language of art, a "vocabulary of forms," from the other artists whose work comprises the history of art; for their part, museumgoers learn it as they learn to "read" paintings.

This description of artistic representation as the negotiation of conceptualizations (the choosing of alternate means of encoding), reveals that cognitive science was already beginning to permeate the aesthetic terrain of art historians and artists. Indeed when Gombrich explains the process of receiving a visual impression by saying that "we react by docketing it, filing it, grouping it in one way or another,"[30] he sounds like a full-fledged information processor.

Three aestheticians, Ernst Gombrich, Rudolf Arnheim, and Nelson Goodman, emanating from the different disciplines of art history, psychology, and philosophy, reflect the productive exchange among disciplines that has been a hallmark of the cognitive revolution. Gombrich's assertion that all artistic discoveries are not of likenesses but of equivalences is echoed in Arnheim's claim: "There is no direct transformation of experience into form, but rather a search for equivalents."[31] Gombrich's assertion that all human communication is through symbols is echoed in Nelson Goodman's advice that his reader substitute the words "Symbol Systems" for "Languages" in the title of his seminal work, Languages of Art.[32]

In his classic essay, What Is Art?,[33] Leo Tolstoy expressed the widely shared view that in art the artist transmits felt emotion to the audience who through the work of art feels the artist's emotion as well. Goodman regards it as unnecessary to think an artist was sad just because his or her drawing expresses sadness, or to assume that a sad drawing will evoke that emotion in its audience. The emotion of sadness can be expressed and recognized without that trademark input or outcome. Goodman's understanding that the properties a symbol expresses are its own, like Arnheim's gestalt vision of the expressed phenomenon as actually present in the object of perception, places a greater emphasis on the symbol itself and describes a different relationship between artist and perceiver as co-constructors of meaning.

The artist is no longer seen as a messenger of meaning, wrapping emotion in a work of art for the recipient to experience upon receipt. Rather the artist is seen now as a maker of meaning, exploiting aspects of ordinary symbols in such a way that the recipient can actively recognize the construction of meaning therein. Goodman illuminates the distinction with the much cited example of a line on an electrocardiogram.[34] To the doctor reading this chart, the line is only significant as the reading on the ordinate and abscissa documents the functioning of the heart; but if that same jagged line is employed by an artist to express the emotion of anger, the angles, width, and direction of that line will have inextricable attachment to the meaning expressed. When such relative properties of the line (which the line will have in any case) are integral to the embodiment of meaning, Goodman considers the line to be relatively "replete." The same line which can be a technical descriptor on the cardiogram and an expressive statement in the artist's drawing demonstrates that symbolic functioning is transient and cannot be adjudged independent of context. As Goodman suggests in his essay, "When Is Art?" (the title clearly counterbalances Tolstoy's), a rock can be a rock when it is lying in a driveway, and a symbol of fortitude when it is exhibited in a museum.[35]

Another important aspect of the meaning of aesthetic symbols is conveyed by their composition. The composition of a drawing is determined by the placement of objects on a page in relation to each other and to the frame (the edges of the page) that surrounds them. Control of composition enables the artist to achieve clarity of statement or what Arnheim calls "unity" or balance. "In a balanced composition," Arnheim tells us, "all factors of shape, direction, location, etc., are mutually determined by each other in such a way that no change seems possible, and the whole assumes the character of 'necessity' in all its parts."[36] As is appropriate to cognitive science, we are reminded of the classical roots of this statement. Aristotle in *The Poetics* described unity of plot: ". . . the structural union of the parts being such that, if any one of them is displaced or removed, the whole will be disjointed and disturbed."[37]

The child as artist is now seen creating equivalences through such strategies as repleteness of line and control of composition. The notion of equivalences as accepted representations for what is known and for what is seen represents a new perspective on an old phenomenon. What has changed is the emphasis from performance itself to the process of performance; from the what to the when, from art as communication of emotion to art as embodiment of emotion through the use of symbols. The field of aesthetics informed cognitive developmental psychology's understanding of art as a cognitive process by affirming that the artist is equipped not only with an "eye," but also with a "mental set"; and by enumerating the components of that mental set as elements of line, composition, and expression.

Effects of the Cognitive Revolution
on Investigation of Child Art

Much of the investigation of children's art that was guided by a symbol-systems approach was carried out at Harvard's Project Zero. Founded by Goodman in 1967, the zero in the title represented a whimsical estimate of the state of "firm" knowledge about art education. Goodman had in mind a particular view of the arts as a cognitive domain and of symbolic functioning as the key component of aesthetic activity. Although our treatment here focuses particularly on drawing, the symbolic capacities explored ranged from composing musical melodies to making poetic metaphors. Researchers sought evidence for Piaget's stage-like development, but toward a different endstate than Piaget's mature logician. In fact, the strong similarities between children's early performances in music, metaphor, and drawing and those of professional musicians, writers, and artists grounded much of the early research in a serious comparison between child and artist. The qualities that Goodman had identified as distinguishing aesthetic from nonaesthetic symbols—like repleteness and metaphoric expression—and the artist's use of composition, which Arnheim had described, provided "adult art" criteria with which children's drawings could be analyzed. Were children actually exhibiting these aspects of nondiscursive symbolic functioning in their drawing? And perhaps as importantly, were young children *intending* to do so?

This question provides the first point of entry to our discussion of this research. It is followed by a few issues which we raised in our sketch of the cognitive revolution and which can be profitably conceptualized in terms of developing differentiation. We first raised the question of differentiation as the effect on drawing development of the challenge of balancing a growing awareness of the details of part with a primary knowledge of the whole. Next, we suggested that differentiation as a developing awareness of another individual's point of view might affect the child as artist both in cultural awareness and in aspects of communication. Finally, we touched upon the interaction between drawing and developing language. Research into children's drawing by colleagues at Project Zero and by cognitive developmentalists in other laboratories has informed each of these areas of inquiry.

THE QUESTION OF INTENTION

A great deal of Project Zero's early effort was directed toward the working out of empirical methods with which to implement research in a developmental psychology of the arts. The question of intention, for example, was approached through various experiments which tested the child's ability to perceive aesthetic properties in the work of others. The underlying hypothesis was that the ability to perceive aesthetic properties in other people's drawing is putative evidence of intention when those aesthetic properties appear in one's own. Accordingly, Carothers and Gardner gave children at different ages the task of completing drawings which were drawn in the style of children and which emphasized repleteness and expression as variations in line. The child's faithful reproduction of the line quality experimentally introduced was considered evidence of the ability to intentionally produce perceived aesthetic properties. Perception of the aesthetic property of expression, as measured through this vehicle, was negligible in the youngest children, but seemed to develop with age, peaking in preadolescence.[38]

In a study of expressivity, William Ives assigned children of different ages the task of drawing representational symbols as trees, and abstract symbols as lines, to express various emotions. Ives observed that children as young as four could depict expressive qualities meaningfully (that is, so that adult judges could perceive them accurately) in abstract form.[39] The combination of Ives's observations of production with Carothers and Gardner's observations of perception presents a curious portrait of the youngest children employing expressive strategies in their own work at a time when they do not perceive them in the work of others. This discrepancy suggests that the expressive quality of young children's drawing may be unintentionally produced; or that children do not, after all, attend to the same aesthetic properties in the works of others that concern them in their own.

Studies of composition also inform the question of intention. Winner et al. have explored Arnheim's description of the use of balance. In a study of children from ages four to ten, Winner found that balanced drawings are preferred to unbalanced ones at all ages, and that preschoolers have at least as strong a tendency toward balance as do older children, if not stronger.[40] Regarding perception and production of composition, then, it would seem that the balanced drawings of young children satisfy the aesthetic preference of the child and may therefore reflect an intentional choice.

Asynchronous development in middle childhood informs the issue of intention differently. As Carothers and Gardner have shown, children at this stage demonstrate increased perception of aesthetic properties like repleteness and expressivity, but at a time when their own work wanes in aesthetic appeal. One explanation offered is that older children's increased perception invites conscious intention to incorporate aesthetic elements into their own work, and the self-consciousness of the effort defeats it.[41] In any case, the development of a more differentiated perspective has been given the credit for increase in aesthetic perception even if it has been named the culprit for decrease in aesthetic production.

THE IMPACT OF DEVELOPING DIFFERENTIATION

Part from whole. Reflecting the orthogenetic principle, the youngest child's drawings may be seen as blessed with an undifferentiated vision of the whole. Lack of differentiation presumes some kind of connection. Connection manifests itself in early drawing between symbol and referent: there is a direct connection between first-order symbols and their referents. It even manifests itself between drawer and drawing. Children's lack of respect for the boundaries between themselves and their drawings can be seen in the example of the preschoolers who responded to Winner and Gardner's directive to draw a "scary house" by drawing a standard house "simultaneously growling at the experimenter in order to scare him."[42] The unity of composition and the fluidity of expression that characterize young children's drawing can also be seen as manifestations of this wholistic connection.

The older child becomes more sensitive to the boundaries that separate part from whole and child from drawing. Vision of the whole becomes obscured by concern with the details of part. Enumerating and outlining the details of physical form supersedes attention to the overall relationship. The number of buttons on a figure's shirt or the configuration of a belt buckle seems more important than the figure's placement on the page. Unity is hereby undermined and the resultant compositions appear disjointed and unbalanced. Self-consciously aware of the boundaries between child and drawing, the older child is inhibited by the challenge of harnessing that separate entity in service of faithful representation of his or her newly acquired more complex lens of vision.

The undifferentiated perspective which translates into powerful production for the youngest child conspires to delimit careful perception. The more differentiated vision of the older child translates into disjointed production while it admits the careful attention to detail that informs aesthetic perception. Developing differentiation appears as a mixed blessing, an acquisition that involves loss. The understanding it allows of a difference between self and other may be seen in the same ambivalent light.

Self from other. An awareness of "other" places the child in the center of a dialogue between culture and the individual. Ives and Gardner present a stage view of development in drawing as it is impacted by culture: I. The Dominance of Universal Patterns (ages 1-5); II. The Flowering of Drawing (ages 5-7); and III. The Height of Cultural Influences (7-12).[43] The child in middle childhood, in the thick of the societal microcosm of school, is producing the same smiley faces that appear on commercial packages—stereotypical schemas that seem to inhibit personal expression while they traffic in a familiar visual language. Project Zero researchers label this period as the "literal stage" in which children's art loses both its flavorfulness and its artistry. Where the preschooler's and the adult artist's drawing exhibits a disregard for convention (the preschooler may be lacking conventions while the artist may be rejecting them), the literal stage child's drawing is dominated by conventions.[44]

The differentiated perspective which attends to the culture of newly recognized others also entitles children to the awareness that other individuals will respond to their work and try to make meaning of it. Diana Korzenik asked children to make drawings for other children so that those other children could "read" the meanings assigned. She observed a developing facility to attend to the visual cues that an observant other would require of the drawer.[45]

Rosenstiel and Gardner explored the less charitable side of that concept in their investigation of the effect of critical comparisons upon children's drawings. In this study, children of different ages produced drawings before and after exposure to drawings that were more and less proficiently executed than their own. Exposure to less proficient drawings was considered a "confidence building" condition; exposure to more proficient drawings, a "confidence undermining" condition. It was found that younger children judged their own work more favorably, and that older children were more affected by the confidence undermining condition. The older children worked harder and improved considerably after exposure to the more proficient drawing.[46] Accordingly, the requirements of another point of view (either the needs of an audience receiving meaning, or the standards of a critic passing judgment) may also contribute to the decrease in unfettered expressivity in the work of older children.

Drawing as a language. Early classification according to prototypical features renders drawing an adequate symbolic language— an apt vehicle for young children's conceptualizations. Gardner and Wolf observed of children from ages three to five that "their conceptual world seems to be organized around basic objects or prototypes, kinds of generalized or modal examples that prove serviceable in representing (or standing for) a range of members of the category."[47] Very young children instinctively fulfill Arnheim's criterion for symbolic meaning: "the sensing of the universal in the particular."[48]

These early equivalences or first-order symbols, referring directly and wholly to their referents, resemble the symbols used by great artists in that they reflect universal understandings. With school, a more culture-specific sort of knowledge is acquired—the knowledge of second-order or notational symbols like numbers, notes, and written words. While first-order symbols may be "richer" and perhaps more telling, notational symbols may be "cleaner" and perhaps more precise.

Dazzled by the precision of these notational symbols, school-aged children engage their new expectations in attempting to apply the discursive aspects of spoken and written language to the nondiscursive realm of drawing. Drawing emerges as lackluster. This disenchantment with drawing was demonstrated in a study of artistic development across symbolic media in which children aged seven through twelve definitely preferred narrative over drawing as a more robust vehicle for the state of their skills and the mandates of their goal of detailed representation.[49]

If drawing has served as an efficient symbolic language for preschool children, the literacies developed in school seem to conspire to erase it. If, as Vygotsky suggested, drawing serves as a link between spoken and written language, the disenchantment of seven-through twelve-year-olds suggests that its work has been completed by middle childhood. Ironically, what children may view as the limitations of drawing as a language may be precisely what artists see as its potential: the construction of allusive symbolic meanings that are not translatable into any other language.

Symbolic Literacies: The Developmental
Portrait Research Has Provided

Development in the visual arts can be described in terms of two aspects of literacy or competency: *perception* and *production*. Perception includes the ability to distinguish the subject matter of a work, the artist's style, and aesthetic aspects like composition and expression. Under perception we also include conceptualization or reflection. This aspect of perception is comprised of an understanding of what is involved in a work of art (such as an individual producing it), as well as an ability to make judgments (as, for example, regarding value). Production is the making of an art (such as the portrayal of a subject) exhibiting stylistic nuances and aesthetic devices. These two dimensions frame the developmental portrait of the acquisition of literacy in the visual arts which synthesizes and further informs our discussion of research.

PERCEPTION

The first aspect of a work of art to which the young school child may attend is the subject matter. However, if that element is controlled or the child is asked to sort works according to style, preschoolers as well as six-year-olds have been found to be sensitive to style. With sufficient scaffolding (left on their own, they apparently show little interest in such pursuits), young children can also display sensitivity to the aesthetic aspects of expression, composition, and texture. In terms of conceptualization, however, young children have very limited understandings of art, thinking, for example, that works of art might be made by machines and increase in value according to size. By middle childhood, children seem to have a single standard for value: "photographic reality." As adolescents, they may reject those rigid standards and adopt the "relativistic view" that is retained by many adults.[50]

Housen[51] and Parsons[52] have researched aesthetic response as perception and as conceptualization, each uncovering quite similar developmental progressions through five stages. A brief overview of Housen's progression can be articulated in terms of the object of the viewer's attention at each stage: (1) the viewer attends to obvious stimuli like subject; (2) the viewer considers how the painting is made, its value, and how faithfully it replicates the natural world; (3) the viewer considers in which stylistic "school" the painting belongs; (4) the viewer explores the symbolism in the work as it relates to his or her own emotional experience; (5) the viewer conceives of the problems confronted and the solutions negotiated by the artist; the viewer may also actively integrate his or her analytic and emotional responses to the work. At stage five, one sees the merging of production and perception through the perceiver's identification with the producer as well as through his or her own active construction of meaning.

The finding of a five-stage sequence by two researchers offers strong support for a developmental sequence of distinct cognitive stages in aesthetic response. It appears that, with exposure to the domain, individuals become progressively more attentive to the aesthetic properties of individual works of art. They also become progressively more aware of the "others" who create works of art working in a domain that has tradition, context, and values. Finally, they also develop the ability to integrate their own personal aesthetic responses with the contextual knowledge they acquire. One quite reasonable explanation for the observed increase in all aspects of aesthetic perception is the development of skills in language which enable children to *tell* the researcher what they perceive and to have dialogue with the relevant culture in the course of conceptualization about drawing. Whether there are individuals equally sensitive yet less articulate is an important question.

PRODUCTION

As for production, the developmental portrait depicts the early enjoyment of scribbling as a mere prelude to early representation or the creation of graphic equivalents. Wolf and Perry credit this depiction to an emphasis on realistic portrayal as an endstate in drawing which limits our ability to view early drawing as anything but preparatory stages for this particular goal. Since realistic art is only one option in the aesthetic gambit of representation, they argue, this view seems especially shortsighted. Challenging the dismissal of the drawings of the youngest children (rampant symbolizers in other domains like play) as "purposeless pencillings," they reconceptualize drawing development as the acquisition of a repertoire of visual languages amongst which scribbling will persist as a resource.[53] Their "repertoire" view admits a similar approach to the less flavorful drawings of the literal stage child. Since future artists like Picasso and Klee wholeheartedly enjoyed a literal stage,[54] the literal stage, like scribbling, may be a time of resource acquisition in spite of its dip in aesthetic appeal. Unfortunately, however, scribbling gives way to a next step in drawing; and for the majority, the literal stage heralds its demise.

The portrait we have provided of literate production is shaped like a U:[55] young children and adult artists balanced at the high points, school-aged children hugging the floor with most of them exiting to the right, transforming the U to an L—perhaps "L" for literal as that Project Zero stage and as the condition of most adults—but certainly not "L" for literate as a competent reader and writer of the language of art. This portrait emerges from research intended to inform the new breed of art education which embraced a cognitive approach—an approach that had already found its way into general education.

Effects of Cognitive Revolution on General and Aesthetic Education

The cognitive revolution was introduced to the field of education at a conference in Woods Hole in 1959. Under the leadership of Jerome Bruner, a group of scientists, scholars, and educators responded to the Soviet challenge of Sputnik by gathering to discuss ways to improve science education in America. Cognitive researchers pondered various issues related to the acquisition and employment of knowledge; but the central issue of these discussions was rooted in Piaget. It was that academic disciplines had schema or *structures* that children could learn to ferret out and use—even across disciplines.

Separated by a decade of thought on the subject, two conferences were to art education what Woods Hole had been to science education: the Seminar on Research and Curriculum Development at Pennsylvania State University in 1965 and a conference entitled "The Arts, Cognition, and Basic Skills" in Aspen, Colorado, in 1977. A movement within art education embraced the Brunerian concept of structures within disciplines. Accordingly, scholars in the field wrestled with the challenge of deciding what these structures might comprise in art education, and how they would be implemented and reconciled with curriculum demands. Bruner had forged the gap between cognitive theory and educational practice, and art educators worked to redefine aesthetic education as the education of a process of thought.

As it had with reference to general education, the cognitivist approach introduced new questions to the field of art education, and new theoretical guidelines were needed for appropriate instruction. The notion of aesthetic thinking was paradoxical. Because it was a process of thought and a way of making meaning through symbols, aesthetic thinking was *like* other cognitive processes; but because the meanings it makes, like the symbols it uses, are unique, aesthetic thinking was also *different* from other cognitive processes. In which ways could aesthetic thinking be taught like other cognitive processes, and in which ways not?

The traditional distinction between a cognitivist and noncognitivist approach relied on a view of expression in art as a cut-off point between emotion and cognition. In fact the field of art instruction had been built in significant measure on a view of the artistic process as a feeling enterprise best accessed through free and untutored expression. However, the new vision was of something called "artistic knowledge"—a way of perceiving, thinking, and forming which was basic and therefore essential to education.[56] The cognitivist notion that literacy had to be gained in the symbolic languages of art resonated in the cry for skills and knowledge to serve art just as vocabulary and syntax served language. The new perspective left behind the "touchy feely" approach to art and invited (not without trepidation) the inclusion of art education in the "back to basics" movement. For researchers, the foremost issue was what was to count as the basics in art education; for practitioners, the question of who was qualified to teach the basics in art education was equally crucial.

In 1982 the Getty Center for Education in the Arts was formed to address such issues and to advocate art as a basic to children's education. The results of this effort and the recommendations that were to rock the boat of art education were presented in 1985 in a volume entitled *Beyond Creating: The Place for Art in America's Schools.*[57] The Getty Foundation recommended Discipline-based Art Education (hereafter DBAE) which attended to four content areas in art instruction. Understanding in art would result from studying and integrating four kinds of knowledge: (1) art production (knowing how—$\pi\rho\alpha\xi\iota\sigma$); (2) art history and culture (knowing about); (3) art criticism (knowing why); and (4) aesthetics (knowing of/within, as through formal aspects).[58] The general consensus among art educators of the early 1980s was that instruction and measurement of student achievement in the arts had historically focused on skill development, with not enough attention given to aesthetics, critical judgment, and cultural context. DBAE would right this imbalance.

In 1988, a group of art educators and researchers applauded the good intention but cited the "ominous flaws" and "potentially dire consequences" of the Getty effort in another volume: *Beyond DBAE: The Case for Multiple Visions of Art Education.*[59] Between these two bookends, a collection of publications presented dueling perspectives, most of which in some way reflected the tenets of the cognitive revolution. Was understanding in art to be skill-based ("knowledge how") or content-based ("knowledge that")? Would it incorporate the integrative nature of information processing, considering aesthetic understanding as a cognitive process of decoding, encoding, and reflecting? In that case, would each part of the process get equal time, or would the field decide which part was most important? Might there even be a way to focus on the interaction, that is, the discipline that grounded the entire process?

The paradox of aesthetic thinking persisted in the attempt to bridge the gap between theory and practice for DBAE. It was feared that DBAE would even be assimilated into a general movement in critical thinking, dissolving the particularities of the special knowledge that is art by focusing on such commonalties with other forms of education as rigor and an interest in excellence.[60] The promise that a cognitive view of art had held, that it might emerge as an essential ingredient in education, appeared as a double-edged sword. Would the recognition that art was as serious a subject as others dilute the differences which were as essential as equal status?

DBAE had introduced a debate that engaged the interest and resources of art educators and researchers. Proponents would explore means of proper implementation; dissenters would devise alternative implementations for a cognitive approach to art education. The spirited cross-fire is reflective of the profound effect that the Getty effort has had on those who think about art education and are now looking for ways to expose ordinary students to aspects of artistic knowledge heretofore reserved for advanced students of art. ARTS PROPEL is one result of this energy and direction.

ARTS PROPEL emerged in 1985 as a joint effort involving Harvard's Project Zero, the Educational Testing Service, and the Pittsburgh Public Schools.[61] The acronym is for perception, production, and reflection, with the final L for learning. Initially conceived to devise assessment instruments for measuring artistic learning in middle and high schools, ARTS PROPEL developed with an equal concern for curriculum modules as with their concordant assessment instruments.

Whereas in DBAE thinking and talking about art carry equal weight as the making of art, in PROPEL the emphasis is on process, primarily process as production which necessarily involves the cognitive components of perception and reflection. Two vehicles propel this process approach. The first is the *domain project*, a set of curricular materials which fit into a regular course. The domain project is a central production experience framed by reflection and perceptual activities, with assessment factored therein. The second vehicle is the *processfolio*. As opposed to the traditional portfolio in which artists collect their best final products in hopes of getting work or a show, the processfolio is a resource for students through which they can retain and review works in progress as tracers of their growth in symbolic activities. Consistent with the cognitive approach, the processfolio seeks to capture the phases in the development of a product or the solving of a problem and to encourage the student to reflect upon his or her processes of learning.

Just as the groundbreaking efforts of DBAE embraced the Brunerian concept of structures within disciplines, ARTS PROPEL encompassed many principles of cognitive developmental psychology. Withal, the cognitive revolution had clearly arrived and promised to remain on the permanent scene of aesthetic education.

Conclusion: What about Everychild?

The parents of Everychild of 1924 were heeding Stern's advice and not mistaking childhood efforts for aesthetic enterprises. The parents of Everychild of today are matting and framing the same efforts, taking Everychild to museums, and hanging Miro prints that look a lot like his or her drawings on the walls—all to assure Everychild that he or she is well on the way to becoming a literate member of the culture of the time. But Everychild of 1924 was making the same drawings as Everychild of today. How do the new tints in the lens we apply to that behavior transform what we see? To answer this question, we return to the three instances of constant behavior and revisit them with a cognitivist lens.

The scribbling. In his discussion of children's earliest marks, Stern reflects on the 1887 drawings we mentioned at the start: "It is not *arte dei bambini*, as Ricci calls it, not children's art. . . . For at first it is not only wanting in all aesthetic aim, but even in any tendency to imitate copies before them."[62] The change in thought effected by the cognitive revolution makes Stern's focus on imitation seem narrow, and his understanding of aesthetic aim limited. His dismissal of the child's activity as drawing what is known (valueless in comparison to drawing what is seen) assumes that what is "known" is of the physical object of representation. Such a claim belies the cognitivist understanding that the child's earliest drawings reveal a crucial understanding of what counts as a satisfactory symbol. A view of aesthetics as standards for beauty may dismiss the child's earliest marks, where a view of aesthetics as effective symbolic functioning will not.

In a cognitivist approach to drawing, the earliest scribbling may reflect the intelligent behavior of Piaget's earliest stage of sensorimotor intelligence—an exploration of physical form that will provide the groundwork for such processing of information as planning, sequencing, and solving spatial problems. It may serve in the acquisition of a facility with line variation—a useful graphic symbolic tool in a growing repertoire. And if it is excessive to suggest that the endlessly joined lines adults call scribbles are in fact apt symbolic representation of the young child's undifferentiated perception of experience, at least it must be acknowledged that the two-year-old is already a user of symbols.

The two-year-old who calls a crescent cookie a moon[63] deserves some credibility when asserting that what you thought was scribbling is really a picture of you. Designating this activity "romancing" suggests a lack of credibility. Naming the drawing after it is completed may express a different sort of intention than naming the object before it is drawn, but it is nevertheless reflective of an awareness that the marks on paper correspond to something in the world beyond them and that it is the child's decision as to what that "something" is. It is unlikely that a child sophisticated enough to have this understanding of both symbol and symbol user, when sitting down to draw, merely babbles on paper.

The child's activity of carefully regarding his or her own marks and "naming" them after the fact as the drawing's subject may even reflect the earliest stage of perception as active construction of meaning. Artists develop the meaning of their work by observing and responding to each mark made on the paper, deciding what next step has been necessitated by the last. Similarly, for perceivers of art, each new perception is determined and facilitated by the last.[64] Indeed the artist anticipates this process by identifying with a perceiver of the work, just as the perceiver comes to participate in the process by identifying with the artist.[65] This activity of the child, so cavalierly dismissed as romancing, could just as easily be described as early active participation in the dialogue between production and perception from which meaning is constructed. In a view of aesthetics as standards for symbolic functioning, any of the above interpretations reflects "aesthetic aim."

The representational drawings of school-aged children. Stern sees the schemes that older children develop in the school years as "real presentations" because physical reality is obviously being presented. In a view of drawing development in which representation is the end in view, the school-aged child who sits engaged in experimentation with variations of inky lines is considered less developed than the child who can produce the caricature of Mickey Mouse that most of the other children are struggling to perfect. A contemporary researcher would recognize the young experimenter, respecting his or her attention to the aesthetic potential of line.

Stern places the emphasis in aesthetics on reference, on the similarity that holds between the drawing and the physical object represented therein. A symbol-systems approach places the emphasis in aesthetics on the symbol itself, on the properties through which it embodies meaning above and beyond the object to which it refers. When the cognitivist approach of applying adult aesthetic criteria to child art is engaged, Stern's "real presentations" may appear lacking in the capture of such replete features as metaphoric expression and unified composition. While Stern celebrates the attention to details of real presentation that developing differentiation allows, cognitivists see it as a challenge to fluid expressive aesthetic functioning.

School-aged children's drawings reflect cultural conventions; and Stern's child is like an artist in deferring to convention. The cognitivist's child is like an artist in transcending them. Young children's connection to their symbolic output equips them with the disregard for boundaries that professional artists strive to achieve. The mastery of conventions by the professional artist is part of the process of acquiring a requisite "vocabulary of forms." Unfortunately, for the developing child as artist, the attempt to master conventions all too often marks the end of the conversation. Beginning with young children's drawings as the low starting point, the stereotypical schemes of middle childhood may have represented the closest Everychild of 1924 would come to real art. Today that starting point is reconsidered as a high period of creative flowering in which the young child intuitively employs many of the cognitive strategies that frame the artistry of the professional artist.[66]

The pivotal difference lies in the different understanding of perception and representation which the cognitive revolution has engendered. Once the preferred view of representation was of "imitation of external reality," a common standard attainable by whomever proved able. The cognitivist view of representation is of an internally constructed version of reality. By virtue of each child's individual perception, production, and reflection, each version represents a unique and valid enterprise. Where once perception was of the necessary physical details to render faithful presentation, now perception is seen as agent to mental representations which transcend the limits of physical reality. Stern's child is limited, making meaning instead of attending to vision; the cognitivist's child more closely resembles an artist by making meaning which incorporates visual perception into a larger whole.

Overall progression. The recognition of graphic symbolization as a means of constructing understanding is crucial in a view of Everychild's overall development in drawing (from universal forms to stereotypical schemes to cessation of the behavior); and of the appropriate aesthetic education for Everychild. The earliest drawings may be valued as first steps in an important process or devalued as a release of motor energy. The drawings of middle childhood may be valued as viable imitations or devalued as flavorless stereotypes. In either case, the Everychild of either era arrives at school enjoying graphic symbolization, and (unless artistically persistent) abandons the activity by adolescence. From Stern's perspective, this exodus is inevitable and of little consequence. Surely there will be artists among us, but they will be few and need to find their own way. From a cognitivist perspective, this exodus marks the abandonment of a way of understanding: a way of producing, perceiving, and reflecting upon meaning not accessed through any other symbol system.

The new view is of the birthright of Everychild to be educated as artist in order always to have access to those understandings that are exclusively extended through aesthetic symbols. Accordingly, educators are struggling to find the appropriate means to teach Everychild to explore the aesthetic potential of the symbol, to value nondiscursive symbols as well as discursive, and to learn the vocabulary of forms as artists come to know them—as part of an ongoing process. The cognitive revolution has entitled us to a view of graphic symbolization as a language in which all children may attain literacy. What in Tolstoy's day was regarded as a language of emotion is today regarded as a language of emotion and cognition. Expression, no longer exclusively viewed as the magical transfer of feeling over time and space, is now also seen as the realization of the possibility for human beings to make meaning out of everyday fare, to enlarge experience that is simultaneously felt and known and thereby given form.

A cognitive approach extends the province of graphic symbolization from representation on paper to representation of understanding.

This is a negotiated understanding, negotiated between two active constructors of meaning, the producer and the perceiver, who are often (as in the process of constructing a drawing) the same individual. In the end, the "when" of art is as dependent on perceiver as it is on producer.

The notion of perception as active construction of meaning has important educational implications. It is not just the child who will develop into a maker of art who will require the symbolic tools of literacy in the visual arts, but also the child who will develop into a maker of meaning through the literate "reading" of the aesthetic symbols of our culture. If education continues to disenfranchise Everychild from the artistic behavior she or he exhibits when arriving at school, the world will be a less artful place not for shortage of works of art produced, but for shortage of those experiences artfully transformed by aesthetic perception.

ACKNOWLEDGMENT. Research efforts described in this chapter have been generously supported by the Rockefeller Brothers Fund, the Rockefeller Foundation, and the Lilly Endowment. We thank the editors for their helpful comments throughout the preparation of the chapter.

NOTES

1. William Stern, *Psychology of Early Childhood Up to the Sixth Year* (New York: Henry Holt and Company, 1924).

2. Rudolf Arnheim, *Art and Visual Perception: A Psychology of the Creative Eye* (Berkeley: University of California Press, 1974, originally 1954).

3. See, for example, Rhoda Kellogg, "Stages of Development in Preschool Art," in *Child Art: The Beginnings of Self-Affirmation*, ed. Hilda P. Lewis (Berkeley: Diablo Press, 1966).

4. Stern, *Psychology of Early Childhood*, p. 370.

5. See Viktor Lowenfeld and W. Lambert Brittain, *Creative and Mental Growth*, 4th ed. (New York: Macmillan, 1964).

6. See Henry Schaefer-Simmern, *The Unfolding of Artistic Activity: Its Basis, Processes, and Implications* (Berkeley: University of California Press, 1947).

7. Herbert Simon and Allen Newell, "Simulation of Cognitive Processes: A Report on the Summer Research Training Institute, 1958," *Items* 12 (1982): 37-40.

8. George Miller, "The Magical Number Seven, Plus or Minus Two: Some Limits on Our Capacity for Processing Information," *Psychological Review* 63 (1956): 81-97.

9. See Noam Chomsky, *Syntactic Structures* (The Hague: Mouton, 1957).

10. Howard Gardner, *The Mind's New Science: A History of the Cognitive Revolution* (New York: Basic Books, 1958), p. 39.

11. Jerome Bruner, Rose R. Olver, Patricia Greenfield, et al., *Studies in Cognitive Growth* (New York: John Wiley and Sons, 1966).

12. Israel Scheffler, "In Praise of the Cognitive Emotions," in Israel Scheffler, *Inquiries: Philosophical Studies of Language, Science, and Learning* (Indianapolis: Hackett, 1986), p. 348.

13. See, for example, Jean Piaget, *The Child's Conception of Time* (New York: Ballantine Books, 1985), and Jean Piaget and Barbel Inhelder, *The Child's Construction of Space* (New York: Norton, 1948).

14. See Jean Piaget and Barbel Inhelder, *The Psychology of the Child* (New York: Basic Books, 1969).

15. See Piaget and Inhelder, *The Child's Construction of Space.*

16. Heinz Werner, "The Concept of Development from a Comparative and Organismic Point of View," in *The Concept of Development*, ed. D. B. Harris (Minneapolis: University of Minnesota Press, 1957), pp. 125-148.

17. See Lev Vygotsky, *Thought and Language*, ed. Alex Kozulin (Cambridge: MIT Press, 1987).

18. Lev Vygotsky, *Mind in Society*, ed. Michael Cole, Vera John-Steiner, Sylvia Scribner, and Ellen Souberman (Cambridge, MA: Harvard University Press, 1978), p. 28.

19. Ibid., p. 115.

20. See Annette Karmiloff-Smith, "Micro and Macrodevelopmental Changes in Language Acquisition and Other Representational Systems," *Cognitive Science* 3 (1979): 91-117.

21. See, for example, Robbie Case, Zopito Marini, Anne McKeough, Sonja Dennis, and Jill Goldberg, "Horizontal Structure in Middle Childhood," in *Stage and Structure: Reopening the Debate*, ed. Iris Levin (Norwood: Ablex Publishing Co., 1986), pp. 1-39; Kurt W. Fischer and Richard L. Canfield, "The Ambiguity of Stage and Structure in Behavior: Person and Environment in the Development of Psychological Structures," in *Stage and Structure*, ed. Levin, pp. 246-267.

22. See, for example, Robert S. Siegler, *Children's Thinking* (Englewood Cliffs, NJ: Prentice-Hall, 1986).

23. See, for example, Norman Freeman, *Strategies of Representation in Young Children* (London: Academic Press, 1980); Claire Golomb, *The Child's Creation of a Pictorial World: Studies in the Psychology of Art* (Berkeley: University of California Press, 1989).

24. See Jacqueline J. Goodnow and Sarah Friedman, "Orientation in Children's Human Figure Drawings: An Aspect of Graphic Language," *Developmental Psychology* 7 (1972): 10-16. See also, Jacqueline Goodnow, *Children Drawing* (Cambridge, MA: Harvard University Press, 1977).

25. Gavriel Salomon, *Interaction of Media, Cognition, and Learning* (San Francisco: Jossey-Bass, 1979).

26. David R. Olson, *Cognitive Development: The Child's Acquisition of Diagonality* (New York: Academic Press, 1970).

27. See Howard Gardner and Dennie Wolf, "Waves and Streams of Symbolization: Notes on the Development of Symbolic Capacities in Young Children," in *The Acquisition of Symbolic Skills*, ed. D. R. Rogers and J. A. Sloboda (London: Plenum Press, 1983).

28. Howard Gardner, *Frames of Mind: The Theory of Multiple Intelligences* (New York: Basic Books, 1983).

29. Ernst Gombrich, *Art and Illusion: A Study in the Psychology of Pictorial Representation*, The A. W. Mellon Lectures in the Fine Arts, 1956 (Princeton, NJ: Princeton University Press, 1960), p. 306.

30. Ibid., p. 297.

31. Rudolf Arnheim, *Toward a Psychology of Art* (Berkeley: University of California Press, 1966), p. 266.

32. Nelson Goodman, *Languages of Art* (Indianapolis: Hackett, 1976), p. xii.

33. Leo Tolstoy, *What Is Art?* (Oxford: Oxford University Press, 1930).

34. Goodman, *Languages of Art*, p. 229.

35. Nelson Goodman, "When Is Art?," in Nelson Goodman, *Ways of Worldmaking* (Indianapolis: Hackett, 1978), pp. 57-71.

36. Arnheim, *Toward a Psychology of Art*, p. 76.

37. Aristotle, *The Poetics*, trans. by S. H. Butcher (New York: Dover Publications, 1951), IX.5, lines 7-10.

38. Thomas Carothers and Howard Gardner, "When Children's Drawings Become Art: The Emergence of Aesthetic Production and Perception," *Developmental Psychology* 15, no. 5 (1979): 570-580.

39. S. William Ives, "The Development of Expressivity in Drawing," *British Journal of Educational Psychology* 54 (1984): 152-159.

40. Ellen Winner, E. Mendelsohn, G. Garfunkel, S. Arangio, and G. Stevens, "Are Children's Drawings Balanced? A New Look at Drawing: Aesthetic Aspects" (Symposium presentation at the meeting of the Society for Research in Child Development, Boston, 1981).

41. See Victor d'Amico, "The Child as Painter," in *Readings in Art Education*, ed. Elliot Eisner and David Ecker (Waltham: Blaisdell Publishing Company, 1966).

42. Ellen Winner and Howard Gardner, "The Art in Children's Drawings," *Review of Research in Visual Arts Education* 14 (1981): 18-31.

43. S. William Ives and Howard Gardner, "Cultural Influences on Children's Drawings: A Developmental Perspective," in *Art Education: An International Perspective*, ed. R. Ott and A. Hurwitz (University Park: Pennsylvania State University, 1984).

44. Elizabeth Rosenblatt and Ellen Winner, "The Art of Children's Drawing," *Journal of Aesthetic Education* 22, no. 1 (1988): 1-15.

45. Diana Korzenik, "Children's Drawings: Changes in Representation between the Ages of Five and Seven" (Doctoral dissertation, Harvard Graduate School of Education, 1973).

46. Anne K. Rosenstiel and Howard Gardner, "The Effect of Critical Comparisons upon Children's Drawing," *Studies in Art Education* 19 (1977): 36-44.

47. Howard Gardner and Dennie Wolf, "First Drawings: Notes on the Relationships between Perception and Production in the Visual Arts," *Perception and Pictorial Representation*, ed. C. Nodine and D. Fisher (New York: Praeger, 1979), p. 373.

48. Arnheim, *Art and Visual Perception*, p. 454.

49. S. William Ives, Jen Silverman, Hope Kelly, and Howard Gardner, "Artistic Development in the Early School Years: A Cross-Media Study of Storytelling, Drawing, and Clay Modeling," *Journal of Research and Development in Education* 14 (1981): 91-105.

50. See Howard Gardner, *Art Education and Human Development* (Los Angeles: Getty Center for Education in the Arts, 1990).

51. Abigail Housen, "Museums in an Age of Pluralism," in *Art Education Here,* ed. Pamela Banks (Boston: Massachusetts College of Art, 1987).

52. Michael Parsons, *How We Understand Art* (Cambridge: Cambridge University Press, 1987). See also chapter 4 in the present volume, where Parsons discusses children's understandings of artworks.

53. Dennie Wolf and Martha Perry, "From Endpoints to Repertoires: Some New Conclusions about Drawing Development," *Journal of Aesthetic Education* 22, no. 1 (1988): 17-34.

54. See David Pariser, "The Juvenile Drawings of Klee, Toulouse-Lautrec, and Picasso," *Visual Arts Research* 13, no. 2 (1987): 53-67.

55. See Howard Gardner and Ellen Winner, "First Intimations of Artistry," in *U-Shaped Behavioral Growth,* ed. Sydney Strauss (New York: Academic Press, 1982).

56. See Rudolf Arnheim, "Perceiving, Thinking, Forming," *Art Education* 36 (March 1983): 9-11. This issue of the journal, edited by Martin Engel, is twice as long as any preceding issue and represents a milestone in the course of the entrance of cognitive science into aesthetic education.

57. Getty Center for Education in the Arts, *Beyond Creating: The Place for Art in American Schools* (Los Angeles: Getty Center for Education in the Arts, 1985).

58. See Elliot Eisner, *The Role of Discipline-Based Art Education in America's Schools* (Los Angeles: Getty Center for Education in the Arts, 1987); Bennett Reimer, *A Philosophy of Music Education,* 2d ed. (Englewood Cliffs, NJ: Prentice-Hall, 1989).

59. Judith Burton, Arlene Lederman, and Peter London. *Beyond DBAE: The Case for Multiple Visions of Arts Education,* sponsored by the University Council on Art Education (North Dartmouth, MA: Peter London, 1988).

60. See Dennie Wolf's remarks in *Issues in Discipline-Based Art Education: Strengthening the Stance, Extending the Horizons* (Report of the invitational seminar sponsored by the Getty Center in Cincinnati, Ohio, May 21-24, 1987).

61. See Howard Gardner, "Zero-Based Arts Education: An Introduction to ARTS PROPEL," *Studies in Art Education* 30, no. 2 (1989): 71-83.

62. Stern, *Psychology of Early Childhood,* p. 369.

63. See Dennie Wolf, "Representation before Picturing" (Presentation at Annual Meeting of the British Psychological Association, 1983).

64. See Clifton Olds, "Wollheim's Theory of Artist as Spectator: A Complication," *Journal of Aesthetic Education* 24, no. 2 (1990): 25-29.

65. As in the highest stages described by Housen and/or Parsons, in which the perceiver, for example, considers the problems of production facing the artist. See Housen, "Museums in an Age of Pluralism" and Parsons, *How We Understand Art.*

66. See Jessica Davis, "The Artist in the Child: A Literature Review of Criteria for Assessing Aesthetic Dimensions" (Qualifying paper submitted to the Harvard Graduate School of Education, 1989).

CHAPTER VI

Aesthetic Learning: Psychological Theory and Educational Practice

DAVID J. HARGREAVES AND MAURICE J. GALTON

Introduction

The ways in which children and adults engage with the arts are diverse, individual, and extremely complex, and this poses formidable problems for psychologists who attempt to understand the underlying processes, as well as for educators who have to encourage and guide the participants. In this chapter we shall discuss the general issues in the specific context of the British education system, which is currently undergoing some radical changes.

The National Curriculum now being adopted in the United Kingdom is based on three "core" and seven "foundation" disciplines, and "art" and "music" are included in the latter category. An integral part of the rationale of the new curriculum is that children should be assessed at regular age intervals in as many subjects as possible. In the case of art and music, this raises issues with which philosophers, psychologists, and others have grappled for many years. How should a piece of art work be assessed—by an expert examiner, or teacher, or by the person who produced it? Can the creative aspects of the piece of work be assessed independently from the skills involved in its creation, and can the creativity of the artist be assessed outside the context of that particular piece of work?

We could formulate many more practical questions like these. It seems reasonable to expect that psychological and educational theory ought to be of some help in answering them, and there are some clear-cut theoretical questions with which they are inextricably linked.

David J. Hargreaves is a member of the faculty of the Department of Psychology, Leicester University, Leicester, United Kingdom. Maurice J. Galton is a member of the faculty of the School of Education at Leicester University.

Two of the most important are: Do age-related stages exist in aesthetic learning, such that we can tailor the curriculum to children's capabilities at each stage? Do generalized developmental changes take place across all art forms, or do specific developments occur such that each artistic domain must be considered in its own right? These two questions are interdependent, as we shall see later in this chapter.

We also need to be clear as to who is asking these difficult questions, and for what purpose. Academics, educational advisors, and administrators have a particular interest in the theoretical as well as in the practical questions; but this interest may well be quite different in character from that of the hard-pressed teacher who has to put theory into practice in the classroom. British teachers are currently mistrustful of the theoretical models being put before them, which they perceive as overly prescriptive, and so it is vital to take their views into account.

In this chapter we attempt to maintain a balance among three sometimes conflicting, sometimes complementary points of view: those of the psychologist, the educator, and the teacher. It will become apparent that the concerns of the first two are currently fairly disparate, but we shall argue that a bridge can be built between them by a careful and reflective consideration of the teacher's point of view.

We begin with the psychological viewpoint by reviewing some of the issues which must be considered in the proposition of any age-related account of artistic development. A Piagetian-style stage theory, incorporating some kind of functional coherence within stages, is almost certainly ruled out by recent theoretical and empirical developments. We shall nevertheless argue that psychological research in this area has now reached a point where it *is* possible to formulate a description of how children engage with the arts at different age levels, and the next part of the chapter is devoted to such a description.

We move next to the educational point of view in undertaking a broad review of the factors that have shaped children's aesthetic learning in British classrooms in recent years. We focus on the prevailing educational ideology and its influence on classroom organization and on assessment procedures. There follows a brief review of the findings of the relatively small amount of observational research carried out on aesthetic learning in British primary school classrooms (age 5-11 years). These findings are contrasted with findings from studies in the secondary school.

In the final part of the chapter we consider the ways we might start to build a bridge between psychological theory and educational practice. We argue first that a consideration of teachers' "working theories" of children's aesthetic development is a very promising starting point. We briefly describe our attempt to put this into practice at the University of Leicester in the DELTA project (Development of Learning and Teaching in the Arts). We conclude with a look at the directions future research might take.

The Psychological Perspective

COGNITIVE THEORIES OF ARTISTIC DEVELOPMENT

The major developments taking place in theoretical explanations of artistic behavior are those within the cognitive or cognitive-developmental approach. In the field of music learning, for example, Hargreaves and Zimmerman have undertaken a detailed comparative analysis of three recent cognitive theories of musical development and have concluded that the similarities among the theories are much more significant than their differences.[1]

One of the crucial questions that must be asked of such theories is the extent to which they deal specifically with developmental progression and in particular with the question "Are there stages in artistic development?" A great deal of thinking about this question is influenced by the predominance of Piagetian and neo-Piagetian stage theories. Piagetian theory postulates a series of discrete developmental stages which are qualitatively different from one another, which unfold in an invariant sequence with age, and which are functionally coherent in the sense that a specified process, or set of coordinated operations, is proposed as the basis for each stage.

There are a number of problems with traditional Piagetian stage theory as it applies to artistic development, and these have been extensively discussed elsewhere.[2] We shall not reiterate these problems here but will instead raise just two specific issues. The first concerns the distinction between *enculturation* and *training*. Piagetian stage theory implicitly describes how mental developments "unfold" with age. This is viewed as a natural process which occurs spontaneously in a given culture, without any conscious effort or direction. The problem with this view is that it pays very little attention to the external influences of teachers, schools, peers, and others. The effects of specific artistic *training* must be an integral part of any comprehensive theory.

Any description of the behavior to be expected at different age levels therefore can at best be only a rough and ready guide to the ages at which such behavior actually occurs in real life. Although modal ages may be set for changes which take place as a result of enculturation, these can easily be swamped by the powerful effects of specific training or experience. This is particularly applicable to a domain such as music, in which the effects of training can be very extensive and far-reaching. A musically gifted child who receives specialist instruction may effectively shortcut the normal processes of enculturation and display adult-like skills at a very early age, as is clearly shown in studies of musical prodigies.[3]

The second issue is closely linked with the first. The postulation of stages of development implies that there are generalized changes that occur across all artistic domains. Gardner has called this the "general-symbolic" view,[4] which has its origins in Piagetian stage theory and finds its clearest recent expression in Parsons's stage theory of the development of aesthetic experience.[5] In direct opposition to this is what Gardner terms the "medium-specific" position, according to which the developments that occur within different artistic domains—in drawing, writing, or in music—do so independently of one another. In this view, children's familiarity with the specific materials and skills involved in particular symbol systems exerts an influence on the course of artistic development that easily outweighs any generalized cognitive changes.

There is room for compromise between these two apparently opposing points of view. Although medium-specific developments with no parallels in other art forms clearly do occur, it is nevertheless possible to identify some common features across different art forms. Wolf and Gardner propose a series of four "waves of symbolization" in the first six years of life.[6] Briefly, these are a wave of enactive representation in infancy, a "mapping" wave in which dimensional relationships can be approximated at around the age of three, a "digital mapping" wave in which representation becomes much more accurate, and the eventual acquisition of cultural symbol systems by the age of five or six. This proposal is intended to complement rather than to contradict more detailed descriptions of medium-specific developments.

FIVE PHASES OF ARTISTIC DEVELOPMENT

We now extend and develop this approach by proposing five distinct phases of artistic development that incorporate general cognitive aesthetic developments as well as those which occur within specific domains. Psychological research in this area has now reached a point where developmental changes can be described with confidence in a number of different art forms, since the descriptions are grounded in empirical data. The current state of the research literature has recently been documented in *Children and the Arts*.[7] Our outline of the five phases draws together the main features of this body of research. We have deliberately described *phases* rather than *stages* so as to avoid the connotations of Piagetian stages. We do not seek here to propose functional explanations for the progression across the phases. Rather, we seek to describe the modes of symbolic thought that are typically displayed by children at different ages in their dealings with the arts.

Our descriptive model is summarized in table 1. The five horizontal rows contain brief descriptions of the phases, which we have labeled the *presymbolic*, *figural*, *schematic*, *rule systems*, and *metacognitive* phases. We have assigned approximate age levels to each phase. The first vertical column, "cognitive aesthetic development," refers to research evidence on general symbolic developments. There are six columns describing domain-specific developments. Four of these deal with developments in music and the other two with developments in drawing and writing. This is not intended to imply that musical developments are in any way more significant or important than those in other domains, but probably reflects the relative diversity of musical behavior and of the research that has investigated it.

We have included singing, which has largely been studied by the analysis of recordings of children's spontaneous output; musical representation, in which children are typically asked to make graphic representations of musical stimuli (usually drawings of tapped rhythm patterns); melodic perception, which is largely based on numerous experimental studies of children's ability to recognize similarities and differences between single-note melodies; and musical composition, an area in which very little systematic data have been collected. We have adopted "composition" as a convenient term for musical invention in its broadest sense. The term is intended to cover improvisation and recordings of original performances as well as traditional written compositions.

The other two main areas of research have been on children's drawings, on which there is a substantial recent literature,[8] and on children's writing, which has a smaller but growing literature.[9] There are several gaps in the table, for which we make no apology; they mostly arise from the lack of research in particular areas.

TABLE 1
Five Phases of Artistic Development

Phase	Cognitive Aesthetic Development	Drawing	Writing	Singing	Domain-Specific Developments Musical Representation	Melodic Perception	Musical Composition
METACOGNITIVE (15+ years)	independence from cultural styles and context	freedom from artistic styles	self-reflection in relation to social roles				enactive and reflective strategies
RULE SYSTEMS (8-15 years)	development of artistic conventions and style sensitivity	"visual realism," viewer-centered	story grammar analysis of structural complexity	intervals, scales	formal-metric	analytic recognition of intervals, key stability	"idiomatic" conventions
SCHEMATIC (5-8 years)	emphasis on realism and subject matter	baselines, skylines	standard narrative forms	"first draft" songs	figural-metric: more than one dimension	"conservation" of melodic properties	"vernacular" conventions
FIGURAL (2-5 years)	concrete, mechanistic	preschematic, 'intellectual realism'	"frame" or outline stories	"outline" songs: coalescences between spontaneous and cultural songs	figural: single dimension	global features: pitch, contour	
PRESYMBOLIC (0-2 years)		scribbling	scribbling, symbolic play	babbling, rhythmic dancing	scribbling: "action equivalents"	recogniton of melodic contours	sensory, manipulative

The presymbolic phase. Our first phase is described as "presymbolic" (0-2 years) since representational symbols are not yet fully formed. Most developments involve physical actions and sensorimotor coordination, and it is only in the second year of life that abstract symbolism begins to emerge. Bruner referred to "enactive" representation at this age,[10] and it takes place in what Piaget described as the "sensorimotor" stage. Thus, to take our final column first, Swanwick and Tillman's description of children's early engagement with music emphasizes mastery.[11] Their spiral model of musical development includes a first "sensory" mode, in which infants are concerned with the exploration of the qualities of sounds (especially timbre), and a related "manipulative" mode in which they gradually master the means of sound production.

Infants' drawings are described as "scribbles," in which the physical action of pencil on paper is most important; scribbles only begin to take on representational meaning toward the end of this phase.[12] There is a clear analogy in musical representation; Goodnow used the term "action equivalents" to describe the marks that preschoolers make when trying to draw sequences of taps on paper.[13] Although the child's actions may match the temporal pattern of the taps, what appears on the paper bears no relation to it.

Early developments in storytelling also take place by means of physical expression. Cowie describes how infants engage in "storying" with pencil on paper; they imitate the flow of a script, so that a graphic or scribbled "text" emerges.[14] There is also a great deal of overlap between early storytelling and symbolic or make-believe play. Smith has suggested that fantasy and sociodramatic play is often the precursor of imaginative writing and that narrative-like and structural features can be observed in early play.[15]

The link with physical action is also a primary feature of infants' singing and their response to music. Moog's observations of some 500 children provide a detailed description of the development of physical responses to music.[16] Babies as young as three to six months were found to sway or bounce rhythmically in response to music, and the coordination between their dance movements and aspects of the music become increasingly accurate in the second year of life. Moog also studied early "babbling songs," which he regarded as a precursor of speech, and demonstrated that singing became increasingly integrated into imaginative play as infants progressed beyond this phase.

Recent research on melodic perception in infants has revealed that their capacity to recognize musical features may be remarkably advanced. Chang and Trehub, and Trehub, Bull, and Thorpe, for example, have shown by means of heart rate measurements that babies as young as five months can recognize changes in melodic contour and rhythmic pattern and that these changes are more salient than pitch transpositions.[17] It appears that infants use a kind of "global" processing strategy to recognize melodic contours, which parallels the strategies adults use to recognize unfamiliar or atonal melodies.[18] This finding is an early pointer to the essence of the second phase of artistic development.

The figural phase. The defining characteristic of the "figural" phase (approximately 2-5 years) is the tendency to make "global" or "outline" representations in various artistic media in which the overall shape, or figure, of the representation is clearly discernible, but the details within that shape are imprecise or absent. This has a good deal in common with Bruner's description of "iconic" representation.[19] Extrapolating from the paragraph above, there is good evidence that preschool children perceive or "process" melodies by attending to their overall shapes or "contours."[20]

This is also mirrored in the spontaneous singing of the preschooler. Some of the work of the Harvard Project Zero group[21] suggests the gradual acquisition of sets of song-related expectations, or "song frames," such that "outline songs" are produced. These are shown most clearly in the gradual coalescences between children's own spontaneous songs and those which they learn from the culture that surrounds them, such as nursery rhymes, playground chants, or pop songs.[22]

There are precise parallels in children's storytelling. Cowie describes how preschoolers produce "frame" stories, which "consist mainly of a beginning and an end—about stock characters who experience unbalancing and unresolved adventures."[23] There are also clear parallels in children's drawings at this age, which might be described as "preschematic." One of their central features is "intellectual realism"; children are said to draw "what they know, and not what they see."[24] Examples include "transparencies," such as people's heads being drawn as visible beneath their hats, and "turning over," where two visual perspectives are incongruously combined in the same drawing. Another feature of this stage is the well-known "tadpole figure"[25] in which children universally draw people without bodies. This latter is a good example of the graphic equivalent of "outlines" in other media.

When children represent music by graphic means at this age, they are once again likely to make figural, or outline representations. In fact, the term "figural" was coined in this context by Jeanne Bamberger in her well-known studies of children's drawings of rhythm patterns.[26] In representing the ten-beat pattern of the second and third lines of "One, two, buckle my shoe," for example, preschoolers are more likely to show the overall two-part shape of the sequence than to depict accurately the rhythmic relationships between each beat. Describing some further work on this topic, Davidson and Scripp point out that the children tend to focus on a single dimension of the task, usually the overall rhythmic pulse.[27]

All these developments are clearly domain-specific. Researchers who have looked more generally at what we have termed "cognitive aesthetic developments," such as Gardner, Winner, and Kircher (1975), Parsons (1987), or Wolf (1989), have discovered a tendency for children to be concerned at this age with the concrete features of art works and with the mechanics of producing them.[28] Gardner, Winner, and Kircher's study also revealed a strong preoccupation with rules, for example, about who is allowed to paint or play an instrument and why; they described these responses as "immature."

The schematic phase. As one might expect, one of the major developments occurring when children's engagements with art works become "schematic" (roughly between the ages of five and eight years) is an increase in the level of organization of "immature" productions, so that they become increasingly congruent with cultural rules and standards. As far as general cognitive aesthetic development is concerned, the researchers mentioned above place a strong emphasis on the subject matter of art works and on the degree of realism of this subject matter. Thus, pictures or drawings are good if they look realistic; *what* they represent is much more important than *how* (that is, in what style) the representation is made. Similarly, in the case of musical composition, Swanwick and Tillman propose a "vernacular" mode of development in which children's output incorporates fairly general musical conventions such as melodic and rhythmic ostinati and sequences and phrasing in 2-, 4-, or 8-bar units.[29]

The acquisition of cultural rules in drawings is clearly evident in children's use of ground lines, or baselines, and skylines. These serve to organize spatially the elements of a drawing which have previously been unsystematically arranged on the paper.[30] Children's stories, similarly, conform increasingly to standard narrative forms with a beginning, a middle, and an end.[31] Their songs at this age have been characterized as "first draft" songs in that they are intermediate between the "outline" songs of the previous part, and the fully accurate songs which occur later in childhood.[32]

One significant and specific development that occurs in the schematic phase parallels Piaget's account of the transition from preoperational to concrete operational thinking. It is embodied in two areas of research on musical development. The first is a direct attempt to create musical analogies of Piagetian conservation tasks. Pflederer carried out a pioneering study of "music conservation" which has stimulated various others to devise and assess similar tasks. She proposed five conservation-type laws for the development of musical concepts.[33] While there is some doubt about the conceptual validity of the Piagetian analogy, the empirical evidence nevertheless lends support to the developmental progression that Piagetian theory would predict.[34] Secondly, studies of musical representation have found that children can typically represent more than one dimension of a rhythmic pattern by graphic means at this age.[35]

The rule systems phase. Although these schematic developments show increasingly fluent use of artistic rule systems, children's output in different domains is still far from completely accurate. Full-scale accuracy in relation to cultural rules only fully emerges between the years of eight and fifteen or so, which we have accordingly labeled the phase of "rule systems." Thus, drawings become "visually realistic," or what Cox has described as "viewer-centered"; objects can be depicted as they might be seen from any angle, or by any viewer, and they are accurate in their use of artistic conventions such as perspective, occlusion, and depth relationships.[36]

The developments that occur in writing have been studied by means of story grammar analysis. Here the emphasis is upon the structural complexity of stories and how this develops with age rather than on the content of those stories.[37] Strictly speaking, this may reflect a development of the *use* of existing rule systems rather than of the acquisition of those systems, since the formal rules of storytelling are less explicit than those in domains such as music.

In singing, musical representation, and melodic perception, the pattern of research findings is fairly similar; children become increasingly accurate at representing and reproducing the precise pitch and rhythmic relationships between notes, so that scales and intervals become stabilized.[38] These "digital" relationships are not only accurate *within* the component phrases of a piece but also in relationship to one another and to the piece as a whole, that is, with respect to its key and time signatures.

In their more general description of the development of children's musical compositions, Swanwick and Tillman propose an *idiomatic* mode of development at around this age which incorporates the fluent use of conventions such as elaboration, call and response, and contrasting sections, all within an authentic harmonic and instrumental context.[39] This is in line with the general finding from studies of aesthetic perception, shown in the first column of table 1, that children become fully aware of stylistic conventions and interpret works of art in terms of those conventions.[40]

The metacognitive phase. In the "metacognitive" phase, which begins in the teenage years, adolescents not only possess a full and mature understanding of artistic conventions, but they may also begin to see the work of individuals, including themselves, in relation to but independent from those conventions. As Wolf puts it, "They become aware that there are no absolute answers, no certain rules; they realize that different minds will construct different worlds and different ways of evaluating those worlds."[41] Many people may never achieve this mature level of artistic understanding.

In visual art, in music, and in other media, artistic styles can be seen in relation to one another, and the creator can draw on each style to varying degrees in formulating the language of an original statement. Swanwick and Tillman have also proposed a final metacognitive mode of musical composition which involves the capacity to be self-reflective and to relate original musical thought to other areas of experience.[42] Albeit at an earlier age level, Cowie suggested that writing can fulfill a reflective function in relation to the social roles of self and others.[43] By adopting the "spectator role," the writer maintains an independent perspective on the network of social relationships of which he or she is a part.

Musical composition is a notoriously difficult area for empirical study, although the cognitive approach is beginning to make some significant inroads.[44] One finding that emerges from two different cognitive studies deserves mention. In a study in which beginning and advanced music students were given a short composition exercise, Davidson and Welsh found that beginning composition students tended to work "enactively" at the piano: they composed in short units and worked sequentially within one phrase at a time.[45] The more advanced students tended to conceive larger musical units internally before trying them out at the keyboard: they worked at a higher-order symbolic or reflective level.

A parallel finding emerged from a study by Hargreaves, Cork, and Setton in which novice and expert jazz pianists were asked to improvise right-hand solos over prerecorded backing tracks.[46] The novices tended to have no clear advance plan, or to focus on a single musical dimension of the backing track, such as its chords or rhythm; only occasionally was there any evidence of change in their improvisations as a result of feedback. In contrast, the experts approached the task with an explicit yet provisional overall plan, which was frequently changed according to what happened as the solo developed.

These two findings are of particular interest because they seem to represent a recapitulation of the shift from enactive to symbolic modes of thinking which was observed in the early phases of artistic development. Although the student composers and improvisers had achieved a high level of mastery of the component skills of the tasks they were set, a similar developmental progression was apparent. This indicates some degree of coherence in our necessarily very brief account of the five phases of artistic development. Since this is our first attempt to sketch the main features of a growing body of research, it is bound to lack completeness, to have many loose ends, and to need further revision as research proceeds.

The Educational Perspective

EDUCATIONAL IDEOLOGY AND SCHOOL PRACTICE

In examining the ways in which the arts are taught in English schools it is necessary to study the prevailing ideology which governs current educational practice. Nowhere is this more sharply defined than in the primary school (5-11 years), although trends are also evident within the secondary range of compulsory schooling, particularly in the lower school (11-14 years). Indeed the situation is even more complicated by the existence of middle schools, seen as a transition stage between the primary and secondary phases. In England, middle schools operate across the 8-12 age range, the 9-13 age range, and the 10-14 and 11-14 age ranges in different parts of the country. The multiplicity of ages of transfer means that the transition view of middle schools as a bridge between primary and secondary practice is oversimplified, and Andy Hargreaves has suggested that middle schools have developed an ideology in their own right, strongly associated with the primary phase.[47] This is particularly true of the more "creative" subjects so that a study of primary teachers' views about teaching creative arts should have implications for a much wider age range.[48]

Recent studies of teachers' thinking have made much use of metaphor as a means of drawing out teachers' beliefs about their work.[49] In the United Kingdom two studies in particular have explored primary teachers' views about their role in fostering what is termed "informal learning," which is generally associated with curriculum areas such as creative writing, art, music, drama, and dance. In Nias's study, teachers were asked to describe how they felt when children were engaged in these kinds of activity.[50] This sample of teachers most often described their roles as facilitators. Indeed, some argued that these kinds of activities could not take place successfully when they were being "the teacher," which they equated with being "the boss figure." Similar findings have emerged from the work of Cortazzi, who used a psycholinguistic model of evaluation to analyze teachers' narratives about their classroom activity.[51] When asked to describe a case where successful learning had taken place within their classroom, none of the teachers mentioned any action of their own which had helped to foster intellectual growth in their pupils. All talked about "being surprised and pleased" at the spontaneous way in which children had acquired new knowledge or new skills. Mostly teachers talked about this knowledge coming in "spurts."

The picture which emerges from such investigations is one where, as Alexander suggests, the horticultural metaphor is prevalent.[52] Teachers are the gardeners whose major task is to create the right conditions for growth to take place in their pupils. Teachers provide a suitable environment and administer a suitable stimulus at the appropriate time. However, the growth in the child, as in the seed, is independent of the teacher-child interaction. The child, like the seed, grows only when it is ready to interact with its environment.

It is not difficult to trace the origins of this ideology to the work of Piaget. The Plowden report of 1967 gave official government approval to this teaching approach in Great Britain and claimed support from Piaget for its prescriptions.[53] However, as noted by Wood and others, Piaget himself had little to say about the implications of his theories for teaching.[54] It was left to others to make the necessary links and in the United Kingdom this was done mainly through a series of papers published by Susan and Nathan Isaacs at the London Institute. Susan Isaacs, in particular, was responsible for much of the formulation described above,[55] which now appears to be an entrenched part of primary teaching ideology. Thus, the creative arts debate which has occupied psychologists has largely been deemed irrelevant by those responsible for training teachers, given the prevailing horticultural imagery of teaching which each generation of new entrants to the profession has been encouraged to espouse. What has, for the most part, engaged teacher educators is the extent to which children, in order to create, need to be free to choose not only *what* they wish to create but also *when* they wish to do so. In its extreme form, the "integrated day" is a manifestation of this approach. Insofar as any external limits are applied to this freedom, it is that children should follow similar procedures as experienced artists.[56] One manifestation of this development has been the growth of the "redrafting" movement in creative writing within primary schools and the use of visiting artists who take up residence in schools for limited periods and work alongside children.

CLASSROOM ORGANIZATION AND THE TEACHING OF THE ARTS

At the time of the 1967 Plowden report, a dramatic change took place in the structure of education within the United Kingdom which had consequences for the teaching of creative arts in schools. During this period selective education was largely abolished. Previously, all children of eleven years had taken an examination, the results of which determined whether they would have an academic or a vocational education in a grammar school or a secondary modern school respectively. In order to prepare children for this "11+" examination, primary schools tended to group their children in classes according to ability. Even progressives such as Nathan and Susan Isaacs did not object to this procedure since, reverting to the horticultural metaphor, different plants need different soil conditions, and it seemed reasonable to group plants (pupils) with similar needs within the same area of the garden (school). The establishment of the comprehensive school, catering to children of all abilities, meant the end of the 11+ examination and the need for streaming in the primary schools.[57] This presented teachers with severe organizational problems which were mainly solved by individualizing tasks and simultaneously grouping pupils involved in similar curriculum areas at the same worktable. Research has shown that, typically, while over 85 percent of pupils are seated in groups, usually of mixed sex and numbering five or six pupils, 85 percent of them are working on individual assignments.[58] Such an organizational pattern, however, presents considerable problems to teachers when they attempt to distribute reasonable proportions of their time among twenty-five pupils or more, the average number in a British primary classroom. Mathematically, each pupil gets just over two minutes per hour but in practice this time is considerably less because of interruptions and loss of time for transition from one curricular area to another. The prevailing ideology that the teacher's role is mainly that of a facilitator and that the children learn spontaneously allows teachers to operate this system with an easy conscience. Teachers tend to concentrate their efforts on helping pupils who are working on the "basic skills" of computing, writing, and reading, which they feel should "be taught," thereby leaving children to paint, draw, and engage in similar activities on their own with little assistance. These findings were first reported in the ORACLE study (Observational Research and Classroom Learning Evaluation), a survey of primary classroom practice based upon systematic observation.[59] They have been confirmed in later studies, notably those of Mortimore et al. and of Tizard et al. covering the junior (7-11) and infant (5-7) age ranges respectively.[60]

ASSESSMENT OF THE CREATIVE ARTS

Another area where the prevailing ideology of primary teaching has had an important impact is in the assessment of the products of creative work in the classroom. In the early 1970s, the switch away from streamed to nonstreamed classes created anxieties among parents who wished to know how teachers could keep track of the progress of twenty-five different children doing twenty-five different things. Great emphasis was placed upon the teacher's role as an expert who knew each of the children intimately. Teachers' judgments were said to be based upon careful observation of children while working, which placed greater emphasis on the process of creating than on the products of the creation. Empirical research such as that cited earlier, suggesting that teachers rarely spent time with children in order to make such judgments, was largely ignored. Little attention was given to the possibility of expectancy effects, although in the ORACLE project Jasman showed that teachers' assessments of creative writing and drawing correlated most highly with their judgments about the same children's reading ability.[61] Generally, therefore, teachers in the primary and middle schools have been encouraged to rely on impressionistic judgments about the quality of pupils' work.[62]

CURRENT CLASSROOM RESEARCH IN ARTS EDUCATION

Music is an exception to these practices because in most British primary schools only one or two teachers have any proficiency with musical instruments. Thus, for the most part, children attend music lessons as a nonspecialist class activity while those learning to play are offered additional tuition by visiting teachers with expertise in the particular instrument. This pattern is revealed in research carried out in the PRISMS study (Curriculum Provision in Small Primary Schools) at the University of Leicester during the period 1982-87. Although the study concerned schools with fewer than one hundred pupils, comparisons with a subsample of larger schools showed very few differences in the data.[63] Music, which accounted for 7 percent and 5.3 percent of all observations in infant and junior classrooms respectively, largely consisted either of singing or moving to an accompaniment, whereas art, accounting for 14.6 percent and 15.3 percent of all observations in infant and junior classrooms respectively, consisted mainly of drawing. In music, all children in the class were engaged in the same activity for most of the time, whereas in art children were working mainly on individual assignments.

To examine the detailed structure of curriculum tasks carried out in these primary classrooms, various criteria of performance were defined. By far the most frequently used criteria were "create," where pupils were required to produce an imaginative response to an idea; "copy," where pupils had to reproduce an original work as accurately as possible in the same medium; and "map," where pupils were required to transfer information from one particular medium to another. Reading aloud would be a simple example of mapping in that the pupil was expected to turn written words into spoken words. Approximately the same amounts of time were spent in creative activities (16 percent) and in mapping (19 percent) in infant and junior classrooms. Copying, however, was more prevalent in the infant classrooms, as might be expected. Over 19 percent of all observations in infant classes involved copying as compared with only 16 percent in the junior classrooms.

When the data were further analyzed the proportion of time allocated to individual aesthetic subjects (music, art and craft, drama, and movement) was found to be so small, in comparison with other subjects, that it was necessary to combine the percentages into a single category to ensure that each cell of the contingency table was filled. This single category was called "fine art." In all, over 27 percent of all observations involved some fine art activity. When such activities did take place, nearly a third of them involved listening, and slightly less than a fifth involved observing. Over a third, mainly in music, involved children speaking. When children were creating they were likely to be either writing or drawing. On average, each observation of a creative activity was associated with three other observation categories, whereas each copying activity was associated with five other categories and each mapping activity with between six or seven. Typically, therefore, a piece of creative work involved fewer subject areas, fewer applications of different media, fewer actions on the part of the pupil and less use of resources than did a piece of copying. Furthermore, a piece of copying involved fewer of these features on average than did a piece of mapping. It follows, therefore, that much creative work in the primary school is less complex an activity in terms of the number of skills, resources, and activities which children are required to utilize. Creative work appears to take place in an environment which is somewhat limited when compared with that required for either mapping or copying. These findings suggest that creative exercises are largely about children expressing themselves "freely" in situations requiring little supervision. They do not seem to involve the development of children's imaginative responses by requiring them to select from a range of different media and resources to achieve a particular form of expression.

Our data on teacher involvement within different curriculum activities also support this view. For each curriculum observation, ten possible behavior observations could be recorded. In just under 50 percent of junior curriculum records and 40 percent of infant records no teacher involvement took place. The data suggest that drawing and art work, in particular, were used as "fillers" for pupils while teachers supervised other activities elsewhere in the classroom. In infant classes there was more supervision of fine art work, greater use being made of play and associated construction activities to occupy children while the teacher was engaged elsewhere. In general, all kinds of creative work appeared to be treated similarly. It was largely seen as something which emphasized the original and unique characteristics of the activity rather than the children's attempts to develop and use a range of techniques more effectively. There was, therefore, little need for supervision, since creative ideas rather than the products of the creation were the criteria used for judging the work. Music, on the other hand, showed a different pattern of results. Although it only occupied some 6 percent of all curriculum observations, compared to 15 percent for art, it was four times less likely to be unsupervised in the infant classroom and nearly six times less likely to be unsupervised in junior classes. In music there was a strong emphasis on vocal work, which was often associated with rote learning. For example, children typically listened to the teacher and repeated the words of a song before learning how to sing it.

TEACHING THE ARTS IN THE SECONDARY SCHOOL

Such findings, based as they are on the analysis of systematic observation data, provide only a limited picture of what actually takes place in the classroom. Fortunately, there exist some small-scale case studies which are largely supportive of the findings of the ORACLE and PRISMS studies.[64] Nevertheless, compared to other areas of the curriculum, there is a dearth of data relating to the arts and, in particular, to music.

While confirming the general emphasis on individuality and spontaneous creation, the limited data available on secondary schools nevertheless suggest that in subtle ways teachers limit this freedom, particularly during periods of transition from one school to another and from one class to another, until teacher/pupil relationships are well established and settled. While there were specialist rooms in middle and secondary schools, pupils were typically marched into these rooms in a controlled way, seated in alphabetical order, given precise instructions on how to use equipment, allocated a single teacher, and given common tasks with detailed instructions.[65] Field notes from the study by Delamont and Galton provide the following examples:

The class have two pieces of work on the go at once, the set work and a piece of pleasure drawing. One or two pupils have had their first pleasure drawing pinned up on the wall. The set work today consists of a pattern with circles and triangles drawn with compasses. . . .

After they have worked for some minutes, Mr. Brearly calls them to attention to explain the next step. . . .

There is a great discrepancy in work rates. The quickest have finished drawing while others are struggling with the measuring and some are still drawing. Two pupils are told to put a water beaker on each tray, one per table. Mr. Brearly then stops everyone and gives instructions for painting—the rules for use of trays and colours that they have: four colours and two neutrals. One boy says "Sir, we've got six colours." Mr. Brearly says they have forgotten what they were taught and gets other pupils to recapitulate why black and white are not colours.

Then Mr. Brearly starts a questioning session on how the primary colours can be used to get secondary colours. A lot of hands go up and pupils say "Sir, purple," "Sir, orange" and so on. Mr. Brearly demonstrates the way they are to mix the paints on the palette—not scooping lots out, just taking small amounts on a damp brush. The drawing they have done is to be coloured with primary colours in the inner segments, and the secondary ones in the outer sections.

The pupils did not have to mix a green, as their palettes had blue, yellow, red, green, black and white powder paints in them.

The boys are now allowed to take their blazers off before they paint. As they begin to paint Mr. Brearly walks round looking at their work. Rex is reprimanded gently for using the wrong brush, Alan for not following his painting instructions, and then Tanya for the same thing (not doing the primary colours first). . . .

A boy shows Mr. Brearly his green, "Sir, is this right?"

11:45. Mr. Brearly tells them to finish what they are doing and gives them the rules on how clearing up is done . . . When they are cleared up Mr. Brearly inspects all the tables and says "Right, well if you tidy up like that every week I see we'll have no problems."[66]

Similar patterns existed for music. For example, one music master was observed in a lesson early in the year.

He asks, "Anyone who didn't take music at the last school" to put up their hands and then to the children who have put up their hands he asks, "Where did you go?" Almost inevitably the answer will be Ashwood Bank from the pupil. One pupil ventures that they did have percussion but they did not have this (meaning this present lesson).

Teacher: (sarcastically) "So you have banged away without knowing why!"

One girl dares to yawn. He rounds on her. "Open that window young lady we'll see if you can be kept awake with fresh air" and then "Here we take music seriously, you haven't come here to relax between maths and English."[67]

This tight control of "creative" activities in secondary schools arises not only because staff have a genuine need to keep the specialist rooms reasonably clean and tidy, so that messy materials such as clay and glue do not spread anywhere, but also because there are pressures on teachers of creative subjects to prove to the pupils that the work is just as difficult and serious as mathematics and English, and not simply a relaxation from the rigors of academic study. As pupils move up the educational scale, therefore, greater emphasis is placed upon knowledge and procedures, and fewer opportunities are offered for pupils to develop their own ideas.

Bridging the Gap between Theory and Practice

TEACHERS' WORKING THEORIES OF ARTISTIC DEVELOPMENT

We pointed out earlier that the prevailing educational ideology in Great Britain has been strongly influenced by Piagetian theory, either directly or indirectly, even though Piaget himself was never concerned to make explicit recommendations for the classroom. This influence has been apparent in two main ways: first, in the formulation of the horticultural model described earlier, in which the teacher is viewed primarily as a facilitator of children's learning; second, in the way in which Piagetian stage theory and its derivatives have led in the past to the view that children can only master certain skills and achievements when they have reached an appropriate level of developmental readiness.

Teaching is an extremely complex and multifaceted activity involving practical issues of classroom organization, timetabling, and discipline, and subject also to external influences such as the demands of national examinations and curricula, as well as the local concerns of parents, educational advisers, and administrators. Teachers cannot translate theory directly into practice because they are subject to all these intermediate influences. Furthermore, "theory" itself is by no means unitary or clear-cut. We have concentrated upon theories of cognitive development as they apply to the arts, but this is only part of a larger picture. Teachers are also concerned with the social and emotional development of their pupils, and the progress of those pupils in the arts cannot be separated from the context of their work in the curriculum as a whole.

What we have termed teachers' "working theories" of their pupils' aesthetic learning are the ways in which they translate all of these disparate considerations into practice. The working theories must incorporate practical and external constraints as well as guidelines from psychological and educational theory. As the first part of the chapter makes clear, however, research on artistic development lags way behind that on the development of mathematical or scientific thinking. Teachers need to be able to make some sense of the small body of knowledge which does exist.

We would like to argue that a generalized description of the course of artistic development, such as that we have outlined, ought to be of some help to them. This might be thought of as a large-scale atlas which indicates the broad landmarks of the terrain rather than a specific map of local features, but it should nevertheless be of some practical use. As the emphasis on assessment and accountability increases in Great Britain, our hope is that current psychological knowledge should serve as a general guide for the working theories of individual teachers rather than as a prescription for detailed directions. As we have seen, the horticultural model of learning is much more prevalent in arts teaching in primary schools than in secondary schools, and it is in the former that this knowledge might be most useful.

THE DELTA PROJECT

The background to the DELTA project is described by Hargreaves, Galton and Robinson,[68] and more detailed publications are currently in preparation. We were concerned from the start to investigate learning and assessment in the arts "from the bottom up," to ground our study in teachers' existing perceptions and practices rather than in "top-down" theory. We concentrated on the junior age range, working mostly with children aged seven to eleven years in some fifteen schools in the English midlands, and we restricted our investigation to children's work in creative writing, music, and visual art. A great deal of interview and informal observational data were collected, which will be reported elsewhere. We concentrate here on the central investigation of teachers' assessments of children's products in the three domains.

After preliminary visits to the schools and informal observations of teaching practices in the arts, we obtained descriptions of activities which teachers described as having been successful with their classes in each of the three areas. A total of 125 descriptions was obtained in this way, from which was taken a representative selection of twenty-four activities in visual art and writing and fifteen in music. Brief descriptions of each were typed onto index cards and were used as the basis of a repertory grid-type elicitation of the teachers' descriptions of the activities. By asking them to suggest how two members of a trio of activities were similar and thereby different from the third, we elicited a series of adjectival descriptions in each art form.

From these we produced a set of bipolar dimensional scales in each of the three areas. There were fifteen dimensions in visual art, of which the most frequently occurring were "own design, imagination—copying from model" and "based on concrete object/ stimulus—based on personal experience." There were twenty-two dimensions in creative writing, of which the two most common were "based in reality (concrete)—imaginary (abstract)" and "directed—

undirected"; and eighteen in music, of which by far the most common was "create new sounds (improvise)—reproduce existing sounds."

Further analysis revealed that a superordinate dimension of what might be called "structuredness" could be identified in the teachers' descriptions of the range of activities in all three art forms. In visual art, for example, a more structured activity might be one in which the artistic *medium, technique,* and *topic* were specified, and in which the pupils were prepared for the task by preliminary discussion. A more unstructured activity would typically not involve such preparation or direction, as for example in an imaginative or abstract piece of art work.

A pilot study was undertaken, and subsequently a main study, in which relatively structured and relatively unstructured activities were carried out in each of the three art forms, in twelve schools in all. At the first of two in-service day meetings that were subsequently organized, representative examples of the pupils' work were used as the basis for a repertory grid-type exercise similar to that which had been carried out earlier with the descriptions of activities. Each teacher made judgments of similarity and difference about selected trios of children's paintings, pieces of creative writing, and videotape recordings of musical activities.

As before, these descriptive judgments were collated and edited to produce a set of bipolar dimensions, this time referring to characteristics of the children's work. There were fourteen scales for pictures, of which the most frequently occurring were "simple—complex" and "formless—ordered"; ten scales for writing, of which the most common were "factual reporting—imaginative writing" and "unevocative—evocative"; and twelve scales for music, of which the most common was "unevocative—evocative." Two evaluative scales were added to each of these lists, namely "aesthetically unappealing—aesthetically appealing," and "technically unskillful—technically skillful."

On the second in-service day meeting, the same teachers rated selected examples of children's work on each of these dimensions using seven-point scales. Somewhat to our surprise, two very clear findings emerged from statistical analyses of the results. First, and most striking, there was a very high level of positive intercorrelation among the ratings of the twelve teachers across the sample of children's work as a whole, and this was accompanied by a similarly high level of intercorrelation between their use of the different rating scales within each art form. In other words, our teachers' ratings appeared to be fairly global, or generalized, rather than differentiated, and these global ratings were made remarkably consistently by the different teachers in our study.

The second finding was that pieces of work from the more unstructured activities obtained significantly higher ratings on the evaluative scales than did those from the more structured activities, although this effect was weaker for the writing products than for those in the other two areas. It appeared that our teachers were inclined to give more credit for original ideas emerging from spontaneous creations than for competent pieces of work which were more constrained and in which teacher expectations were more explicit. This provides direct support for the argument, advanced earlier in this chapter, that teachers perceive themselves primarily as *facilitators* in the creative arts.

Although these are preliminary findings from a small-scale, exploratory, and local study, their clarity and consistency is quite striking. While they urgently require replication and further development, they inspire some confidence in the view that teachers *can* make reliable assessments of pupils' artistic products even when they have not been involved in the process of creation, so that we have some grounds for optimism about the validity of consensual assessment in the arts.

Conclusion

The DELTA project has been described in some detail because it highlights our contention that it is important to work from the teacher's point of view, and to try to make that point of view explicit. In the project, this goes no further than their views of specific arts activities and pieces of work. It nevertheless leads to the suggestion that teachers' explication of their working theories in other areas of aesthetic learning and teaching may be a vital foundation of the bridge between theory and practice. We still have a very long way to go, however, and will conclude by identifying three directions for further research.

First, as we have already argued, psychological theories of developmental change in the arts ought to form an important and more explicit part of teachers' working theories of their pupils' progress. This general framework should form the background to specific individual developments; considerably more research should be devoted to teachers' implicit and explicit notions of developmental progression, and to how this progression might be monitored in the context of classroom activity.

Second, and closely related to the first aim, we need to investigate the *process* of artistic development alongside its *products*. This is reflected in the distinction between *formative* and *summative* assessment; both are equally important, and observational studies are needed to complement the product-centered approach we have adopted in the DELTA project.

Third, as the second section of the chapter has demonstrated and the DELTA research has confirmed, we lack an adequate theoretical base to inform the pedagogy of arts teaching. Current recommended practice tends to "deskill" teachers, reducing their role to that of a facilitator rather than an active participant in the child's artistic development. Psychologists have tended to reinforce this pedagogic model by largely researching children's development in the arts from outside the classroom. It is now time to redress this balance, as we have tried to do in a modest way within the DELTA project.

This is not to say that the pupil's perspective should be neglected, and we have said very little about the child's point of view. At the opening of the chapter we surmised that the creator of a piece of art work is in one sense the only person who is truly qualified to assess it, and research so far has hardly scratched the surface of this issue. We need to consider *children's* working theories of their own artistic development, and of the world of the arts more generally, and try to map these onto the constructs of the teacher, as well as those of the psychologist. Paradoxically, this was the essence of Piaget's approach, even though certain aspects of his theory have been adopted as the source of what has turned out to be an overly prescriptive developmental model. Perhaps we should let Piaget have the last word:

The child is of considerable interest in himself, but interest in psychological investigations of the child is increased when we realize that the child explains the man as well as and often better than the man explains the child. While the adult educates the child by means of multiple social transmissions, every adult, even if he is a creative genius, nevertheless began as a child, in prehistoric times as well as today.[69]

ACKNOWLEDGMENT. We wish to thank Linda Hargreaves and Janet Mills for their helpful comments on earlier drafts of this chapter.

Notes

1. David J. Hargreaves and Marilyn Zimmerman, "Cognitive Theories of Music Learning," in *Handbook for Research in Music Teaching and Learning*, ed. Richard Colwell (New York: Macmillan, 1992).

2. Howard Gardner, "Developmental Psychology after Piaget: An Approach in Terms of Symbolization," *Human Development* 22 (1979): 73-88; David Hargreaves, *The Developmental Psychology of Music* (Cambridge: Cambridge University Press, 1986).

3. John Radford, *Child Prodigies and Exceptional Early Achievers* (Hemel Hempstead: Harvester Wheatsheaf, 1990).

4. Howard Gardner, *Developmental Psychology*, 2d ed. (Boston: Little Brown, 1982).

5. Michael J. Parsons, *How We Understand Art* (Cambridge: Cambridge University Press, 1987).

6. Dennie P. Wolf and Howard Gardner, "On the Structure of Early Symbolization," in *Early Language Intervention*, ed. Richard Schiefelbush and D. Bricker (Baltimore: University Park Press, 1981).

7. David J. Hargreaves, ed., *Children and the Arts* (Milton Keynes: Open University Press, 1989).

8. See Norman H. Freeman and Maureen V. Cox, eds., *Visual Order* (Cambridge: Cambridge University Press, 1985).

9. See Helen Cowie, ed., *The Development of Children's Imaginative Writing* (London: Croom Helm, 1984).

10. Jerome S. Bruner, "The Growth of Representational Processes in Childhood," in Jeremy Anglin, ed., *Beyond the Information Given: Studies in the Psychology of Knowing* (New York: W. W. Norton, 1973).

11. Keith Swanwick and June Tillman, "The Sequence of Musical Development: A Study of Children's Composition," *British Journal of Music Education* 3 (1986): 305-339.

12. Glyn V. Thomas and Angèle M. J. Silk, *An Introduction to the Psychology of Children's Drawings* (Hemel Hempstead: Harvester Wheatsheaf, 1990).

13. Jacqueline J. Goodnow, "Auditory-visual Matching: Modality Problem or Translation Problem?" *Child Development* 42 (1971): 1187-2101.

14. Helen Cowie, "Children as Writers," in *Children and the Arts*, ed. David J. Hargreaves (Milton Keynes: Open University Press, 1989).

15. Peter K. Smith, "The Relevance of Fantasy Play for Development in Young Children," in *The Development of Children's Imaginative Writing*, ed. Helen Cowie (London: Croom Helm, 1984).

16. Helmut Moog, *The Musical Experience of the Preschool Child*, trans. Claudia Clarke (London: Schott, 1976).

17. Hsing-Wu Chang and Sandra E. Trehub, "Infants' Perception of Temporal Grouping in Auditory Patterns," *Child Development* 48 (1977): 1666-1670; Sandra E. Trehub, Dale Bull, and Leigh A. Thorpe, "Infants' Perception of Melodies: The Role of Melodic Contour," *Child Development* 55 (1984): 821-830.

18. W. Jay Dowling, "Melodic Information Processing and Its Development," in *The Psychology of Music*, ed. Diana Deutsch (New York: Academic Press, 1982).

19. Bruner, "The Growth of Representational Processes in Childhood."

20. Dowling, "Melodic Information Processing and Its Development."

21. Lyle Davidson, Patricia McKernon, and Howard Gardner, "The Acquisition of Song: A Developmental Approach," in *Documentary Report of the Ann Arbor*

Symposium: Applications of Psychology to the Teaching and Learning of Music (Reston, VA: Music Educators National Conference, 1981).

22. A number of examples of these so-called "pot-pourri" songs can be found in Moog, *The Musical Experience of the Preschool Child* and in Hargreaves, *The Developmental Psychology of Music*.

23. Cowie, "Children as Writers," p. 23.

24. G. H. Lucquet, *Le Dessin Enfantin* (Paris: Alcan, 1927).

25. Norman H. Freeman, "Do Children Draw Men with Arms Coming Out of the Head?" *Nature* 254 (1975): 416-417; idem, *Strategies of Representation in Young Children* (London: Academic Press, 1980).

26. Jeanne Bamberger, "Revisiting Children's Drawing of Simple Rhythms: A Function for Reflection-in-Action," in *U-Shaped Behavioral Growth*, ed. Sydney Strauss (New York: Academic Press, 1982).

27. Lyle Davidson and Lawrence Scripp, "Education and Development in Music from a Cognitive Perspective," in *Children and the Arts*, ed. David Hargreaves.

. 28. Howard Gardner, Ellen Winner, and Mary Kircher, "Children's Conceptions of the Ats," *Journal of Aesthetic Education* 9 (1975): 60-77; Parsons, *How We Understand Art*; Dennie P. Wolf, "Artistic Learning as Conversation," in *Children and the Arts*, ed. David Hargreaves.

29. Swanwick and Tillman, "The Sequence of Musical Development."

30. David J. Hargreaves, Philip M. Jones, and Diane Martin, "The Air Gap Phenomenon in Children's Landscape Drawings," *Journal of Experimental Child Psychology* 32 (1981): 11-20.

31. Cowie, "Children as Writers."

32. Davidson, McKernon, and Gardner, "The Acquisition of Song."

33. Marilyn Pflederer, "The Responses of Children to Musical Tasks Embodying Piaget's Principle of Conservation," *Journal of Research in Music Education* 12 (1964): 251-268.

34. See reviews by Mary Louise Serafine, "Piagetian Research in Music," *Bulletin of the Council for Research in Music Education* 62 (1980): 1-21, and by David Hargreaves, *The Developmental Psychology of Music*.

35. Davidson and Scripp, "Education and Development in Music from a Cognitive Perspective."

36. Maureen V. Cox, "Children's Drawings," in *Children and the Arts*, ed. David Hargreaves.

37. B. M. Kroll and C. M. Anson, "Analyzing Structure in Children's Fictional Narratives," in *The Development of Children's Imaginative Writing*, ed. Cowie.

38. Dowling, "Melodic Information Processing and Its Development"; Davidson and Scripp, "Education and Development in Music from a Cognitive Perspective."

39. Swanwick and Tillman, "The Sequence of Musical Development."

40. Howard Gardner, "Style Sensitivity in Children," *Human Development* 15 (1972): 325-338.

41. Wolf, "Artistic Learning as Conversation," p. 33.

42. Swanwick and Tillman, "The Sequence of Musical Development."

43. Cowie, "Children as Writers."

44. See John A. Sloboda, ed., *Generative Processes in Music: The Psychology of Performance, Improvisation, and Composition* (Oxford: Clarendon Press, 1988).

45. Lyle Davidson and Patricia Welsh, "From Collections to Structure: The Developmental Path of Tonal Thinking," in *Generative Processes in Music*, ed. Sloboda.

46. David J. Hargreaves, C. Cork, and T. Setton, "Cognitive Strategies in Jazz Improvisation: An Exploratory Study," *Canadian Journal of Music Education*, in press.

47. Andy Hargreaves, *Two Cultures of Schooling: The Case of Middle Schools* (London: Falmer Press, 1986).

48. Les Tickle, "The Arts in Education and Curriculum Research," in *The Arts in Education: Some Research Studies*, ed. Les Tickle (London: Croom Helm, 1987).

49. James Calderhead, ed., *Exploring Teachers' Thinking* (London: Cassell, 1987).

50. Jennifer Nias, *Primary Teachers Talking* (London: Routledge, 1989).

51. Martin Cortazzi, *Primary Teaching: How It Is—A Narrative Account* (London: David Fulton, 1990).

52. Robin Alexander, *Primary Teaching* (London: Holt, Rinehart and Winston, 1984).

53. Department of Education and Science, *Children and Their Primary Schools: A Report of the Central Advisory Council for Education in England*, vol. 1: *The Report* (London: HMSO, 1967).

54. David Wood, *How Children Think and Learn* (Oxford: Basil Blackwell, 1988).

55. Susan Isaacs, *The Psychological Aspects of Child Development*, Institute of Education Yearbook (London: London University Press, 1935).

56. Michael Armstrong, "The Case of Louise and the Painting of Landscape," in *A Teacher's Guide to Action Research*, ed. J. Nixon (London: Grant McIntyre, 1981).

57. Joan Barker-Lunn, *Streaming in the Primary School* (Slough: National Foundation for Educational Research, 1970).

58. Maurice Galton, Brian Simon, and Paul Croll, *Inside the Primary Classroom* (London: Routledge and Kegan Paul, 1980).

59. Ibid.

60. Peter Mortimore, Pamela Sammons, Louise Stoll, David Lewis, and Russell Ecob, *School Matters: The Junior Years* (London: Open Books, 1987); Barbara Tizard, Peter Blatchford, Jessica Burke, Clare Farquhar, and Ian Plewis, *Young Children at School in the Inner City* (Hove and London: Lawrence Erlbaum, 1988).

61. A. Jasman, "Teachers' Assessments in Classroom Research," in *Research and Practice in the Primary Classroom*, ed. Brian Simon and John Willcocks (London: Routledge and Kegan Paul, 1981).

62. Malcolm Ross, "Against Assessment," in *Assessment in Arts Education*, ed. Malcolm Ross (Oxford: Pergamon Press, 1986).

63. Maurice Galton and Helen Patrick, eds., *Curriculum Provision in the Small Primary School* (London: Routledge, 1989).

64. See Sara Delamont, "Teachers and Their Specialist Subjects," in *Moving from the Primary Classroom*, ed. Maurice Galton and John Willcocks (London: Routledge and Kegan Paul, 1983), and Tickle, "The Arts in Education and Curriculum Research."

65. Sara Delamont and Maurice Galton, "The Oracle and the Muses: Aesthetic Activity in Six Schools," in *The Arts in Education*, ed. Tickle.

66. Ibid., pp. 41-43.

67. Ibid., p. 45.

68. David J. Hargreaves, Maurice Galton, and S. Robinson, "Developmental Psychology and Arts Education," in *Children and the Arts*, ed. David J. Hargreaves (Milton Keynes: Open University Press, 1989); idem, "The DELTA Project," *Bulletin of the BPS Education Section* 14 (1990): 47-53.

69. Jean Piaget and Barbel Inhelder, *The Psychology of the Child* (London: Routledge and Kegan Paul, 1969).

CHAPTER VII

Teaching through Puzzles in the Arts

MARCIA MUELDER EATON

I still get angry when I think about the visual art classes I had in grade school. My elementary classes in art made that subject seem so vapid that I avoided all other classes in the visual arts until my senior year in college when I finally took a course in art history. As my interest in and love of art has grown since then, I view those empty years with not just regret, but with irritation.

In my school, art was taught by a person who came to our classroom twice a month. "Art" thus was something that was outside the regular, "serious" curriculum. Absolutely no attempt was made to relate it to the rest of our daily activities. (We also had a special bimonthly music teacher, but music was a part of the regular curriculum, and at home music was a central part of our family life. Furthermore, radio and television occasion many more musical experiences in ways that integrate it into daily lives. The same is true of literature, theater, and film. Even dance gets more regular exposure than the visual arts.)

The education we received from the teacher who appeared twice a month was seriously deficient. With one exception, art periods were times to "mess around" with our hands. For six years we did drawings of what we did on summer vacation, seasonal scenes, holiday activities. No advice was given about how to proceed—except for an occasional strategy, such as using "dough-people" to depict squatting instead of standing. For the minority of my classmates with innate drawing skills, such freedom afforded an opportunity for satisfying self-expression and a competitive edge over the rest of us. But for most of us, art class merely afforded the opportunity to goof off legally. No attention was given to helping us achieve some standard of performance. The one exception to which I referred above

---

Marcia Muelder Eaton is Professor of Philosophy at the University of Minnesota.

(the only time in six years when I took great pleasure in the art period) was a class devoted to "laws of perspective." Here, using pencil and ruler, we were *taught* how to draw telegraph poles alongside a railroad track. *Everyone* in the class produced pictures that successfully provided the illusion of three-dimensional space. Some were neater, more carefully designed; but all of us made something of which we could be proud.

I have taken this opportunity to complain because my own experience (which I have learned was widely shared by people of my generation and, unfortunately, too often continues to be shared in our schools today) points to two "lessons" of bad art education: (1) art is not connected to the important aspects of life, and (2) art is mindless activity; one handles art either passively or purely manually. Thought plays no role.

Although there are signs that the situation is changing, the questions of how thinking, and, more importantly, *critical thinking*, can be a part of art education, and how art can be rightfully positioned at the core, not at the periphery, of life (and hence of education) still need attention. The role that the critical analysis of aesthetic puzzles might play here is the subject of this chapter.

Elsewhere I have argued that art criticism and the teaching of art can helpfully be viewed as *invitations.*[1] Both activities have as a central goal encouraging others to participate in worthwhile pursuits, namely, attending to and reflecting upon intrinsic features of objects and events. Properties such as arrangements of color, space, or line are pointed to because they are considered valuable—likely to reward discovery and contemplation. Art teachers as inviters have obligations of the sort that accompany any responsible issuing of an invitation. One must consider what will give pleasure to those one invites and must do what is necessary to make enjoyment more likely. The good host or hostess will not simply say, "Enjoy!" and be done with it. He or she will make the effort required to make the enjoyment possible or, preferably, probable. In the case of visual art, the teacher-as-inviter will do what is necessary to engage the kind of attention that will repay the student-as-invitee's effort.

There are a variety of ways in which attention can be engaged or directed so that there is some payoff. One way is the use of puzzles.

According to Webster, puzzles cause people difficulty with regard to a course of action or choice; they confuse, embarrass, bewilder, perplex. All these states are discomfiting for most individuals. At the same time, human beings enjoy some puzzles. We seek out the puzzle page of the newspaper, buy jigsaw puzzles, entertain children and friends with riddles. Perplexity is pleasurable when it is controlled and when seeking for the solution provides as much, if not more, satisfaction than reaching the solution itself. In general, puzzles engage our minds in ways that yield positive experiences. When we offer puzzles to others, we invite them to use their heads—and compliment them by implying that they have a head to use.

Using puzzles (often promoted to the rank of "case studies") to teach is by no means new. There is, however, a new book, *Puzzles about Art: An Aesthetics Casebook*, that provides a systematic pedagogical approach to using puzzles to introduce students to basic issues in philosophical aesthetics.[2] The book contains puzzles contributed by thirty-eight scholars in aesthetics and related fields. It will, I am sure, be a great help to both aestheticians and art teachers who want to include an aesthetics component in their courses. It is also very timely for the increasing number of art educators who are convinced that Discipline-based Art Education (DBAE)—art education that includes aesthetics, history, and criticism as well as manipulation of materials— is "the way to go." Though specific details of the DBAE approach are controversial, there is increasingly widespread agreement that the disciplines of aesthetics, art criticism, and art history have much to contribute to art education. I shall suggest ways of using a few of the particular puzzles from this book later in this chapter. For now I wish to consider more generally the use of aesthetic puzzles to invite people to think critically about art.

Let me begin by describing a puzzle that I use the first day of my introductory aesthetics class to give students a sense of the issues and problems that we will be investigating. My intention is to get students themselves to suggest and challenge a wide range of theories.

I bring in a shopping bag full of small objects: plastic toy car, piece of driftwood, cake pan, small painting, ceramic pot, rotten apple, and so forth. Students are asked to "vote" on which are art and which are nonart. The tallying of votes invariably indicates wide disagreement within the group and in itself stimulates interest. We then turn to a discussion in which individuals are asked to explain their votes, that is, to give reasons for their responses. Their justifications can be turned into statements of rough definitions or theories. For example, some people reject some of the objects because they are not beautiful, others insist that something is a work of art because it was created with the intention of making a work of art. Others emphasize the importance of the expressiveness of an object. These opinions suggest the following general proposition: x is a work of art if and only if it is beautiful, or x is a work of art if and only if it is created with the right sort of intention, or x is a work of art if and only if it is expressive. Once stated, these principles are always challenged. It is pointed out that artworks are not always beautiful or that sometimes objects created for a very practical purpose become works of art. Problematic terms are identified; questions are asked about the meaning of "expressive," for instance.

When people feel torn by competing viewpoints, when they are challenged by others about their opinions, they are engaged. There is a strong sense in which the engagement really amounts to accepting what I have called an "invitation." They are brought to think, and, just as importantly, to see that there is a role for *thinking* in aesthetic experience. Principles begin to be formulated, revised, and even ranked (expressiveness is declared to be more important than beauty, for example). As the editors of *Puzzles About Art* write,

If a theory is complete and consistent as an account of art, it should eventually decide hard cases . . . and if it is inadequate to do so, the theory will thus reveal itself to be in need of extension or repair. Thus, by using cases, we can identify and address difficulties within aesthetic theory itself, and reveal the sources of confusion as well as illumination in what we think about art.[3]

All this is done in the context of *justification.* Thoughtful persons ask others and themselves to justify or explain or give reasons for their positions. As soon as this happens, art becomes an object of thought, not just of passive perception or manual manipulation.

Since art involves thinking, the study of art can be used to teach skills of critical thinking as well as perceptive and manual skills. Aesthetic questions do not merely elicit answers that reflect subjective personal preferences but generate attempts to articulate objective principles about the nature of art and aesthetic experience. Puzzles about what art is or the role of expression or intention in artistic production should encourage students not to stop once they have stated their own opinions. As I am using the phrase, critical thinking is reasoning culminating in judgments which can be justified and which are consistent with other judgments that one believes are true. A common definition of knowledge is "justified true belief." Rational people demand *reasons.* Knowledge is not merely a matter of believing things that happen to be true. One must expose beliefs to criticism by asking for justification, that is, for the reasons supporting them. The reasons given must in turn be exposed to criticism, and beliefs must be compared with one another to see if they are consistent. If they are not, one must be prepared to reject some as false. Which ones are rejected depends upon analysis of the support provided—by scrutinizing reasons that are used to justify a claim. The negative connotations of "criticism" are quite apt here, for, as it has been said, education is a matter of learning to distinguish "rot from nonrot." In the shopping bag puzzle about what counts as art, for example, students find that they must justify their votes by giving reasons, not merely reiterate their opinions by referring to personal preferences.

An obstacle frequently encountered in discussions of art is the widespread view that there is no *fact of the matter* in art. A pervasive relativism ("It's all relative—just a matter of opinion or the way you were brought up") colors many, if not most, people's attitudes toward aesthetic judgments. What is "rot" (or "nonrot") when everyone's opinion is as good as everyone else's? And if there is no way to distinguish truth from falsity here, what role can critical thinking play? How can we demand the reasons that justify a belief if aesthetic judgments are neither true nor false? Rationality seems to be relevant only to those things that are objective. If matters of art are all subjective, rationality seems to have no role to play. A basic question of aesthetics is whether there is anything objective, anything to be rational or critical toward.

A puzzle contributed by Ronald Moore to *Puzzles About Art* is one way of getting at the questions of the extent to which giving reasons is a legitimate component of aesthetic discussion. Moore uses a *New Yorker* cartoon that shows a couple leaving a movie theater. One of them says of the film, "I never said it wasn't good, I merely said I hated it." Moore asks whether this is a philosophically defensible remark.[4] What is the relation between liking or not liking an artwork and its being good or not good? If liking and being good are equivalent, then it would make no sense for you to say that a film is good but you hate it. If liking and being good are different, then perhaps judging something to be good is objective and depends upon reasons and principles.

I have learned that most people come to believe that there is a role for giving reasons when they are asked to contrast cases where preferences are stated with cases of value judgments. The question "Why?" seems to be far more appropriate with respect to value judgments than it does with respect to statements of personal preferences. That is, we tend to be ready to give reasons for our value judgments easily while we are not so prepared to do so with respect to our personal preferences. And this suggests an answer to the puzzles about "hating good films." *Being good* is backed by reasons, *hating*, at least sometimes, is not.

Consider the following statements.

The sun is shining today.
Brussels sprouts taste terrible.
Casablanca is a great movie.

In the first we have a clear statement of belief. If someone says it in a room with no windows we might very well ask for his or her reasons. "I just came in from outside," or "I heard it on the radio," or "I got it from a reliable source" would to some degree justify the belief of the speaker and give the hearer some grounds for believing it as well. Were the speaker unwilling or unable to give reasons in support of the belief, we would rightly accuse him or her of irrationality. "I just feel that the sun is shining even though I have no evidence" would strike us as very odd and suggest that the speaker has serious problems.

In the second utterance we have a clear statement of personal preference. It would be very unlikely that we would ask for someone's *reasons* for saying that Brussels sprouts taste terrible. Even if we did, it would not be at all surprising if the speaker were unwilling or unable to give any. "They just do, that's all!" would be the most probable reply. Someone who does not like Brussels sprouts is not considered irrational. Part of the explanation for this lies in the fact that we expect genuine reasons to be generally applicable. A real reason will be a reason for you as well as for me. Hearing it on the radio does not simply give the speaker reason to believe that the sun is shining outside; it gives everyone (at least everyone who trusts the radio) some justification. There are no general reasons for believing that Brussels sprouts taste bad, for it is clear from experience that they taste bad to some people and good to others. Belonging to the same nationality, class, or family, sharing scientific beliefs about the nutritional value of Brussels sprouts—none of these things counts for or against the likelihood of assenting to the statement "Brussels sprouts taste terrible." Therefore, asking for reasons is inappropriate. Furthermore, it is not at all unusual for someone to agree that Brussels sprouts are good for you, but still hate them. Thus, "I didn't say they aren't good (valuable), I just said I hate them" is not at all odd.

Is the statement "*Casablanca* is a great movie" more like "The sun is shining" or "Brussels sprouts taste terrible"? Even people who initially are inclined to liken it to the second begin to have doubts when they see that asking for and giving reasons in support of claims about the goodness or badness of works of art is appropriate. "I don't have any reasons for saying that *Casablanca* is a great movie; I just think so, that's all" will strike us as an odd or uncooperative response. Someone may not have any reasons for liking the film, but then they will not be likely to believe that it is a great movie. When we do feel ready to support our own preferences we seek general principles that will be acceptable by others. We point to the structure of the plot, the characterization, the lighting, the use of musical background, the role of the film in the history of art, the acting, and so forth.

It is far more likely that I will expect you to appreciate good acting than that I will expect you to share my dislike of Brussels sprouts. Thus something like general reasons function in statements about the value of art works. Saying that something is a great work of art is rather like saying that Brussels sprouts have nutritional value. And thus it is possible to believe that a movie is great, but still hate it. Most people who see movies with fine acting, intricate plot, and original camera work like them; but not all do. Fine acting is a reason in support of the claim that a movie is great; it will not insure personal favorable response. Nonetheless, the *New Yorker* cartoon and the discussion it provokes show that there is a genuine role of reason giving and hence rationality and critical thinking in aesthetics.

The cartoon itself acts as an "invitation" of sorts, and once again I think it is helpful to compare aesthetic judgments with invitations. If I invite you to dinner, I will, as responsible inviter, try to predict what will please you. Having invited children to a party, I am unlikely to serve Brussels sprouts, not because I have reason to believe that Brussels sprouts are bad, but because I have reason to believe that children often do not like them. If I invite you to go to a movie, I will legitimately look for reasons to support my choice.

One important objection to claiming that reasons play a role in aesthetic discussions, particularly in evaluations, must be considered. (I shall discuss descriptions and interpretations later.) Reasons, I have argued, only operate effectively when they are supported by principles or generalizations. For example, "I heard it on the radio" serves as a reason justifying "The sun is shining today" only if there is a general, lawlike statement that lies behind it, such as "Radio weather reports are reliable" or, more specifically, "If one hears on the radio that the sun is shining today, then the sun is shining today." It is precisely the lack of this sort of general principle or law in the

Brussels sprouts case that makes reasons irrelevant. There is no law that provides a foundation for getting to "Brussels sprouts taste terrible" via an appropriate reason. That is, we would have to have an argument of the following sort:

1. Anything green tastes terrible. (General principle or law)
2. Brussels sprouts are green. (Reason)
3. Therefore, Brussels sprouts taste terrible. (Claim or conclusion)

And statements such as (1) are simply not forthcoming.

Reasons play a role in factual judgments such as "The sun is shining today." They do not play a role in personal preference judgments such as "Brussels sprouts taste terrible." If they play a role in making aesthetic judgments such as "*Casablanca* is a great movie," then there must be a general principle (for example, "Movies with tight plot structures are great.") that operates as a major premise in the argument. The trouble is, of course, that there do not seem to be any such principles to which all or even most people would assent.

This point has been made clearly by the philosopher Arnold Isenberg in a paper entitled "Critical Communication."[5] The breakdown of the general principle-reason-conclusion model in personal preference judgment cases like the Brussels sprouts case also characterizes aesthetic judgments, he argues. There are, he believes, no general aesthetic principles or laws, and hence criticism cannot correctly be explained as consisting of giving reasons that will justify beliefs.

This breakdown does not worry Isenberg, however. For he thinks that aesthetic judgments do not have as their goal bringing others to share our beliefs; rather, they have as their goal getting others to see what we see in a work. Critical communication is an elaborate form of *pointing*. If I say, "*Casablanca* is a great movie" and go on to mention its plot structure or characterization, I am not giving you reasons to believe that this is a great film. Rather, I am trying to get you to perceive the features that I see.

Isenberg's position is very appealing, but the upshot of it is to turn aesthetic discussion into activity that is essentially irrational. For if there is no role for reasons, there is no possible way for one to justify one's aesthetic judgment by citing one's reasons for it. If someone asks me why I like *Casablanca*, I will not be able to give reasons. All I can do is what I do in the Brussels sprouts case—shrug my shoulders and simply say, "I just like it, that's all." It does not help to point to the smell or shape or color of Brussels sprouts, for these are precisely features that their fans admire. If appreciation of *Casablanca* is like this, then it would be futile to point to features of the film to explain my favorable judgment. And this seems wrong to me. Aesthetic judgments do not seem completely analogous to those of purely personal preference. The incredibly large body of critical writing supports the intuition that we do feel compelled to give reasons in support of our aesthetic judgments. People generally do not respond, "Oh, no reason" or "I just do (or don't)" when asked why they like or dislike works of art.

Aesthetic judgments in a sense seem to straddle the fence that marks a boundary between statements of fact and statements of personal preference. Isenberg is right in asserting that there are no aesthetic laws that achieve anything like universal assent. It is frustratingly easy to find counterexamples to generalizations such as "All graceful vases are beautiful," or "All suspenseful novels are good," or "All symphonies in classical form are great." At the same time, I believe that there is a genuine pull in the direction of justifying our aesthetic judgments by doing something very much like giving reasons for them. "Because it's graceful," "because of the buildup of suspense," or "because of its use of classical form," and other such statements do play a significant role in aesthetic discussions. We may sometimes utter such things just to hear ourselves talk; but not always.

Isenberg thinks we say things like "It's graceful" in order to point. And he is partly right. However, more is going on than mere pointing. Pointing is done in order to *invite* people to see what we see. And if there is no role for reasons in pointing, there certainly is a role for reasons in inviting. Responsible invitations are issued with the goal of providing an opportunity for others to engage in activity that we find worthwhile and believe they too will find worthwhile. Our own enjoyment of gracefulness or suspense or classical forms gives us a reason to believe that other human beings will also take enjoyment in the works that have these features. As teachers, we must presuppose that most people, once they learn to perceive gracefulness or classical form or the buildup of suspense or unity or harmony or any of the other properties of objects we hope to bring them to be able to discern, will benefit from the experience. There is no guarantee that someone who perceives gracefulness or buildup of suspense will like it or the work in which it is located. Nonetheless, the expectation that appreciation will increase and life will thereby be enriched lies behind all educational invitations.

Now we can see how puzzles and invitations and reasons come

together. Puzzles are one way of issuing invitations to perceive and reflect upon features of objects that we have reason to believe will give satisfaction to others. In particular, aesthetic puzzles, by getting people to think about works of art, draw their attention to features of these objects that one believes worthy of that attention.

Puzzles about art thus have a double function: they get people to philosophize by doing aesthetics per se, and they get people to pay closer attention to works of art per se. In a philosophy class, the main goal is to get students to do philosophy, and there is a sense in which one can do *philosophy* of art without actually looking at or listening to particular works of art. One can attempt, for instance, to answer the question "What is art?" by just thinking—without looking at actual physical objects. (My own preference, however, even in doing "pure" philosophy, is to do it in the presence of specific, concrete examples.) But aesthetics as the philosophy of *art* is a different matter. Since the usefulness of aesthetics in art education lies in its capacity to direct attention to specific works, philosophical puzzles about art are interesting philosophically, but are also valuable because they engage people aesthetically.

The nature of aesthetic experience has been debated endlessly. Just what it is or how one identifies it in oneself or others is a matter of controversy. Sometimes attempts to delimit aesthetic experience emphasize attention to something for its own sake alone, that is, attention to an object or event without an ulterior purpose. One's experience of a sunset is thought to be aesthetic if one just enjoys it as it is, without worrying about its scientific causes, for instance. One appreciates a car aesthetically, it is often thought, if one thinks about its appearance, not about how much mileage it gets, whether it will start in cold weather, or how efficient the engine is.

However, it is better to try to understand aesthetic experience not in terms of what it lacks (an external goal, for example) but in terms of positive features that distinguish it. My own view is that aesthetic experience can best be characterized as follows: *An experience is aesthetic if and only if one pays attention to intrinsic features of things or events, and those features have been traditionally or culturally identified as worthy of perception and reflection.*[6] I will say more below about which intrinsic features matter. First I want to turn to two more puzzles and show how they focus attention on these features.

The puzzle about the man leaving the movie theater dealt with evaluation. I chose it because I wanted to show that there is a role for reason giving, that is, for rationality in aesthetic discussion, and likes and dislikes provide the hardest case for this. But evaluation is only one part of aesthetic activity, and although it is often thought to be the central part, probably in sheer quantitative terms it takes a back seat to two other aspects: description and interpretation of works.

Successful description requires a vocabulary that allows one to pick out relevant properties of something. We describe a tree, for example, in vocabulary familiar to us; we use words like "branch," "leaf," and "trunk." Imagine what it would be like if we were not familiar with trees or tree vocabulary and suddenly were asked to talk about them. The more extensive one's vocabulary, the better able one is to produce a description that is truly "descriptive," that is, one that gives detailed information. But, of course, an extensive vocabulary gives only information to hearers who share that vocabulary. Someone who knows the terms for various shapes of leaves will learn a lot from a description that utilizes them. But information will not be exchanged if the hearer is ignorant of the meanings of the special words. And lacking words for leaf-shapes, we are likely to overlook details of the leaves themselves.

Suppose you are asked to describe the taste of a fine wine, a task which feels like a "puzzle" to many people. Possession of the wine experts' terminology will make the task relatively easy. But most of us are not experts and are left with simplistic choices like "fruity" or "tastes like wine." An expert who tells you to notice the tannin or acid or structure will probably only leave you frustrated. One is confronted with a circle into which it seems impossible to break. On the one hand, you have to be familiar with something before you can talk about it; on the other hand, you have to know how to talk about it before you can become familiar with it. You have to recognize the tannin taste before you can say that a wine has a strong tannin taste. But until you know the meaning of "tannin," you cannot identify it by taste.

Experts who are also good teachers know where to begin with novices so that they can break into the circle. For example, building on the novice's use of "fruity," the expert can urge the novice to look for subtle fruit differences. Does it taste like an orange or a grape? Really like a grape, or—and now we approach understanding one of the basic terms of wine assessment—more like a black currant? Of course, for those who have never tasted a black currant, descriptions in terms of this fruit will not be helpful. The expert may have to provide grapes and black currants themselves in order to bring the novice to perceive the latter taste in a glass of wine.

The frustration of feeling left out because one lacks the vocabulary or the acquaintance and hence does not know where or how to begin also characterizes the experiences of many people when they approach art forms with which they are unfamiliar. Technical words like "dentil" or "Ionic order" used to talk about ancient Greek temples often leave novices cold. Even apparently obvious terms such as "symmetrical" may elude beginners. Detailed analysis of various orders is not merely a memory exercise; it allows viewers actually to see details that they would be likely to miss without the appropriate terminology. Instead of playing the "put-down game" that merely confuses, embarrasses, bewilders, or irritates, teachers should demonstrate that acquisition of new vocabulary (and knowledge in general) provides for richer experiences.

This brings us to the second puzzle that I promised to provide as a way of drawing attention to intrinsic properties of works of art. One term that gives people a lot of trouble is "style"; and the puzzle "What is style?" provides an excellent way of helping students to see via philosophizing. Cognates of this word turn up frequently in descriptions of artworks: "in the classical style" or "highly stylized" are just two examples. I have found the following exercise very helpful in bringing people to understand what style is and why it is important aesthetically and artistically.

First, as with the wine example, it is important to start at a point that will make sense to the person perplexed. I work with the term "stylish," because people in our culture from a remarkably early age are acutely aware of what it means to be stylish. I begin by choosing four or five people in the classroom dressed in different styles— someone preppy, someone punk, someone conservative, someone artsy, for example. We then try to answer several questions:

1. Are the people dressed in the same style? If not, describe the differences.

2. Is the choice of clothing an accident?

3. If not, what lies behind the choice? What "statement" or feeling is being made or expressed?

4. Are the individuals successful in making what you take to be their intended statement? If not, suggest changes that would make for greater success.

5. Could the clothing of one person be used to make the same statement that someone dressed differently makes? What changes would have to be made?

Following a discussion of these questions, one can turn to showing artworks done in different styles—Egyptian, Greek, and contemporary statues of human figures, for instance. Adaptations of the five questions asked about clothing can be asked about these styles of art (for example, "Are all of these works done in the same style?"). Following this discussion one can now ask what is meant by "classical style" or "highly stylized." Finally, the students can be asked to write their own definition of the term "style." And they are usually quite pleased to be told that they have now become "philosophers"! Most importantly, they will now have learned a vocabulary that will allow them to see, point to, and invite others to enjoy features of the world that aesthetically enrich one's life.

It is also important to have students write as a part of their art education. An exercise such as defining a term or presenting their own solution to an aesthetic puzzle demonstrates further that art can be cognitively approached. And it cannot be emphasized too often that students need all the practice at writing that they can get.

Another puzzle from the "puzzle book" foregrounds an additional component of aesthetic activity: interpretation. The meaning of a work, often even how it is to be correctly described, is almost always open to question. Here is how David E. Carrier introduces a puzzle about interpretation:

Commenting on Caravaggio's *Conversion of St. Paul*, the nineteenth-century critic Jacob Burckhardt wrote: "How coarsely Caravaggio could compose and feel . . . *The Conversion of St. Paul* . . . shows, where the horse nearly fills the whole of the picture."

The art connoisseur Bernard Berenson described the picture thus: "We are to interpret this charade as the conversion of Paul. Nothing is more incongruous than the importance given to horse over rider, to dumb beast over saint . . . no trace of a miraculous occurrence of supreme import." Writing a few years later, the art historian Rudolf Wittkower asserts: "In his *Conversion of St. Paul* he rendered vision solely on the level of inner illumination. . . . [Like the Counter-Reformation religious] reformers, Caravaggio pleaded through his pictures for man's direct gnosis of the Divine. Like them, he regarded illumination by God as a tangible experience on a purely human level." If Wittkower is right, Burckhardt and Berenson have completely misinterpreted the work by making too much of the horse. If Burckhardt and Berenson were right, Wittkower is wrong, and the horse cannot be ignored. How do we decide which of these great writers is right?[7] Questions like these are at the heart of philosophical puzzles about the nature of interpretation.

The questions "Are there right and wrong interpretations?" or "Are some interpretations better than others?" require one to look carefully at the work as well as to think about these general problems. The fact that Caravaggio's painting is not reproduced here shows, I think, how essential it is to raise these questions in the presence of specific works. Even if one is familiar with *Conversion of St. Paul*, as one reads this passage it is impossible not to become frustrated by being unable to see again for oneself just how the horse and St. Paul are related. This frustration supports what I have said repeatedly: good aesthetic discussion, by engaging attention, invites viewers to look carefully. This particular example also shows how important history is to the understanding of a work. Students who do not know, for example, the story of St. Paul's conversion, or are unaware of the controversy about the church's role in human access to the divinity, will not have a full experience of this work. This is why knowledge of *history* is a crucial component of the full experience of a work of art (and why in a discipline-based art education curriculum it plays an important role.)

My own view is that although there are rarely, if ever, single correct interpretations of artworks, it is possible to discriminate between good and bad ones. Adequate interpretations must:

1. Direct attention to the work.
2. Point to details (the more the better, usually).
3. Account for the organization or structure of the work.

If an interpretative remark directs the viewer away from the work (to think, for instance, about psychology or religion rather than about the work of art), then there is no way that the features or details of the work will be noticed. Or if an obvious feature of the work is left out, then the interpretation will fail on both statements 2 and 3 above. Someone who says that the horse is not important in Caravaggio's painting simply does not give a good interpretation—unless, of course, a strong case is made for this on the basis of a significant number of other features of the work.

One of the important lessons of puzzles about interpretations is that students are shown that even experts disagree. But done correctly, the lesson will not send the message that "anything goes." For one will insist that interpretative conclusions be backed by premises that point to features of artworks. Another important goal of such exercises is demonstrating that aesthetic activity and looking at works of art are not passive—that it is not enough to look at a work, decide if you like it, and then go on to something else. One must look at artworks carefully, and more than once. One must think about what one sees, and make various parts cohere. One looks for patterns of organization. All these actions are cognitive.

I have repeatedly used the term "intrinsic" to describe the features of a work that I believe are relevant aesthetically. I must now say more about what I mean by it. Essentially, intrinsic features of something are properties that are located "in" it. More specifically, a property is an intrinsic property of a thing if and only if one must perceive (see, hear, feel, smell, taste) the thing for oneself in order to know if it has that property, and, if one knows the meaning of a word used to refer to an intrinsic property, then all one needs to do is perceive it in order to know if the thing has that property or not (although one must sometimes pay very close attention). One can know that a work was painted in Spain without looking at it (via historic documents, for example), but one cannot know that something is in the Spanish style without looking. One can know that a song was first performed in London without hearing it; but one cannot know if a song is lyrical without listening to it. In general, knowing whether an artwork possesses a particular aesthetic quality requires direct perception of properties *in* the work. We saw above that one must first know the meaning of a term before one can know whether a particular object possesses the property named by that term—"tannin" or "Ionic," for example. But once one does know the meaning of these terms, all one need do is direct attention to intrinsic properties of wine or buildings to know if they apply. This is always the case with intrinsic properties. If one knows the meaning of the phrase "in the Spanish style," then one can discover whether it correctly describes a painting or not by looking at the painting. It is *intrinsic* properties or features that matter aesthetically—the features that one perceives and reflects upon in an aesthetic experience.

Not all intrinsic features matter aesthetically, however. The precise measurements of a painting may not matter aesthetically; its smell almost never does. Which of an object's intrinsic features are aesthetically relevant depends upon traditions, practices, conventions, and institutions that shape the way a community treats the objects it designates as artworks.[8] As these change, so will what matters aesthetically. The size of the horse matters more when the convention of proportion dominates, less when an allegorical convention does, for example.

In the West during much of the twentieth century, art theorists and critics often have argued that the only properties of an object that are aesthetically significant are its formal properties—shape, color, spatial organization of these, and so forth. However, more and more theorists are now ready to admit a much broader range of features. The philosopher Aristotle taught that in order fully to understand anything, one must know four things about it (four "causes" he called them, though this term can be misleading): one must know who made it, what it is made of, what its form is, and why it was made. He used the example of a statue to explain what he meant. "Knowing" a statue demands that one know its material (bronze, for example), who made it (the sculptor), its form (runner-shape), and why it was made (to commemorate the opening of an athletic club). All these things can figure importantly in aesthetic discussions—as long as they direct attention to intrinsic features of objects. Referring to extrinsic facts, as well as to intrinsic features, will be relevant as long as intrinsic features become the focus of attention.

I invite my students to do what I call "FRETing" over works. (Fretting and puzzling are clearly related.) One "FRETs" by considering four aspects of works: *f*ormal properties, *r*epresentational properties, *e*xpressive properties, and *t*echnical properties. First one looks for such things as shapes, colors, and handling of space. Second, one considers the things or ideas represented by a work which are usually important. Even when works are abstract and have no realistic content, they can still be discussed in terms of the statements that an artist is attempting to make by way of shapes and colors. Third, one asks what a work expresses—either a feeling or thought. Like "representation," "expression" has been variously interpreted. Advanced students can indeed be invited to try to define these terms for themselves. Fourth, one considers the techniques used by the maker. Finally, one asks how all these are related. What techniques did the artist utilize in order to create the formal properties that result in the representations and expressions presented? If you look back at the exercise about style, you will see how "FRETing" took place. The order in which one considers these various aspects does not matter; nor does it spoil things to skip around. What is important is to use this as a strategy for engaging attention in a not completely random way.

Puzzles About Art is a very helpful book and fills a need that the mindless activity of my grade school years never did. It provides clear problems that will engage students' attentions and make them *think* about art and artistic activity. However, puzzles about art are all around us. Nearly every week one finds a difficult case reported in a newspaper or on television. Forgeries are uncovered that make us ask whether it really matters who painted something as long as we enjoy it. Canvases bring millions of dollars at art auctions, confronting us with the question of how aesthetic and market value are related. "Artists" produce things that only the makers recognize as art. All these provide exciting occasions for introducing conceptual and critical aesthetic thought into discussions of art.

Of course, excitement and extent of discussion are no guarantees that the frustration of not being able to give final and definite answers will go away. Philosophy rarely produces answers that generate universal agreement. But that does not put philosophers in the category with people who tell riddles without answers. It is "impolite," to say the least, to tell someone a riddle and then announce that you don't know the answer yourself. "Why did the chicken climb the tree?" "I don't know—why?" "Gee, I don't know either!" Hardly a way to win friends! Philosophy sometimes seems like this. Philosophers are often accused of presenting puzzles that they then leave unanswered.

All the examples we have looked at (What is art? What is the connection between liking a work of art and its being good? What is style? and Are there good or correct interpretations?) continue to be controversial. I have indicated some of my own views along the way, but by no means will everyone agree with them. There is no way, short of ignoring the activity altogether, to make the frustration go away altogether. But puzzling over things lies at the root of being human. As teachers we can exploit this aspect of human nature in ways that make for more precise, thoughtful, and coherent individuals. Or we can ignore it and leave students to random, scatterbrained, and desultory bull sessions. Enriching art experiences by raising philosophical questions may spare students from the kind of emptiness that I experienced in my own art classes. They will, I believe, be rewarded with increased perceptivity and insight and heightened awareness of the central and integral role that art can play in human experience.

Introducing puzzles without knowing the answer oneself, even if not impolite, can be frightening. It is best, of course, to have thought about the puzzles oneself before engaging others in them. But experts disagree, and one must always be prepared to be challenged in ways that may force one to throw out one's own views. At the very least, we come to appreciate the frustration by remembering, with Socrates, that "the unexamined life is not worth living."

NOTES

1. Marcia Muelder Eaton, "James' Turn of the Speech-Act," *British Journal of Aesthetics* 23 (Autumn, 1983): 33-45.

2. Margaret P. Battin, John Fisher, Ronald Moore, and Anita Silvers, *Puzzles About Art: An Aesthetics Casebook* (New York: St. Martin's Press, 1989).

3. Ibid., pp. vii-ix.

4. Ibid., p. 203.

5. Arnold Isenberg, "Critical Communication," *Philosophical Review* 58 (July 1949): 330-44.

6. For more on this definition, see Marcia Muelder Eaton, *Aesthetics and the Good Life* (Cranbury, NJ: Associated University Presses, 1989), chap. 7.

7. Battin et al., *Puzzles About Art*, p. 91.

8. For more on this topic, see Eaton, *Aesthetics and the Good Life*, chap. 6.

CHAPTER VIII

Arts Education, Human Development, and the Quality of Experience

MIHALY CSIKSZENTMIHALYI AND ULRICH SCHIEFELE

Introduction: Do the Arts Really Matter?

   A generally held view is that knowledge in the natural sciences and mathematics is more important for the well-being and survival of humankind than any other area of knowledge or experience. This commonsense view is also reflected in the policies of governments and major research foundations which invest the larger part of their funds in the "hard" sciences. In the context of this cultural atmosphere it seems absurd to give public support to people just to enable them to live as painters, sculptors, or musicians. The educational system, which usually mirrors the values of society, also gives only marginal importance to arts and music instruction.[1]

But this minor role assigned to the arts in society and education needs to be questioned. There are at least three major reasons for rethinking these political and educational priorities. The first reason is that the technical progress made possible by intensive research in physics and the other sciences is at least as threatening for man's future as it is beneficial. At the very least, it seems desirable to slow down the development and production of energy-consuming goods and to direct human creativity increasingly to other fields of meaningful activity and production.[2] Second, the increasing automatization of production, the decreasing amount of working time, and the increasing average age of the population pose problems about the use of free time.[3] The reception as well as the production of artistic products (e.g., pictures, photographs, poems, prose, music) should

---

Mihaly Csikszentmihalyi is Professor of Psychology and of Education, University of Chicago. Ulrich Schiefele is on the faculty of Social Sciences, University of the Bundeswehr, Munich, Germany.

provide people with a valuable alternative to watching TV, to being bored, or to engaging in dull, energy-consuming, or environmentally damaging leisure activities. The third reason for assigning more significance to arts education lies in its possible value for human evolution and for the development of the individual human being. The last assertion will be scrutinized now more closely.

Aesthetic Cognition and Human Development

Artistic activities, cognitions, and experiences appear to have significant functions in the course of phylogenetic and ontogenetic development.[4] Past accounts of human evolution have, however, clearly favored the acquisition of rational knowledge as it is represented by the sciences and mathematics. It is true that rational cognition has unequivocally proved its function as a tool for adaptation to the world around us. Rational cognition has made it possible for humankind to predict external events and thus master obstacles and make use of the environment for its own purpose.[5] Its power is very much based on the precision with which phenomena can be analytically defined and labeled, and on the assumption that things in the world can be assigned to single, mutually exclusive categories (i.e., Aristotle's principle of noncontradiction).

These features of rational thought, which contribute a great deal to its usefulness, are at the same time responsible for its constraints. When it comes to basic human affairs, such as feelings and social relationships, a rational system based on precise analytic assumptions ceases to be an adequate representation of reality. A straightforward quantitative approach would disguise these complex and ambiguous phenomena rather than clarify them. Furthermore, seemingly contradictory feelings like love and hate can be experienced almost at the same time. Thus, it seems questionable that the assumption of noncontradiction, which excludes the possibility that a thing can at the same time be its opposite, is a correct model for describing all aspects of reality. The obvious constraints of rational thought led Wittgenstein to demand that "What we cannot speak about we must pass over in silence."[6] He maintained that the rationality of science is not able to deal with those issues that are the most essential to everyday life—such as death, religion, ways of living, the meaning of work and life. It follows that the development of more and more specific rules for scientific reasoning results in the exclusion of ever larger amounts of thought and experience. Although reasoning has proved itself adaptive, there is justified doubt that increasing the powers of reason at the expense of other modes of knowing will ultimately lead to greater understanding.

Some theorists have explored the role of aesthetic cognition as a complementary alternative to rational cognition.[7] It is generally agreed that both science and art are symbolic systems that provide knowledge. However, their respective procedures and the nature of the resulting knowledge are quite different. Unlike science, art represents experienced reality that is ambiguous, contradictory, and partly unconscious. Artistic cognition is based on symbolic rules that are holistic, idiosyncratic, and implicit rather than explicit. The products of art do not represent unequivocal pictures of reality that can be tested empirically.

Were mankind to rely only on this type of knowledge, it would not be able to survive. The merits of aesthetic cognition, however, are as a corrective to an exclusively rational approach. Aesthetic cognition gains its evolutionary value by providing models or descriptions of internal and external realities which cannot be represented by purely rational means. As Getzels and Csikszentmihalyi have shown, artists most often deal with basic existential questions that cannot be answered by scientific reasoning.[8] In *A Portrait of the Artist as a Young Man*, James Joyce provides a nice example for this basic aspect of the artistic endeavor when at the end of the book Stephen Daedalus says: "Welcome, O life! I go to encounter for the millionth time the reality of experience and to forge in the smithy of my soul the uncreated conscience of my race."[9]

In dealing with as yet unexpressed existential human problems, the artist might be regarded as part of the avant garde that creates new concepts and new rules of thinking, and thus may lead rational thought to expand its borders and to reach higher levels. While rational cognition gains control over reality by drastically reducing it to its basic quantifiable aspects, art models phenomena in a more global and analogic way that also tolerates contradictions between constitutive elements.

The contribution of artistic models of reality to the evolution of human thought also appears on the level of individual development. This is especially true for those who actively engage in the creative production of art. Getzels and Csikszentmihalyi have provided numerous examples of painters and sculptors who use their work to express personal problems and basic life themes.[10] The process of visual expression clearly helps gain some control and understanding of barely conscious internal tensions, diffuse problems, or felt ambiguities. "The key to creative achievement is the transformation of an intangible conflict into a tangible symbolic problem to which the creative solution will be the response."[11]

A second function of arts-related activities at the level of individual development is helping the person to maintain the cognitive structure of the self. The sum of all activities a person is engaged in defines a great deal of the person's self. This is especially, and perhaps only, true for intentional and self-determined activities.[12] As the creation of art is by definition an intentional and self-determined activity, it should contribute to what a person defines as his or her being. This contrasts with other ways people strive to reassure themselves that their self is an autonomous and powerful agent, for example, through the possession of material objects, the control of physical energy, and the control of other people's psychic energy.

In this section we have shown that there are important differences between rational thought, as it is represented by the sciences and mathematics, and aesthetic knowledge produced by creating or responding to art. It was our intention to show that the two domains complement each other, by fostering cognizance of different dimensions of reality. Our analysis suggests that creating, responding to, or learning about art have more relevance for people's everyday life experience and their existential struggles than do the natural and technical sciences. If one wants to find a suitable way of living or to understand how another person feels, mathematical equations, physical laws, or sophisticated computer programs won't provide much help. It may be argued that psychological knowledge will bring helpful advice. While this is certainly true for some well-defined problems, psychological knowledge cannot solve many basic existential problems with which we have to struggle. In addition, it is interesting to note that many therapeutic techniques encourage the patient to engage in activities that resemble those of an artist: interpretation of dreams, illogical associative thinking, mental visualization, holistic thinking, painting, psychodrama, and focusing on inner mental and bodily states.[13]

Jung wrote that when rationalizing and "normalizing" cease to help the client then therapy has to follow the client's idiosyncratic and "irrational" thought patterns.[14] In this phase of the therapy, the therapist is no longer treating the client but seeks to facilitate the development of the client's creative potential. To achieve this goal, Jung relied mainly on dreams. Moreover, it is a crucial part of the process of dream analysis that the client paints or draws his or her dreams. According to Jung, this is the only means of decoding the hidden meaning of a dream and of turning it into a subjectively helpful insight. It is not necessary that the therapist understand the client's dream intellectually; what counts is that the client arrives at a subjectively meaningful interpretation.

Finally, perhaps the major difference between rational knowledge and artistic knowledge is in terms of their outcomes. Whereas we use reason generally as an instrumental tool in order to achieve some external good (a better prediction, a more efficient procedure), the use of artistic representation is an end in itself; it generates its own enjoyment and its own meaning regardless of future consequences. The enlightenment a work of art produces in the artist and in the viewer enhances the quality of life here and now, and needs no further justification. To the extent that the quality of life is the highest good toward which all our activities tend, it can be argued that art contributes to it directly, whereas sciences and technology do so only indirectly.

If there is validity to these distinctions between rational and artistic cognition, then one would expect that the quality of experience is rather different in these realms. More specifically, we assume that young people engaged in arts-related activities have a more positive experience than when engaged in solving mathematical problems or when learning about physical facts. Whether this is true or not, and what the resulting consequences are for teaching, is the question addressed in the following sections.

The Significance of Arts in Everyday Life: Evidence from Case Studies

The empirical data reported in this chapter are part of a large-scale longitudinal study of talented adolescents.[15] The study involves 208 freshmen and sophomores from two high schools who were studied for a period of five years to determine some of the causes of disengagement from talent. These students were among 535 nominated by teachers as having outstanding talent in either arts, athletics, music, mathematics, or science (74 percent were nominated in one area only, while 26 percent were nominated in two or more areas). Data were obtained through questionnaires, interviews, and the administration of the Experience Sampling Method (ESM).

The ESM consisted of the following procedures. Each student was asked to carry for one week an electronic pager and a booklet containing fifty identical response sheets. About eight times a day, at a randomly chosen moment, a signal was sent to all the pagers. When the signal activated the pager, students would take out their response booklet and fill out a page, indicating what they were doing, where they were, and what they were thinking about. In addition, each time they also rated their feelings on thirty scales along a variety of dimensions (e.g., happy-sad, strong-weak, clear-confused). This technique allows precise description and comparisons of the quality of experience.[16]

Besides the ESM several other measures were taken (e.g., personality test, self-concept questionnaire, ability test) and all students were intensively interviewed at the beginning of the study. Before we turn to the results based mainly on the ESM, we want to introduce the reader to some of our students who showed high interest in the arts. The following cases are based on the interviews. The cases we have selected are intended to highlight the relationship between the arts and quality of experience.

CASEY

Casey is a fifteen-year-old girl who has been nominated as being talented in arts. She has already won an art contest. Her self-description shows her as a normal teenager who likes to be with friends, finds school sometimes boring, and has a good sense of humor. Her greatest problem is being "shy around people that I don't really know." Also, she seems to get easily upset and wishes to be better able to control her emotions. Casey wants to get good grades so she can go to a good liberal arts college and become a commercial artist. Since she does not know whether she will be good enough to make a living as an artist, she needs a job that allows her to "do fine art . . . in my spare time."

What makes it meaningful for her to paint or draw pictures? "In art I like being able to feel some way and have someone else feel the same way." For Casey art seems to be a tool to express her own feelings and to communicate them to other people. Moreover, in doing art she seems to be able to gain more control of her emotions. She says: "I'm more interested in emotions than anything else. I'm not interested in logical thinking. I'm not interested in the laws of nature. I'm just interested in surroundings, the way things look, the way I feel, the way other things feel." But doing art isn't just fun, it also involves becoming more competent and skilled. In fact, Casey regards enjoyment and skill development as being closely related. She not only likes art more than ever but also believes that she has "improved a lot from last year." She thinks that the more she puts into art the more she gets out. Obviously, the reward of becoming more and more competent in the arts is the artistic activity itself (and not the "good life" in the future). It is not surprising then that she states: "No, I never really thought about quitting art. I didn't think it was something that you could actually quit. Once you get started with it you don't just stop."

PAUL

Paul is fifteen years of age and his talent and interest are in art, especially drawing and sketching. Paul does not want to be popular. In stark contrast to most of his peers, Paul likes being alone. The one thing Paul most dislikes about himself is, like Casey, "being shy—mostly with girls." He also believes that he should take school more seriously, because he is not doing as well as he thinks he should.

The expression of emotions is for Paul an important part of drawing. "I normally draw my emotions and feelings," he says. A vivid example of using art as a means to overcome a personal problem or to cope with strong negative feelings is given by his description of what he did over the weekend after his beloved grandmother died. At that time he had to do an assignment: "I was really depressed—and the assignment was to do something strange with a shoe, so I made the shoe shaped like a little boy that hung himself with a shoelace." But art in Paul's life is not solely important during times of personal crises. He generally enjoys doing art and attributes high significance to it: "It gives me freedom, I guess. It makes me more creative. It makes me think more." He feels that his interest in drawing is "the strongest thing I have right now."

As we will see below, the major constituents of optimal experience are the perceptions of high skills and high challenges. When these conditions are present, an experience of "flow" becomes possible. When asked whether he ever experienced doing something where his concentration was very intense, his attention wrapped up in what he was doing, and where he became totally unaware of things around him, Paul named drawing as his foremost flow activity. He indicated that at least once a week drawing helps him experience flow.

KENDALL

Kendall is fourteen years old and has been nominated as a talented musician, a singer. Like many of her peers Kendall expresses confusion about who she really is as a person. Otherwise, she describes herself as being grown-up and "really understanding, really logical."

One of the things Kendall likes about herself is that she is a good singer: "It's not conceited to say, I just am. I've worked really hard at it. . . . I'm pretty much to the point where I can sing almost anything. I just have to work at it." She has already sung in the chorus of "South Pacific." Singing is also her main and most enjoyable activity. Her most ambitious goal for the future is to get a lead part to sing. "Right now, nothing is as important as accomplishing my music, and being able to sing really well." In her case, the desire to be competent and the enjoyment of singing are not contradictory forces. "I've been enjoying myself more than ever in chorus class, because we've been singing really hard music that I really had to train myself hard to sing." Singing is her greatest challenge right now, more important to her than all other things in school. Kendall exhibits a strong need to become competent which is accompanied by a strong sense of self-determination: "It's [singing] the one thing I have that's really mine right now, something other people don't tell me how to do or what to do with it. When other people tell me how to do it, it's like they're taking away the only thing right now that's being independent." Another consequence of being intrinsically motivated is that one becomes less dependent on extrinsic rewards: "I don't like compliments, or comments right after I finish singing. . . . First I like to dwell over it and figure out if I thought it was good or not. Then I don't mind some comment."

As has been true for Casey and Paul, Kendall seeks to have a job that allows her to follow her interest in singing. She has realized that a career as a singer is improbable, "because you can't make it just as a singer." But even with these external obstacles, music will not lose its significance for Kendall: "I really do think that I'll pursue it all the way through my life."

The cases described above have several points in common. First, the talent areas in which Casey, Paul, and Kendall are involved provide a great deal of positive experience. They are not only important in the context of school but own a central place in the lives of these teenagers. Second, probably as a consequence of the positive experience, all three students exhibit high levels of intrinsic motivation to learn. Obviously, they want to learn to become more and more skilled in their craft and to experience the enjoyment that acting on a high skill level provides. They are not primarily motivated by getting good grades, by praise, or by the goal to be better than others. The needs for self-determination and competence are essential aspects of their behavior. According to Deci and Ryan, these needs are the basis of every intrinsically motivated activity.[17] Third, enjoyment of the activity and hard work or effort do not exclude each other. Rather, the two go hand in hand and the one seems not to be conceivable without the other. On the one hand, the liking for art motivates the acquisition of skill and knowledge, and, on the other hand, the mastery of new challenges facilitates interest and enjoyment. Fourth, as we have argued above, artistic activities function as a means to express and communicate emotions, which is particularly important during adolescence when emotions swing between extremes and can disrupt interaction.[18] Fifth, all three students wish that they could continue being involved in art or music throughout their adult lives. They realize, however, that this is rather difficult and have thus made plans to strive for professions which will allow them to stay on as active artists in their spare time. Finally, despite the fact that Casey, Paul, and Kendall are regarded as being talented, their problems, attitudes, and expectations show that they are pretty much "normal" teenagers. This suggests that their experience might be accessible to almost every student.

Of course, there are some teenagers in our sample who seem to have similarly positive experiences in mathematics or science. But these cases are very rare. The interviews we conducted suggest that for most students engaged in art or music a high level of quality of experience is available. However, this conclusion might be premature and in the next section we will present the results of a more objective and quantitative analysis.

Arts and Quality of Experience:
A Systematic Analysis

We report here on comparisons made between the quality of experience of students talented in mathematics and science and those talented in arts and music when these groups were actively engaged in their respective talent area. The analysis is based on data obtained by the Experience Sampling Method.

In this report quality of experience in different talent areas is compared by means of four dimensions of experience: affect, potency, self-esteem, and intrinsic motivation. These dimensions have been measured by means of rating scales. Affect was represented by the scales happy-sad, cheerful-irritable, and sociable-lonely. Potency comprised the scales alert-drowsy, active-passive, strong-weak, and excited-bored. Self-esteem was based on ratings of the following questions: Did you feel good about yourself? Were you satisfied with how you were doing? Were you living up to your own expectations? Intrinsic motivation was measured by the question: Do you wish you had been doing something else?

In order to simplify the presentation of results, we have combined the four talent areas into two subgroups, mathematics and science on the one hand, and art and music on the other hand. It should be noticed that all subsamples are independent. If a student, for example, was nominated in two or more talent areas, he or she was assigned to that group which represented his or her *preferred* talent area. The math/science group consists of twenty-nine students talented in mathematics and fourteen students talented in science. The art/music group is made up of fourteen talented art students and forty-nine talented musicians.

First, the results revealed that across all situations the students' feelings were almost exactly the same regardless of the area of talent.

The comparison of experience between specific talent areas is based on only those reports that were made in response to signals received while the students were engaged in school in their respective talent areas. The responses included were as follows: for mathematics students, responses while in mathematics classes; for science students, while in chemistry and biology classes; for art students, while in art class, the studio, and the art room; and for music students, while in music class, the music room, and during rehearsals with a band or orchestra. The number of completed experience sampling forms for individual students ranged from one to five. On the average, every student filled out two or three forms. All analyses are based on individually aggregated scores. In order to outweigh individual differences in general levels of experience, individual z-scores have been computed.[19] Thus, positive z-scores indicate that quality of experience is above the person's weekly average, while the reverse is true for negative z-scores.

The analysis of talent-related experience reveals clear differences (see Table 1). When doing science and mathematics, the teenagers gifted in these subjects tended to feel *worse* than they usually felt. Conversely, when teenagers gifted in art or music were involved in their subjects, they felt *better* than their weekly average. The differences are especially marked for self-esteem and intrinsic motivation. The level of intrinsic motivation is not only a significant educational goal in itself; it also facilitates learning processes especially when deeper levels of comprehension are required.[20]

TABLE 1

MEANS ON MEASURES OF QUALITY OF EXPERIENCE WHEN STUDENTS
WERE WORKING IN THEIR OWN TALENT AREAS

DIMENSIONS OF EXPERIENCE[a]	MATH/SCIENCE STUDENTS ($n = 43$)	ART/MUSIC STUDENTS ($n = 63$)	t-TEST[b] t	$p <$
Affect	− .05	.28	2.39	.05
Potency	− .06	.26	2.51	.05
Self-esteem	− .21	.21	2.83	.01
Intrinsic motivation	− .21	.19	2.74	.01

[a] All mean values reported are based on individual z-scores.
[b] Two-tailed.

What happens when students who are talented in mathematics or science do art or music, and vice versa? As the following results show, the quality of experience shown in table 1 is reversed. When engaged in art-related activities, the quality of experience for math/science students became at least as positive as their weekly average, as shown by the following group means: affect, $M = .06$; potency, $M = .23$; self-esteem, $M = -.01$; intrinsic motivation, $M = .28$. On the other hand, when arts/music students were doing mathematics or science, they reported a quality of experience consistently lower than their weekly average. However, it is only for "potency" that a statistically significant difference between math/science and art/music students emerges (t = 2.99, $p = < .01$). It should also be noted that because not many math/science students were enrolled in arts or music classes there were few of them to respond while in those settings. Despite these restrictions, it seems that subject matter can modify the quality of experience. Interestingly, the results also indicate that even without having an outstanding talent in art or music talented students in mathematics and science can have a positive experience in art and music classes.

The results correspond with our theoretical discussion of the differences between scientific and aesthetic reasoning. The domains of mathematics and science are characterized by their functional and logical approach, while in the arts thought processes do not follow a formal logic and cannot be regarded as means toward a clearly specified end. Our empirical data confirm that engagement in art activities provides more intrinsic rewards than engagement in mathematics or science.

What might be the reason for these compelling results? It seems as if the sciences are learned because they are useful and of high instrumental value, not primarily because they provide positive experiences. It is true that many expert mathematicians and scientists end up enjoying their craft and derive profound joy and satisfaction from it.[21] But such intrinsic enjoyment of science is relatively rare and usually confined to its most skilled practitioners. As our results suggest, however, for most high school students doing science provides only few immediate rewards. Its practice must be extrinsically motivated (e.g., social recognition, promising career prospects) if it is to be done at all. The arts classes, by comparison, seem to provide intrinsic rewards for both high- and low-skilled students. Even a child a few years old can experience profound joy and satisfaction from scribbling on a piece of paper, or from humming a tune. In fact, the domain of arts and the domain of science seem to possess quite different amounts of inherent rewards for the student.

The explanation given above is, however, quite speculative. There are at least two alternative (but not contradictory) reasons that could explain why the arts provide enjoyment, and the sciences do not. The first possibility is that mathematics and science are taught in ways that deter young people from getting involved in these subject matters. The second possibility has to do with the central position attributed by the educational system to mathematics and science compared to all other school subjects. For some students, the achievement of good grades in mathematics and science seems to be more important than getting good grades in other subject areas. As a consequence, the concern of those students for academic success might override the possible enjoyment of doing mathematics and science.

The Conditions of Optimal Experience

The preceding section suggests that involvement in the arts is more enjoyable than engagement in mathematics and science. It is likely that the differences in experience produced by these domains are at least partly a function of their nature. To be able to give further support to this assertion it is useful to specify more clearly those factors that contribute to the quality of subjective experience.

Most people, when they are asked to describe what makes them happy, will first think of something easy and relaxing, like watching TV, having a beer with friends, or having sex. But if they have more time to think, they usually come up with experiences of a different kind, experiences that involve meeting an unusual challenge and require a certain level of skill, such as hiking a treacherous mountain, bowling a perfect game, hearing an outstanding concert, or having an exhilarating conversation with a stimulating friend. None of these activities depends on external reinforcement. People get involved in them because of the quality of experience they provide. Therefore, experience functions in these cases as an autotelic (or intrinsic) reward. But what are the characteristics of such optimal experiences that lead people to get involved in activities just for their own sake?

A line of research that bears on this question was started in the early 1970s at the University of Chicago.[22] In numerous studies hundreds of people have been interviewed who pursued intrinsically rewarding activities such as painting, rock climbing, dancing, playing basketball, playing chess, and composing music. It was found that whenever people deeply enjoy what they are doing, they report a rather similar experiential state. This state has been called a *flow experience*, because many of the respondents said that when what they were doing was especially enjoyable it felt like being carried away by a current, like being in flow. Consequently, the theoretical model that describes optimal experiences is known as the flow model.

At the core, the flow model states that the perception of high challenges (or action opportunities) and high skills can lead people to a state of consciousness (flow) in which high levels of control, concentration, unselfconsciousness, and a strong sense of involvement are experienced. This "negentropic" state of consciousness contrasts with an "entropic," confused, or random state of consciousness. Persons in flow are deeply concentrated and feel a merging of action and awareness, their attention is centered on a limited stimulus field, and they may experience a "loss of ego" and feel in control of their actions and the environment. A further crucial component of the flow experience is its autotelic nature. In other words, the person in flow does not strive for goals or rewards beyond the activity at hand. The activity provides its own intrinsic rewards.

There is some evidence that flow is most readily experienced in certain kinds of activity. For example, games and play are considered to be ideal flow activities. In our view, typical flow activities provide the acting person with clear goals, well-defined rules, and unambiguous feedback on performance. This also explains why many rituals and other religious practices enable people to go off into trance-like states. However, the experience of flow is by no means restricted to games and play. Almost every kind of activity can be structured so as to facilitate the experience of flow.

Research has shown that flow is only possible when a person feels that the opportunities for action in a given situation match his or her ability to master the challenges. The challenge of an activity may be something concrete or physical like the peak of a mountain to be scaled, or it can be something abstract and symbolic, like a set of musical notes to be performed, a story to be read, or a puzzle to be solved. Similarly, the skill may refer either to a physical ability or to the mastery of manipulating symbols. More recent research has shown that balance of skill and challenge alone does not necessarily produce a flow experience. Both the challenges and skills must be relatively high (i.e., above a person's average) before a flow experience becomes possible.[23]

Let us now examine the experience of skills and challenges in the two groups of our study. We found rather strong differences with regard to these dimensions. The results show that there is a considerable discrepancy between the experiences of skill ($M = -.27$) and challenge ($M = .90$) in the math/science group. Contrastingly, skill ($M = .27$) and challenge ($M = .52$) seem to be well balanced in the art/music group. The high challenge ratings in mathematics and science indicate that students experience these subjects as rather difficult. The differences between the math/science and the art/music group with regard to perceived skills and challenges are significant at the .01 level (two-tailed t-tests).

The results cannot reveal, however, whether individual students actually experienced similar amounts of skills and challenges at the same time. Therefore, we performed a more direct analysis of varying skill-challenge fits.

Figure 1 depicts a model of different "channels" of experience based on differing degrees of skill and challenge. The center of the figure corresponds to the average intensity of challenges and the average strength of skills as measured by the ESM during the week. A flow experience is expected when both challenges and skills are above average. Thus, the respective quadrant is called the "flow channel." A person is in the "anxiety channel" when challenges are high and skills are low. When challenges are low and skills are high, the condition is one of boredom. Finally, experience is characterized as apathy when both skills and challenges are below average.

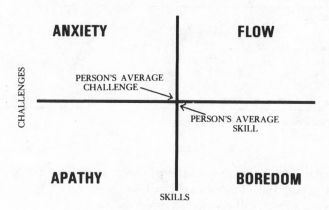

Fig. 1. A model of the quality of experience in terms of the balance of challenges and skills.

For every student we determined the frequency of being in the apathy, boredom, anxiety, and flow channels while engaged in their respective talent areas. Table 2 shows the group means for percentage of time in each of the four channels of experience. The results indicate that when students are engaged in their respective talent areas flow seems to be the most frequent experience for art/music students, while the most frequent experience for math/science students is anxiety. Math/science students are significantly more prone to experience anxiety than are the art/music students, and they are less frequently in the boredom channel than are the art/music students. Art/music students tend to be in the flow channel more frequently than math/ science students, but this difference is not significant. The difference between group means with regard to being in the apathy channel is also not significant.

The Representation of Experience in Personality

Our theoretical assumptions suggest that if a student enjoys doing mathematics or music, that student is more likely to cultivate and develop his or her talents in the subject. Indeed, analyses by Csikszentmihalyi et al. and by Wong and Csikszentmihalyi confirm

TABLE 2

GROUP MEANS FOR PERCENTAGE OF TIME IN FOUR CHANNELS OF EXPERIENCE

| TALENT AREA | FLOW | CHANNELS OF EXPERIENCE[a] | | APATHY |
		ANXIETY	BOREDOM	
Math/Science (n = 43)	.38	.48	.05	.09
Art/Music (n = 63)	.48	.21	.17	.14
t-Test[b]				
t	− 1.25	3.39	− 3.06	− 1.63
p <	ns	.01	.01	ns

[a] Values indicate weighted frequencies.
[b] Two-tailed.

that quality of experience is a valid predictor of engagement in one's area of talent, and of school achievement in general.[24] In order to explain the influence of experiential states on scholastic outcomes, it is useful to assume that people create enduring internal representations of their experiences. Only when a person is able to remember previous interactions with an object or a domain, will experience become a motivator for engaging or not engaging with them in the future.[25] Since students, for example, have rather different experiences in different domains (as we have seen above), the conclusion seems justified that people develop *domain-specific* motivational orientations. Most previous measures designed to tap different motivational orientations[26] are based on the idea that students are either intrinsically or extrinsically motivated, regardless of the content of the task. According to this view, some students just like to learn, whether the subject matter is English or chemistry. In contrast, we believe that a domain-specific concept is more appropriate and has greater power to explain why students are engaged in some subject-matter areas but not in others.

A line of recent research on how motivation affects text comprehension has made extensive use of the concept of interest.[27] Interest implies that people develop specific relationships with different subject areas. The subjective representation of a person-object relationship, as part of the enduring cognitive structure of a person, is called interest. More precisely, interest is defined as a relatively long-term orientation of a person toward an object (e.g., an area of knowledge) or an activity. According to Schiefele, this orientation or relationship is composed of feeling-related (emotional) and value-related valences that are stored in long-term memory.[28] Feeling-related valences refer, for example, to the association of object-related activities (e.g., solving mathematics problems) with feelings that either precede, accompany, or follow these activities. If personal significance is ascribed to an object or activity, one speaks of a "cognitive" or a value-related valence. In addition to these components, a third important feature of the interest concept is its intrinsic character. This means that interest-based involvement with a certain object is not instrumental for the achievement of goals that are external to that object (e.g., passing an exam) or for receiving any positive rewards.

Although there is not much research on the relation between quality of experience and interest, it seems justifiable on logical grounds to assume that experience affects the strength of interest in a certain domain.[29] The research reported in this chapter indicates that students have a more positive experience when they are involved in art than in mathematics or science. This leaves unanswered, however, the question of whether students also exhibit covarying levels of interest. Fortunately, some relevant data have been gathered as part of the present project. Specifically, students responded to a questionnaire that taps a number of intrinsic and extrinsic reasons for their choice of courses in their respective talent area.

The results are reported in Table 3. They reveal clear-cut and interesting differences between the two domains of talent. First, in both talent domains intrinsic reasons are rated higher than extrinsic reasons. Second, art/music students rated most of the intrinsic reasons significantly higher than math/science students. Third, math/science students rated the three extrinsic reasons having to do with require-ments, earning a living, and getting good grades significantly higher than art/music students. This result strongly confirms our hypotheses and the preceding findings.

Some interesting deviations from the general line of results occurred. Art/music students indicated that company of friends and impressing other people are important reasons for them to choose a course. This corresponds with findings from the interviews where art/music students often reported that they enjoy their activities especially when they are with friends or classmates. This is not surprising, especially for music, since most musical activities involve either the presence of listeners or of fellow musicians (e.g., in the school orchestra).

The finding that art/music students put more emphasis on

TABLE 3

MEAN RATINGS FOR IMPORTANCE OF REASONS FOR CHOOSING A COURSE IN
ONE'S TALENT AREA

REASONS FOR STUDYING[a]	MATH/SCIENCE STUDENTS (n = 43)	ART/MUSIC STUDENTS (n = 63)	t-TEST[b] t	p <
INTRINSIC REASONS				
I enjoy it.	4.76	5.66	4.49	.001
It's interesting to me.	4.76	5.49	3.15	.01
I get satisfaction from getting better or learning more.	4.76	5.08	1.33	ns
EXTRINSIC REASONS				
It's required.	3.10	.93	6.28	.001
It's something that will be useful for earning a living.	4.49	2.49	5.78	.001
My friends do it and I like their company.	1.37	2.53	3.57	.001
It's something I get good grades in.	4.41	3.66	2.07	.05
It's something that impresses other people.	2.71	3.76	3.39	.01
It's a way to get away from my problems.	1.20	3.46	6.92	.001

[a] Range of values: 0 = not at all important for choosing a course; 6 = very important for choosing a course.
[b] Two-tailed.

impressing other people is also quite understandable. It probably reflects the fact that teenage peers are less impressed by a friend who solves an equation with several unknowns than by someone who is able to perform music. Music, of course, is extremely important to adolescents.[30]

Finally, engaging in art and music can be a means to escape from or to cope with one's problems. And, if a student has a problem (for example, with engaging in activities in mathematics and science), experiences in those areas are not likely to be helpful to the student in overcoming other problems.

Consequences for Teaching the Arts

Clifford's comprehensive account of the history of research on teaching the arts reveals some interesting parallels with our discussion of the differences between rational and aesthetic thinking.[31] Her analysis suggests that research on teaching in the arts has been very rare and was almost without any influence on the practice of teaching.[32] Those art teachers who are very skilled in their domain have been found unresponsive and even resistant "to the general pedagogical currents which press insistently against American public education."[33] Art and music teachers also have often been described as lacking necessary classroom techniques. This might reflect the fact that teachers in arts and music often see themselves as artists rather than teachers. It seems as if the relation between research and teaching in the arts is almost nonexistent, with the exception of some recent developments.[34]

One obvious reason for this state of affairs is that scientific research on teaching processes is based on logic and rationalism, while the subject matters of music and art are different in nature. They do not lend themselves easily to a straightforward and rational analysis. In order to investigate the effect of teaching methods, research has to rely on seemingly objective outcome or criterion measures, such as achievement tests or grades. While this kind of research tends to work for mathematics and science, it creates considerable problems when applied to art or music. Specifically, it has been argued that "artistic production does not lend itself to objective evaluation."[35] It is much easier to agree on the outcomes of teaching in mathematics and science (as well as in languages or history) than to agree on the outcomes of teaching in arts and music. A case in point is the development of musical aptitude tests,[36] which have been criticized as covering only very limited aspects and as being atomistic and mechanistic. In our view, the desired outcomes of art education should include enhancement of subjectively meaningful experience and enhanced creativity and originality. To summarize, the gap between research and teaching in the arts is primarily due to the fact that it seems doubtful whether rational or empirical educational criteria are applicable to the teaching of the arts, which deal primarily with matters of feeling and creativity.

These fundamental differences between scientific and artistic thinking partly explain why art and music teachers might resist looking for help from educational research. It seems obvious that an atomistic and reductionistic approach is far from being helpful to instructors who seek to increase feeling-based, intuitive, and holistic thought processes in their students.

In the following, we want to draw some conclusions about teaching arts from the perspective of our research. Whatever the real accomplishments of students in art and music classes might be, the outcome measure of experience in our study shows that students generally seem to enjoy these subject areas. Whenever art and music students engage in activities related to their talent, they seem to be in a much more positive experiential state than science and mathematics students. Although we are not able to disentangle precisely the causal conditions for this finding, our study suggests that teaching in arts and music is at least not detrimental to the students' experience.

In recent years there has been an increased effort to put more emphasis on arts education in our schools (e.g., the Getty Center for Education in the Arts).[37] This effort is at least partially based on the concept of discipline-based art education, which means that students are expected to learn about art through four different approaches: art history, aesthetics, art performance, and art criticism. While there are certainly many good points to such initiatives, there is also some danger in such ambitious art programs.[38] The danger is that art education will become more like science and mathematics teaching, and as a result, students will lose their interest in art. A large part of the negative experience associated with science and mathematics is due to their impersonal, instrumental, achievement orientation. There has been much concern about how much students learn in mathematics or science, but not about how much they get to like these subjects. The importance of art and music education rests primarily upon the quality of experience they provide. Thus, any reform to renew the teaching of art and music should be careful to maintain these positive features. To put it in Arnheim's words, "The experience of art . . . must be the beginning and the end of all such [historical, aesthetic, social] explorations."[39]

Art assumes an even greater importance in schools as long as science and mathematics classes are unable to provide a positive experience for many students. To the extent that art classes make it possible for students to have positive experiences in school, they may compensate for the negative feelings experienced in mathematics and science classes.

Educational psychology has relied almost exclusively on cognitive outcome measures. Yet, as has been argued previously,[40] the major obstacles to learning are not primarily cognitive in nature. It is not that students *cannot* learn; the real problem is that they don't *want* to. Moreover, we have seen from the perspective of an evolutionary epistemology how absolutely essential is the education of the emotions, or the prerational intuitions and understandings that lead to creative transformations of knowledge.[41] As a consequence, research on teaching should concentrate on emotional and motivational variables.[42] When this is done, the importance of the arts for the total educational curriculum will become apparent, instead of being overshadowed, as it is at present, by a naively simplistic reliance on rational-empirical subject matter for the content of instruction.

ACKNOWLEDGMENT. The research reported in this chapter was supported by a grant to the first author from the Spencer Foundation. The opinions expressed are our own and do not reflect the positions or policies of the Spencer Foundation. In preparing this chapter the second author was supported by a scholarship from the Deutsche Forschungsgemeinschaft.

NOTES

1. Geraldine J. Clifford, "An Historical Review of Teaching and Research: Perspectives for Arts and Aesthetic Education," in *The Teaching Process and Arts and Aesthetics*, ed. Gerard L. Knieter and Jane Stallings (St. Louis: CEMREL, 1979), pp. 11-39.

2. Mihaly Csikszentmihalyi and Eugene Rochberg-Halton, *The Meaning of Things* (New York: Cambridge University Press, 1981).

3. See, for example, Robert Kubey and Mihaly Csikszentmihalyi, *Television and the Quality of Life: How Viewing Shapes Everyday Experience* (Hillsdale, NJ: Erlbaum, 1990) and W. Nahrstedt, "Allgemeinbildung im Zeitalter der 35-Stunden-Gesellschaft (General Education in the Age of the 35-Working Hours Society)," *Zeitschrift für Pädagogik* 32 (1986): 683-692.

4. Mihaly Csikszentmihalyi, "Phylogenetic and Ontogenetic Functions of Artistic Cognition," in *The Arts, Cognition, and Basic Skills*, ed. Stanley S. Madeja (St. Louis: CEMREL, 1978).

5. Donald T. Campbell, "Evolutionary Epistemology," in *The Library of Living Philosophers*, vol. 14, ed. P. A. Schilpp (LaSalle, IL: Open Court, 1974), pp. 413-463; Jean Piaget, *Biology and Knowledge* (Chicago: University of Chicago Press, 1971).

6. Ludwig Wittgenstein, *Tractatus Logico-Philosophicus* (London/New York: Routledge & Kegan Paul/Humanities Press, 1969), p. 151. Originally published in 1921.

7. Robert Collingwood, *The Principles of Art* (New York: Galaxy Books, 1958); John Dewey, *Art as Experience* (New York: Minton Balch, 1934); Howard Gardner, *The Arts and Human Development* (New York: Wiley, 1973); idem, *Arts, Mind, and Brain: A Cognitive Approach to Creativity* (New York: Basic Books, 1982).

8. Jacob Getzels and Mihaly Csikszentmihalyi, *The Creative Vision: A Longitudinal Study of Problem Finding in Art* (New York: Wiley, 1976).

9. James Joyce, *A Portrait of the Artist as a Young Man* (New York: Penguin, 1976), p. 253. Originally published in 1916.

10. Getzels and Csikszentmihalyi, *The Creative Vision*. See also, Mihaly Csikszentmihalyi and Olga Beattie, "Life Themes: A Theoretical and Empirical Exploration of Their Origins and Effects," *Journal of Humanistic Psychology* 19 (1979); 45-63.

11. Getzels and Csikszentmihalyi, *The Creative Vision*, p. 246.

12. Edward L. Deci and R. Michael Ryan, "A Motivational Approach to Self: Integration in Personality," in *Nebraska Symposium on Motivation*, vol. 38, *Perspectives on Motivation*, ed. Richard A. Dienstbier (Lincoln, NE: University of Nebraska Press, 1991).

13. See, for example, Eugene Gendlin, *Focusing* (New York: Everest House, 1978).

14. Carl G. Jung, *Seelenprobleme der Gegenwart* (Psychological Problems of Our Time) (Olten: Walter, 1935).

15. Mihaly Csikszentmihalyi, Kevin Rathunde, and Samuel Whalen, *Disengagement from Talent in Adolescence* (New York: Cambridge University Press, forthcoming).

16. Mihaly Csikszentmihalyi and Reed Larson, *Being Adolescent* (New York: Basic Books, 1984); idem, "Validity and Reliability of the Experience-Sampling Method," *Journal of Nervous and Mental Disease* 175 (1987): 526-536.

17. Edward L. Deci and R. Michael Ryan, *Intrinsic Motivation and Self-determination in Human Behavior* (New York: Plenum Press, 1985).

18. See, for example, Csikszentmihalyi and Larson, *Being Adolescent*.

19. Cf. Reed Larson and Philip Delespaul, "Analyzing Experience-Sampling Data: A Guidebook for the Perplexed," in *The Experience of Psychopathology*, ed. Martin de Vries (New York: Cambridge University Press, 1990).

20. R. Michael Ryan, J. P. Connell, and Edward L. Deci, "A Motivational Analysis of Self-determination and Self-regulation in Education," in *Research on Motivation in Education*, vol. 2: *The Classroom Milieu*, ed. Carole Ames and Russell E. Ames (London: Academic Press, 1985), pp. 13-51. See also, Ulrich Schiefele, "The Importance of Motivational Factors for the Acquisition and Representation of Knowledge," in *Regulation of Learning*, ed. P. R. J. Simons and G. Beukhof (Den Haag: SVO Selecta, 1987); idem, "Topic Interest and Levels of Text Comprehension," in *The Role of Interest in Learning and Development*, ed. K. A. Renninger, S. Hidi, and A. Krapp (Hillsdale, NJ: Erlbaum, 1991).

21. Mihaly Csikszentmihalyi, *Flow: The Psychology of Optimal Experience* (New York: Harper and Row, 1990); Moritz Schlick, "The Foundation of Knowledge," in *Logical Positivism*, ed. Alfred J. Ayer (New York: Free Press, 1959), pp. 209-227. Originally published in 1934.

22. Mihaly Csikszentmihalyi, *Beyond Boredom and Anxiety* (San Francisco: Jossey-Bass, 1975; idem, *Flow: The Psychology of Optimal Experience*; Mihaly Csikszentmihalyi and Isabella Csikszentmihalyi, eds., *Optimal Experience: Psychological Studies of Flow in Consciousness* (New York: Cambridge University Press, 1988).

23. Fausto Massimini and Massimo Carli, "The Systematic Assessment of Flow in Daily Experience," in *Optimal Experience: Psychological Studies of Flow in Consciousness*, ed. M. Csikszentmihalyi and I. Csikszentmihalyi, pp. 266-287.

24. Csikszentmihalyi, Rathunde, and Whalen, *Disengagement from Talent in Adolescence*; Marion Wang and Mihaly Csikszentmihalyi, "Motivation and Academic Achievement: The Effects of Personality Traits and the Quality of Experience," *Journal of Personality*, in press.

25. See also, John Dewey, *Experience and Education* (New York: Macmillan, 1938).

26. See, for example, Susan Harter, "A New Self-report Scale of Intrinsic versus Extrinsic Orientation in the Classroom: Motivational and Informational Components," *Developmental Psychology* 17 (1981): 300-312; Teresa M. Amabile, "Work Preference Inventory (College Version)," Unpublished manuscript, Brandeis University, Department of Psychology, 1987; John G. Nicholls, Michael Patashnick, and Susan B. Nolen, "Adolescents' Theories of Education," *Journal of Educational Psychology* 77 (1985): 683-692.

27. Ulrich Schiefele, "The Influence of Topic Interest, Prior Knowledge, and Cognitive Capabilities on Text Comprehension," in *Learning Environments: Contributions from Dutch and German Research*, ed. J. M. Pieters, K. Breuer, and P. R. J. Simons (Heidelberg: Springer, 1990), pp. 323-338; idem, "Topic Interest and Levels of Text Comprehension."

28. Schiefele, "Topic Interest and Levels of Text Comprehension."

29. M. Prenzel, "The Selective Persistence of Interest," in *The Role of Interest in Learning and Development*, ed. K. A. Renninger, S. Hidi, and A. Krapp (Hillsdale, NJ: Erlbaum, 1991).

30. Csikszentmihalyi and Larson, *Being Adolescent*.

31. Clifford, "An Historical Review of Teaching and Research."

32. See also, Robert M. W. Travers, ed., *Second Handbook of Research on Teaching* (Chicago: Rand McNally, 1973).

33. Clifford, "An Historical Review of Teaching and Research," p. 21.

34. See, for example, Roger D. Gehlbach, "Art Education: Issues in Curriculum and Research," *Educational Researcher* 19, no. 7 (1990): 19-25; Beverly J. Jones and June K. McFee, "Research on Teaching Arts and Aesthetics," in *Handbook of Research on Teaching*, ed. Merlin C. Wittrock (New York: Macmillan, 1986), pp. 906-916.

35. Harry A. Greene, Albert N. Jorgensen, and J. Raymond Gerberich, *Measurement and Evaluation in the Elementary School* (New York: Longmans, Green, 1953), p. 526.

36. Elliot W. Eisner, "Art Education," in *Encyclopedia of Educational Research*, ed. Robert L. Ebel (New York: Macmillan, 1969), pp. 76-86; Charles Leonhard and Richard J. Colwell, "Research in Music Education," in *Arts and Aesthetics: An Agenda for the Future*, ed. Stanley S. Madeja (St. Louis: CEMREL, 1977), pp. 81-108.

37. For a review, see Jones and McFee, "Research on Teaching Arts and Aesthetics."

38. See Philip W. Jackson, "Mainstreaming Art: An Essay on Discipline-based Art Education," *Educational Researcher* 16, no. 6 (1987): 39-43; and Elliot W. Eisner, "Discipline-based Art Education: A Reply to Jackson," *Educational Researcher* 16, no. 9 (1987): 50-52.

39. Rudolph Arnheim, *New Essays on the Psychology of Art* (Berkeley: University of California Press, 1986), p. 10.

40. Mihaly Csikszentmihalyi, "Literacy and Intrinsic Motivation," *Daedalus* 119 (1990): 115-140.

41. See also, Arnheim, *New Essays on the Psychology of Art*.

42. Paul R. Pintrich, "The Dynamic Interplay of Student Motivation and Cognition in the College Classroom," *Advances in Motivation and Achievement* 6 (1989): 117-160; idem, "Implications of Psychological Research on Student Learning and College Teaching for Teacher Education," in *Handbook of Research on Teacher Education*, ed. W. Robert Houston (New York: Macmillan, 1990), pp. 826-857.

Section Four
AESTHETIC KNOWING AND THE
CULTURE OF SCHOOLING

CHAPTER IX

Toward a Place in the Curriculum for the Arts

JOHN I. GOODLAD

The rhetoric of school reform during the 1980s offered little hope for a surge in the place of the arts in the K-12 curriculum during the 1990s. The national educational goals emerging out of the education summit called by President George Bush in the fall of 1989 gave high priority to mathematics and the natural sciences: Our schools are to lead the world in these fields by the year 2000. There is no mention of the arts.

It is difficult to imagine a real debate arising out of the following resolution: Be it resolved that a child born today will enjoy a richer life in adulthood because of his or her early education in the arts rather than mathematics. Nonetheless, I believe not only that we should be seriously and continuously engaged in such debate but that a strong case for the pro side can be made. Of course, the sharp edges of such debate would be flattened immediately (except in jousts between formal debating teams) by the observation that we need not choose; we can have both.

So goes the rhetoric but it simply does not square with reality. School curricula mirror a society's values. Look into that mirror and we do not see the arts. Ironically, however, one of the indices included in the never-ending polls and surveys to determine America's most livable cities is the richness of cultural life as measured by their support of symphonies, dance companies, art galleries, theaters, and the like.

John I. Goodlad is Professor of Education and Director of the Center for Educational Renewal, College of Education, University of Washington.

The arts are something to be enjoyed *after* one is "successful," to be supported after one becomes affluent. Artists are to come into full flower by some form of immaculate conception, not through being nourished in public schools. Likewise, the ability to enjoy art blossoms late, when one has the time and money to participate in those experiences that hone appreciation. Cultivating the arts becomes a kind of finishing school for the much educated and well positioned, and has little place in the lives of the masses, presumably.

During the past decade in particular, policymakers have hammered home the message: better schools mean better jobs. This message has been translated into the curriculum perceived to be instrumental to that end: language skills plus the mathematics and sciences basic to finding employment in a highly technological market place. A work force so prepared is essential to a healthy economy. Yet, the largest number of new jobs created during the past ten years—millions of them—has been in service occupations demanding more in dependability and good human relations. For these and many more millions, education for productive, satisfying living outside of jobs looms as having profound implications for the K-12 curriculum and beyond.

Daily life experiences make my point. The second-floor custodian in the building where I once occupied an office took the job because the work demands little, and he chose the night shift because he prefers natural daylight for his painting in oils. Brief encounters with the man who picks up our garbage are enriched by conversation about the sets he designs for a local theater. Ordering dinner in one of our favorite restaurants is interspersed by comments from the waitress regarding a new show at the Henry Art Gallery. The young woman who cleans our house in times of need keeps us posted on new books worth reading. The window washer who shows up periodically is into acrylics now; he hopes we will come to his first show next month. The arts are not required for any of these jobs; nor is much mathematics. The work they do provides a living; the arts in their lives make living more than getting by.

There are jobs not listed under the arts in the yellow pages that require artistic expertise. The talented man who repaired the wounded gelcoat "skin" of my boat did an extraordinary job of matching an unusual blue and of blending the new into the old. His days are spent mostly in restoring vibrant colors to beautiful things—for which he is rather well paid. He was lucky in school; the arts were his lifeline: "Without the arts, I'd never have made it." And then he speaks angrily of his wife's enforced change in career. "She was an arts teacher in an elementary school," he said, "but the district wiped out the program a couple of years ago and she couldn't find another job. She's close to finishing a program in special education at the university and is sure of a job."

Research and exhortation have been directed over the years to the plight of the arts in schools. The research findings, although disagreeing on average percentages of time devoted to the arts, cluster around a common conclusion: programs are starved of time and resources, particularly with respect to the participation of highly qualified teachers. This general starvation pales somewhat in significance when compared with data on variability. Some schools have virtually no arts programs; some students have no encounters with the arts (except in some relatively superficial integration of the graphic arts with other subjects in elementary schools) throughout their entire schooling. And yet, the arts score at the top in students' liking of and interest in school subjects—even when many of those polled have had no school-based courses in the arts![1]

I have joined with arts educators over the years in envisioning just over the dry hills a green valley made even more beautiful by colorful schools with the arts at their center. Always the valley lies beyond the next dry ridge. I shall eschew attempting to contribute still one more time to the utopian literature of the arts paradise unrealized.

Instead, I shall attempt in this chapter to do three things. First, I shall seek to show how the dominant conception of the role of schools in this country creates an inhospitable context for the arts. Second, I shall seek to show how the conduct of teacher education perpetuates organizational and curricular arrangements and reinforces an ethos in schools that is disadvantageous to the arts. Third, using a concrete example of a faculty group in a junior high school, I shall endeavor to show the obstacles innovative proposals—such as those that include the arts—confront because of community expectations and the regularities of schooling. I conclude on a somewhat upbeat note by suggesting how arts educators might join the mainstream of teacher preparation in the simultaneous renewal of schools and the preparation of teachers.

An Inhospitable Context for the Arts in Schools

Only a few countries have equalled the United States in placing education close to the center of personal and national well-being. Even fewer have so equated schooling and education. As Cremin states it, universal schooling "is as radical an idea as Americans have embraced."[2] Immigrants pouring into the United States in the late nineteenth and early twentieth centuries perceived the common school as offering entry into the work force and economic advancement. Indeed, at the time, the school was so defined.[3]

There has been a downside to the centrality of universal schooling defined instrumentally that arguments for schools committed to education for its own sake have not been able to counter—a downside not favorable to the arts. We have only to look at the standardized tests used to determine the health of our schools to realize that the arts simply do not count; what is not measured is not important. The impact of this instrumental paradigm on the place of the arts in schools is exacerbated by other popular perceptions. For example, the arts are "soft" and better suited to the nursery school and kindergarten years where women teachers dominate. They are to be left behind for the "tough" subjects—mathematics and sciences—in the more masculine world of schooling that tends to follow. Also, the arts are to a considerable extent tactile—more of the hand than of the head—and so, goes the thinking, are not within the core of truly intellectual subjects. And as for talent and giftedness, the classic sorting machine is the intelligence test and its dependence on linguistic and quantitative abilities as the determinants of I.Q. Let us take a look at the essence of schooling—curriculum and instruction—to see how these perceptions and practices contribute to the neglect of the arts.

BACK TO THE BASICS IN ELEMENTARY SCHOOLS

The instrumental model of education that ties schooling to jobs and economic aspirations creates a highly pressured curriculum, reminding us of the two-wheeled curricle being pulled furiously around a race track. It is stripped of everything seen as not basic—including a seat for the driver. In schools, only the fastest curricles are permitted to dally and, perhaps, while waiting for the others to catch up, to dabble in the arts. But the slow never catch up and, therefore, never get to dally and dabble. An unfortunate by-product is that the dallying time is not taken seriously; dabbling is rarely disciplined into rigor. And nothing of importance is lost by those who never get to dally.

What holds for individuals holds for entire schools. Our earlier studies revealed enormous variation among elementary schools in regard to the hours of opportunity they provided each week for students to have encounters with school subjects—from just over eighteen to more than twenty-seven. In other words, some schools managed to get approximately 50 percent more instructional time out of a school week than did others. The explanation appears to be that some school staffs simply take care of their business better than do others:[4] they manage to be more successful in getting parents to have their children at school on time, get the day started promptly, hold recesses and lunch periods to the times scheduled, clean up quickly at the end of the day; and more.

Even though one can argue reasonably for our not having to choose between mathematics and the arts in the curriculum, something inevitably is sacrificed in schools with short instructional weeks. Since the language arts (including reading) and mathematics are the king and queen in the early grades, their place is not threatened. It appears that about the same amount of time is devoted to these two subjects in schools with short instructional weeks as is the case in schools with twenty-five or more hours. But the arts virtually disappear in the former group.[5]

The teachers in this group would support the importance of the arts but would argue that there is no time for them. Yet, ironically, when the states took on the tasks of defining "basic" education during the 1970s, most found themselves pressured to include the arts. And Ernest Boyer concluded from his staff's surveys that we want it all.[6] However, when we return, as we always do, to placing schooling at the heart of our economy, the arts tumble quickly to the bottom of our priorities. Those who recommended a longer school day and year in *A Nation at Risk* did not have in mind creating more time for the arts.[7]

I concluded from our data on the use of school time that the arts begin to secure some attention in the elementary school curriculum when the instructional week begins to go above twenty-three hours— slightly more than the average for our sample. There is, apparently, a kind of built-in cultural expectation for mathematics and the language arts—an hour a day for the former and an hour and a half for the latter. By getting the use of time up to twenty-five hours—something accomplished by a few of the schools in the sample—there are now twelve and a half hours to spread around among the other subjects. Claiming even three or four hours each week for the arts—hardly generous but nonetheless not inconsequential—still leaves a solid share for the social studies and science.

But fewer than a third of the elementary schools in our small representative sample managed to achieve even twenty-three hours of instructional time for a week. These schools, boasting the longest instructional week of the group, averaged 4.1 hours per week in the arts. The same number of schools at the bottom end—not one of them getting even twenty hours out of the week—devoted on the average only 2.7 hours to the arts.

We begin to see that the problem of assuring a good arts education program for students in elementary schools goes beyond determining a curriculum and preparing teachers for it. Indeed, the best of curricula on paper accomplish nothing when sloppy practices in schools waste valuable time that might otherwise go to the arts. It is apparent, too, that teachers prepared for and committed to infusing the arts into elementary school programs must possess the skills and abilities necessary to joining with their colleagues in designing a productive work week or the arts will go by the wayside in the competition of the subjects for scarce time.

THE SHOPPING MALL HIGH SCHOOL

The general neglect of the arts in secondary schools stems in large part from their low ranking in the model that connects schooling and economic advancement, as with elementary schools. But high school teachers, unlike most elementary school teachers, have little or no autonomy with respect to the distribution of daily and weekly time among the school subjects. Most of the decisions in this regard are made for them—customarily beyond the school site. Nonetheless, circumstances unique to the school one happens to attend play a significant part in determining whether or not a given student will gain access to the arts.

Whether or not the arts are offered in high schools depends heavily on dominant values in the larger society. A good indicator of prevailing values is the allocation of teachers to the school subjects. The schools of our sample were widely distributed across the United States. At the junior high level, one teacher in ten was allocated to the arts; the ratio dropped to one in just under twelve at the senior high level.[8]

What is most striking in our data is variability among schools. At one high school in the sample, only one teacher in thirty-three was assigned to the arts; at another this ratio jumped to one in just over eight. Variability steadied markedly in the four basic subjects required for college admission, with most high schools allocating from 15 percent to 25 percent of their teachers to English, 12 percent to 18 percent to mathematics, about the same for social studies, and from 10 percent to 14 percent for science. Variability is conspicuous in regard to vocational education, with the range spreading from 13 percent to 42 percent of the total number of teachers allocated to this field.

We see that shopping mall high schools, as Powell and his associates designated secondary schools,[9] have in common several steadily frequented shops. These stock the goods most generally valued—those viewed as most instrumental to higher education and, of course, the professions. The presence and popularity of the other shops in the mall depend on the more particularized interests of the immediate community. Hence, two of our shopping mall high schools opted for allocating over 40 percent of the teaching force to vocational education. (Both were located in blue collar communities where the educational level of parents was below and their income level above the averages for our sample.) In so doing, they pulled clientele— students—away from English, mathematics, social studies, and science and, of course, the arts. Two others devoted only 13 percent of the teaching force to vocational education, pushing up the allocations not only in the first four fields but also in the arts—to 11 percent and 12 percent of the teaching force, respectively.

The arts in secondary schools, as in elementary schools, are not a clear option for students. The priorities of nation and state and the vagaries of local circumstances conspire to make their presence in the curriculum quite uncertain. What is less apparent and understood, however, is the way in which the sheer weight of our top curricular priorities serves not merely to give to the arts a small shop on the mall but to bar some prospective clients from entering its door. Awareness of this phenomenon requires considerable understanding of certain regularities governing the mall as a whole.

One of these regularities is the need to present certain credentials prior to seeking entry. The entire high school mall is open to young people who learned how to use the elementary school mall well. Large parts of it are closed to the others. I move away now from the shopping mall analogy. There are in most high schools three divisions of subject matter divided into tracks. The most academically able students who completed their reading and mathematics assignments quickly and spent some time drawing and painting find themselves in the track characterized by the high-status subject matter most valued in college. Many arrive at their senior year with most of the required courses behind them and have ample space in their programs for elective courses, including the arts.

Slow students find themselves not only in the low-track classes featuring lower status and more immediately utilitarian subject matter, but also in additional remedial courses in the basic subjects. Since entry into college is viewed by counselors and, ultimately, by these students, as unlikely, the need to think about future employment opens up the vocational education alternative. The combination of taking the courses required for graduation and a sequence of vocationally oriented courses pushes the arts to the margins for most. These are students predominantly from economically marginal backgrounds and many are also members of minority groups.[10] Artistic talent among these young people is as widespread as it is among those students who enjoy the luxury of greater choice. Most of these curricularly disadvantaged students not only are deprived of the opportunity to prepare for lifetime enjoyment of the arts but also are cut off from initial access to the long road that could lead to development of this talent.

. On the surface, then, the arts appear to be an undernourished part of the curriculum, available as electives to those who seek them but not yet established as basic and required. In actuality, however, there is not free and equal access.[11] The low standing of the arts among our educational priorities and the pervasive dominance of other subjects conspire with certain regularities in contributing to serious pathology in the conduct of schools. Those students who take least well to the favored subjects not only are denied the best of their contents but also are denied access to alternatives that possess great intrinsic value as well as potential for holding some of them through the school years to graduation. We make the same educational mistakes in each successive era of school reform.

I would like to believe that implementation of currently popular proposals for schools of choice[12] would change these circumstances; that enlightened parents and teachers would ensure for all children and youth comprehensive education in all the major systems of knowledge and knowing.[13] I am not optimistic. The values that have shunted the arts aside in schools generally are likely to determine the curricula of schools specifically. And there has been little in national behavior over recent decades to make me confident that the future well-being of all children and youth will dominate in local decision-making groups. Members of minority groups tend to trust the courts over the majority group in seeking justice and equity.

I shall not enter here into age-old arguments regarding the relative dangers inherent in state and school district prescription of the curriculum as compared with those inherent in unrestricted local freedom to choose.[14] But I am convinced that the latter is unlikely to be a universal option for the foreseeable future. By the time the plebiscite regarding a voucher plan for schooling in California was ready to go to the people, it included a long list of restraints designed to protect against abuse—restraints not unlike those already in place for the public schools of the state. It is naive to believe that states will leave schools of choice to go their unfettered way free of regulations governing their operation.

Similarly, it is naive to believe that parents with common interests who come together for purposes of shaping an entire school of choice will agree on the components sufficiently to provide stability. The so-called "free schools" of the 1960s, joined in a loose nationwide network, never numbered more than three hundred. Just as one opened, another closed because the fragile initial agreements among parents broke down at the level of particulars: curricula, organization, teaching methods, and more.

For schools—whether chosen by parents and managed at the site or controlled by school boards at state and district levels—to assure for our young people the comprehensive general education they will need tomorrow for effective, satisfying living, there must be in the surrounding context an ongoing dialogue and some closure with respect to a present consensus. This consensus will evolve as dialogue proceeds. In *A Place Called School*, I recommended that this dialogue begin with some presuppositions regarding the components of this general education and the balance of attention to be given to each. At the secondary school level, time would be distributed as follows: up to 18 percent for literature and language, 18 percent for mathematics and science, 15 percent for the arts, 15 percent for vocational education (completely redefined), and 10 percent for physical education. Variation of up to 20 percent of the percentage of the program allocated to any of these categories would be acceptable. This leaves a minimum of 9 percent to be devoted to the development of special talent and for this I would provide vouchers to be used in any approved educational program, public or proprietary. Students taking the approved minimum might be able to free up as much as 20 percent of their time for the development of special talents. The proposed distribution assures the arts for all.

I am not sanguine about securing for the arts a firm place through exhortation. The arts must be protected by firm overall curricular requirements, just as mathematics and English are now protected, or they will fall by the wayside.

Teacher Education and Arts Teachers in Schools

The educational reform movement of the 1980s carried into the 1990s a fundamental agreement on the part of policymakers and grassroots reformers alike: the individual school is the most promising unit for improvement.[15] This proposition asks much of teachers and principals, whether or not the school stands free and independent of a district or enjoys much decentralization of authority and responsibility to empowered teachers. The sample of elementary schools described earlier operated within quite comparable district circumstances. Yet, they varied widely in their ability to take care of school-wide business, less than a third achieving sufficient efficiency to assure substantial time for all the major subjects of the curriculum. The arts suffered disproportionately to the other fields. Findings such as this raise questions regarding the potential outcomes of schools charged with site-based renewal. How well are today's teachers prepared for such a responsibility?

The findings from a five-year study of a representative sample of teacher-preparing institutions are not encouraging.[16] First of all, my colleagues and I concluded that proposals for the reform of schools and of teacher education have been promulgated quite separately from one another over the years.[17] What appears to be a natural connection between the two has gone largely unattended to. One looks in vain for such joining in the work of James B. Conant, for example, whose reports on secondary schools[18] and teacher education programs[19] in an earlier reform era were separated by only four years. This general failure to connect the two, we found, has left teacher education free to define a mission independent of the schools and, of course, independent of the wrenching that schools experience during eras of reform.

Several more specific findings emerging from our massive body of data lead to the conclusion that new teachers coming into the schools are not ready to assume the responsibilities of stewardship. The so-called foundations courses introduced years ago for the purpose of acquainting students with issues of school function and scope had been seriously eroded in the settings we studied.[20] Similarly, we found little or nothing that addressed either the school curriculum as a whole or how to go about designing a comprehensive elementary or secondary school program.[21] The bulk of the program for prospective elementary school teachers focused on methods of teaching in several subjects and on classroom management. Because of omission of all else, prospective high school teachers might well have assumed that their respective subjects constituted the only ones in the curriculum. At best, only a few class periods were devoted to moral issues pertaining to the inequities regarding access to knowledge characterizing most schools.[22]

Future teachers moved through their preparation programs as individuals, with little informal opportunity to interact. There was virtually no deliberate use of cohort groups (such as the class of 1996 in medicine or law) to socialize students into the profession of teaching.[23] And then students in our sample went singly into student teaching placements where they were socialized by cooperating teachers into the regularities of classrooms. Rarely did any join the school faculty as a whole as junior colleagues engaged in school renewal. These findings were so consistent in setting after setting that it is difficult to imagine that a different or larger sample would have produced significantly different results.

We were struck by the lack of common learnings among future teachers, such as a common set of cases as in law. Clusters of prospective high school teachers took courses together in mathematics, for example, but shared little with students of other subjects. They appeared to be developing an allegiance to the subject, more than to its teaching or to teaching in schools as a profession. The lack of coherence of program components around a common mission operated against the development of shared values with respect to the responsibilities inherent in school teaching.[24] At the elementary school level, there was further splintering into sometimes almost completely separated programs in early childhood education, special education, and the arts. On one campus, we found six different schools or colleges preparing teachers—agriculture, fine arts, health and physical education, business, education, and the arts and sciences.

And now this polyglot of future teachers is to come together in a collegial team to redesign our schools and bring them triumphant into the twenty-first century—with all the goals of President Bush's Education Summit accomplished! Presumably, they will go beyond these goals and include the arts for all. Nonsense.

The separation of the arts from much of the rest of teacher preparation is particularly deleterious to the place of the arts in schools because of the lack, as we have seen, of a firm place for them in K-12 curricula. This is particularly the case with music as part of the general education curriculum—a field which has successfully and understandably lobbied for the large number of music credits deemed essential to developing proficiency in playing an instrument. In general, the field and its teacher-students have set themselves up as specialists. The common consequence is that the arts are not securely embedded as a necessary part of general education in schools. At the secondary school level, student choruses and orchestras are good for community relations but are readily classified as frills at budget-cutting time.

Special teachers and special hours for the arts in elementary schools do little to convince grade-level classroom teachers that the arts are an integral part of a balanced curriculum. Some appreciate being relieved of their classes a time or two each week. But others resent the time lost for the "basic" subjects included in the achievement tests. Some wonder why the school structure prohibits them from teaching just one subject such as mathematics or reading in the same way that arts teachers are able to specialize. Some elementary school principals have found themselves in bloody battles when they attempted to bring specialists, including those in the arts, into teaching teams collectively responsible for the whole of instruction in a clutch of classrooms. Many specialists have resisted such moves, even when it was clear that this would reduce class size and student-teacher ratios overall. In so doing, they have not endeared themselves to fellow teachers.

It is interesting to note that a significant part of the literature in arts education has ignored the larger issues of community context and school organization and their negative effect on the standing of the arts in school programs. (There are notable exceptions.)[25] The issues more commonly discussed—such as the balance between appreciation and performance, and particularly that classic, the virtues of the arts in pure form over some kind of integration with other fields—are important, of course. But these become irrelevant if the arts have not secured a place in school programs. The questions of curricular content and organization and of teaching on which arts educators prefer to concentrate will become more salient when the arts have a secure, protected place in schools and have been brought into their mainstream as general and not special education.

Toward the Redesign of Schools and Teacher Education

One need not read between the lines of what precedes to conclude that I am pessimistic about communities demanding a place for the arts in their schools and about schools themselves becoming strong advocates of an arts curriculum. Nor am I optimistic about arts educators bringing off a coup that will change these inhospitable circumstances in the near future. But I believe there are some promising strategies that can benefit by riding piggyback on certain elements of the ongoing educational reform movement. These include growing impatience with the continuation of things as they are.

I already have indicated my support for and recommendation of a substantial place in the general education curriculum for the arts— more time than has been recommended in any other school reform report, I believe. And I also have recommended a backdrop of curriculum specifications that leaves open for all high school students 9 percent or more of school time for developing talent. What I propose now is not, then, my only position with respect to the place of the arts in schools. What follows must be placed beside what precedes.

Preceding pages have addressed elementary and primarily the senior level of secondary schools. It is appropriate, then, to select the junior high school in discussing the redesign of schools so as to give attention to the arts.

REDESIGNING A JUNIOR HIGH SCHOOL

My interest in the role of education in the arts goes beyond both reserving a place for them in the curriculum and providing opportunities to all for the development of artistic talent, however. I identify closely with the theory of multiple intelligences elaborated so well by Howard Gardner.[26] Consequently, to have been denied the arts is to have been denied opportunity for the full development of human intelligence. The education of most of us has been sadly neglected.

But the development of musical, spatial, or bodily-kinesthetic intelligence means much more than filling in a discrete component of one's total repertoire of intelligences. It means the enrichment or augmentation of other frames of mind; the sum is greater than the parts. Elliot Eisner stated this position succinctly: "Perhaps the most important contribution that my immersion in the visual arts has made to my views of education is the realization that neither cognition nor epistemology can be adequately conceptualized if the contributions of the arts to these domains are neglected."[27]

My interpretation of what Eisner then goes on to write is that there is enormous potential in the arts not just for preparing one to participate in the artistic or aesthetic part of the human conversation but for rounding out the contribution of the other fields of knowledge and knowing. Or, leaving out the man-made categories, the arts enrich one's capacity to perceive, to inquire, to think—even to transcend

cognition. We have a long way to go, of course, before such justification of the arts will be confirmed by achievement tests.

The above brings me to what might best be described as a glancing
episode in my life—and the considerable consequences in which I was
only peripherally involved. In late fall of the 1984-85 academic year,
the principal and a teacher from a nearby junior high school came to
me with a request: Would I meet with the entire faculty at a school
"retreat" during the coming winter? "We think we have a good
school," said the principal. "But it's good in the conventional sense. I
think we're on a plateau and have grown complacent."

They had read my *A Place Called School* which says, in essence, that
the junior high school is a good concept gone astray in practice. They
had been struck particularly by my comments on the abrupt transition
in the regularities and the anonymity students experience in moving
from the elementary to the junior high school.

For the week preceding the Friday evening I met with this faculty,
I had been ill—quite ill—and was sustained largely by antibiotics. I
had little appetite for food and was on a schedule of eating lightly
more frequently. The students learning the restaurant business in the
technical institute where we were meeting were slow and careful in
preparing and serving our food. The long wait exacerbated my
discomfort. My address was harsh—too harsh, I feared later. I
described the general failure of junior high schools to fulfill the initial
ideal expectations for them. "If the shoe fits, wear it," I said.

Apparently, the shoe was perceived by many to fit only too well.
On Tuesday morning (Monday was a holiday), I called the principal
to apologize. "For what?" he asked. I spoke of my unhappy after-
thoughts and offered a date to meet again for purposes of responding
to questions and concerns. "I'll take you up on that but there is no
need for apologies. You hit sensitive nerves and stirred up what we
had hoped for. Several teachers were waiting for me this morning.
They had continued meeting over the weekend and have come up
with an interesting proposal for redesigning part of the school."

Things moved quickly. By April, when I met with the faculty
again, this small group of teachers had come together many times,
involving the principal and other colleagues. In brief, five teachers
representing language arts, mathematics, social studies, science, and
the arts were now quite far along in planning for the 1985-86 year a
school within the school for ninety boys and girls who were to be
offered the option of coming together as a cohort group under the
guidance of this team of teachers for their junior high years.

Communication with feeder elementary schools already was under way.

Several aspects of the plan implemented during the following year were quite remarkable. First, it was politically wise for these teachers to put up front the subjects required for college admission. The arts became a bonus. Second, the arts were not elective; they were embedded in the general education of all students. Third, the concept of team teaching opened up the opportunity for new learning on the part of all teachers—each became a teaching participant in subjects from which they are barred in the usual departmentalized structure of secondary schools. We have ample evidence of the degree to which many teachers become intellectually stagnant because of the way schools are organized.[28] Fourth—and exceedingly important—the plan anticipated the need to do everything possible to preserve the integrity of the several fields, including the arts, while seeking to enhance each by adding the arts perspective.

Perhaps most remarkable of all was the degree to which a common core of learning was created out of the identification of the intellectual skills and abilities presumably sought in the education process regardless of the field. The arts specialist brought into the dialogue the schema developed by Charles Fowler and promulgated by the Pennsylvania department of education.[29] Although processes such as perceiving, understanding, creating, and evaluating are addressed to the arts, it is easy for teachers in other fields to recognize and accept them as their own. The arts became instrumental to enhancing the development of these intellectual traits in all the subjects.

Many purists in the art education field grow uneasy in the face of proposals for integrating the arts and other subjects—and rightly so. The arts have been savaged in programs seeking, for example, to integrate them with the social studies. Drawing pyramids in a unit on Egypt or building covered wagons in the unit on westward migration may help students gain understanding of concepts in the social studies but such does little for enhancing their understanding and appreciation of the arts.

A critical element in the plan was that all the teachers had credible credentials in their fields. The arts teacher was fully qualified—not a teacher of some other subject who dabbled in the arts. On the serendipitous side was the degree to which three of the four other teachers already had brought into their classrooms modest use of the arts. The language arts teacher had used drama and literature for purposes of generating creative ideas for writing and for enlightening certain language concepts. The mathematics teacher had made use of the visual arts; the social studies teacher had enriched lessons because of a background in drama. All participated in a short in-service immersion on infusing the arts into the curriculum. Throughout the 1985-86 year, drama and the visual arts became major components of the other subjects.

Subsequent stumbling blocks arose out of the circumstances of schooling, not waning enthusiasm or incompetence on the part of teachers. Indeed, by the end of the third year, the whole school had adopted the plan, admittedly with some compromises with respect to team teaching and subject integration.

A continuing problem had not been anticipated. Part of our American fabric is the expectation that schooling will become harder and tougher as students progress upward. Kindergarten is not seen as real school. A major signal to the effect that the junior high is not mere continuation of the more soft and tender ambience of the elementary school has been adoption of most of the regularities of the senior high school, especially the schedule of six or seven classes and teachers each day. Many parents and even some of the students perceived the seamless curriculum of their junior high school to be more like elementary than secondary school.

More serious, students who might otherwise be in honors classes were now folded in with average students—and, indeed, the handicapped and learning-disabled. Teachers who had formerly taught in the honors program feared loss of status in the community; they were now teachers of ordinary children. Redesigning this school according to sound educational principles—long recommended by thoughtful reformers—ran into trouble because the new configurations did not reinforce the rituals we have come to associate with schooling.[30]

A body blow came from newly enacted state certification requirements. Teachers prepared in a given field were disallowed from teaching in another—a sad commentary on the perceived state of general education in college. The four-hour block schedule initiated by the teaching team during 1985-86 was severely strained by the need to account for teachers' time subject-by-subject and to conform to lunch and bus schedules. Teachers enthused by apparent opportunities to innovate find themselves overwhelmed by the regularities of schooling.

Another phenomenon surrounding the change process had troubled me from the beginning. Its impact is subtle and pervasive. It is referred to in business and industry as the "rate-buster" syndrome. We encountered its power in a study of school change and improvement involving the League of Cooperating Schools conducted in the late 1960s and early 1970s.[31] The one school in each of eighteen districts chosen to be a member of the League and freed of some of the usual restraints was regarded almost at the outset as a "funny farm," endangering the placidity of the other schools as a rate-buster bent on changing established regularities of schooling. Even some of the superintendents who had selected and blessed their schools at the outset were ebullient about innovation but cautious regarding changing anything fundamental. The rate-buster syndrome attached to a given school can be powerfully intimidating.

From the day the principal and his colleagues first spoke with me, the debilitating power of this phenomenon was what I most feared. I was somewhat reassured by the fact that the district was in the midst of one of those "schools for the 21st century" projects so popular in the post-*A Nation at Risk* era of the 1980s. Deviance was being encouraged, at least rhetorically. But some teachers' union leaders were eyeing developments somewhat suspiciously, given the aura of a top-down, community-driven activity.

Early on, the principal and the team of teachers were jolted by the admonition from the district office to keep those test scores up. This was countered, in part, by promising an alternative approach to evaluation, geared to the program's goals. The schema developed with the aid of my colleague, Kenneth Sirotnik, ultimately revealed evidences of greater verbal fluency and originality of the experimental group when compared with a control group. Participating teachers agreed on such outcomes as increased student motivation, increased retention of subject matter, and active participation in learning activities on the part of a larger percentage of students. The teachers' enthusiasm was such that they ultimately opted to infuse music and dance as well as drama and the visual arts. Although the whole was modified over the years to conform somewhat more closely with the established ways of schooling and district regularities, a good deal of what had been sought at the outset was attained and permeated the school.

The available data confirm for me how difficult it is to buck and then change the tyranny of the existing norms of schooling—standardized testing, state and district regulations, divisions of the school day into subjects and periods—and the regularities seen as right and proper by the community that serve also to provide a sense of security for many teachers. It is hazardous to the health of a school to attempt to go it alone. We learned in earlier studies of educational change that ground-breaking schools require close connections with schools similarly engaged—preferably close by so that face-to-face communication is easy to come by. Further, they need a prestigious, legitimating alternative drummer. In the League of Schools, for example, the connection with the University of California, Los Angeles, was sufficiently compelling for some parents to try to smuggle their children across attendance lines in order to get them into a League school—long before anything new of significance was under way. A number of schools joined in a network articulating together alternative values goes a long way toward closing down the "funny farm" derogations. And redesigned teacher education programs could contribute much to socialize teachers in such ways that assuming responsibility for renewing schools would become the norm. To this possibility we now turn.

RENEWING SCHOOLS AND THE EDUCATION OF EDUCATORS

Some readers may still be pondering the question, "What does the foregoing have to do with education in the arts in schools?" An implicit theme is that the struggle to include the arts in the curriculum in some legitimate, nonbastardized way has created for them not only an aura of "special" and "precious" but a considerable degree of separation to the point of isolation from the other school subjects and those who teach them. This has been accompanied by, and to some degree has exacerbated, naivete with respect to the logistics and politics of changing the status of arts in schools from marginal to central. Evidence for this is found in the fact that the arts have received short shrift in the school reform era that accelerated during the 1980s.

One of my proposals for rectifying this situation is that arts educators become more deeply involved in preservice teacher education generally, not just in the preparation of those who will teach music, drama, or the visual arts in schools. For the first time this century, the reform of schools and of teacher education are being conceptually joined. The Carnegie Forum on Education and the Economy envisioned teachers educated in such ways that our schools would become the bastions of a democratic society we want them to be.[32] In its initial, unpublished report, the Holmes Group assumed for its member institutions considerable responsibility for addressing the problems of the schools. Its published report recommended, somewhat more timidly, the joining of universities and school districts for purposes of creating professional development schools for teacher education.[33] And in 1985, my colleagues and I created the National Network for Educational Renewal, now consisting of thirteen school-university partnerships in as many states, each committed to the simultaneous renewal of schools and the education of those who work in them.[34]

The central idea in our work is that future teachers must be socialized into teaching by experienced teachers joined with university-based personnel as partners in this enterprise, in which all engage together in renewing their elementary, middle, or senior high school. Instead of only making recommendations for others in books and articles, they will assume responsibility for designing and continuously revising exemplary schools—exemplary in curriculum, organization, teaching, and accompanying regularities. In a setting preparing one hundred new teachers each year, there might well be ten partner schools, each with ten teacher interns, comprising a center of pedagogy. This center will embrace the necessary faculty in the arts and sciences, education, and the partner schools.[35]

There are not to be several such centers in a university setting—one each for agriculture, health and physical education, and the arts—but one only, as there is now only one school of medicine, law, or dentistry. The curricula of all future teachers will have a great deal in common, just as each will be specialized in a given domain. All will be professionally educated to be responsible moral stewards of schools. What the junior high school faculty group described earlier attempted to do against the odds will be expected as the norm.

In spite of repeated exhortations for faculties in education and in other university schools and colleges, especially the arts and sciences, to join in the education of teachers, progress toward productive collaboration has been minimal. Professors of art, history, and English have demonstrated no more enthusiasm for this kind of collaboration than have professors of education. But villain theories get us nowhere.

So far, however, those talking about and even beginning to plan for professional development or partner schools are predominantly in the field of education. They are confronted by such a mind-boggling array of perplexing problems that such schools are still largely nonevents.[36] The university reward system looms as one of the most formidable obstacles.[37] The creation of school-university partnerships as a collaborative umbrella under which these schools might thrive proceeds much more slowly than some of the "gee-whiz" reports might suggest.[38] Given all this, it is not likely that education professors gingerly getting closely involved with partner schools will think to invite university colleagues who move in different intellectual and professional circles.

But taking the initiative and getting involved in action programs designed to enhance the place of the arts in schools is not novel behavior for arts educators. Current stirrings regarding the reform of teacher education through hands-on involvement in schools for purposes of their becoming laboratories for the preparation of teachers offers the best opportunity in many years to build the arts into the culture of schooling.

NOTES

1. John I. Goodlad, *A Place Called School* (New York: McGraw-Hill, 1984), p. 219.

2. Lawrence A. Cremin, *Popular Education and Its Discontents* (New York: Harper and Row, 1990), p. viii.

3. James S. Coleman, "The Concept of Equality of Educational Opportunity," *Harvard Educational Review* 3 (1968): 11.

4. Paul E. Heckman, *Exploring the Concept of School Renewal: Cultural Differences and Similarities Between More and Less Renewing Schools*, Technical Report No. 33, Laboratory in School and Community Education (Los Angeles: Graduate School of Education, University of California, 1982).

5. All the above data are from Goodlad, *A Place Called School*, chapter 5.

6. Ernest L. Boyer, *High School* (New York: Harper and Row, 1982).

7. National Commission on Excellence in Education, *A Nation at Risk* (Washington, DC: U.S. Government Printing Office, 1983).

8. Goodlad, *A Place Called School*, pp. 136-137.

9. Arthur Powell, Eleanor Farrar, and David K. Cohen, *The Shopping Mall High School* (Boston: Houghton Mifflin, 1984).

10. Jeannie Oakes, *Keeping Track: How Schools Structure Inequality* (New Haven: Yale University Press, 1985).

11. John I. Goodlad and Pamela Keating, eds., *Access to Knowledge* (New York: College Entrance Examination Board, 1990).

12. John E. Chubb and Terry M. Moe, *Politics, Markets, and America's Schools* (Washington, DC: Brookings Institution, 1990).

13. John I. Goodlad, "The Learner at the World's Center," *Social Education* 50 (October 1986): 424-436.

14. An excellent recent treatment of the pros and cons is found in M. Frances Klein, ed., *The Politics of Curriculum Decision-Making: Issues in Centralizing the Curriculum* (Albany: State University of New York Press, 1991).

15. Kenneth A. Sirotnik, "The School as the Center of Change," in *Schools for Tomorrow: Directing Reform to Issues That Count*, ed. Thomas J. Sergiovanni and John H. Moore (Newton, MA: Allyn and Bacon, 1989).

16. John I. Goodlad, *Teachers for Our Nation's Schools* (San Francisco: Jossey-Bass, 1990).

17. Zhixin Su, "Teacher Education Reform in the United States (1890-1986)," Occasional Paper No. 3, Center for Educational Renewal (Seattle, WA: College of Education, University of Washington, 1986).

18. James B. Conant, *The American High School Today* (New York: McGraw-Hill, 1959).

19. James B. Conant, *The Education of American Teachers* (New York: McGraw-Hill, 1963).

20. Kenneth A. Sirotnik, "On the Eroding Foundations of Teacher Education," *Phi Delta Kappan* 71 (May 1990): 710-716.

21. Phyllis J. Edmundson, "A Normative Look at the Curriculum in Teacher Education," *Phi Delta Kappan* 71 (May 1990): 717-722.

22. John I. Goodlad, Roger Soder, and Kenneth A. Sirotnik, eds., *The Moral Dimensions of Teaching* (San Francisco: Jossey-Bass, 1990).

23. Zhixin Su, "The Function of the Peer Group in Teacher Socialization," *Phi Delta Kappan* 71 (May 1990): 723-727.

24. Our data here aligned closely with those of Kenneth R. Howey and Nancy L. Zimpher, *Profiles of Preservice Teacher Education* (Albany: State University of New York Press, 1989).

25. See, for example, Jerome J. Hausman, ed., *Arts and the Schools* (New York: McGraw-Hill, 1980).

26. Howard Gardner, *Frames of Mind* (New York: Basic Books, 1983).

27. Elliot W. Eisner, "What the Arts Taught Me about Education," in *Reflections from the Heart of Educational Inquiry: Understanding Curricula and Teaching Through the Arts*, ed. William Schubert and George Willis (Albany: State University of New York Press, 1991).

28. See, for example, Dan C. Lortie, *Schoolteacher* (Chicago: University of Chicago Press, 1975).

29. Charles Fowler, *The Arts Process in Basic Education* (Harrisburg, PA: Pennsylvania State Department of Education, 1974).

30. Thomas Timar, "The Politics of School Restructuring," *Phi Delta Kappan* 71 (December 1989): 269.

31. See particularly Mary M. Bentzen, *Changing Schools: The Magic Feather Principle* (New York: McGraw Hill, 1984); and John I. Goodlad, *The Dynamics of Educational Change* (New York: McGraw-Hill, 1975).

32. Carnegie Forum on Education and the Economy, *A Nation Prepared: Teachers for the 21st Century* (Washington, DC: Carnegie Forum, 1986).

33. Holmes Group, *Tomorrow's Teachers: A Report of the Holmes Group* (East Lansing, MI: Holmes Group, 1986).

34. Kenneth A. Sirotnik and John I. Goodlad, eds., *School-University Partnerships in Action* (New York: Teachers College Press, 1988).

35. For further details, see Goodlad, *Teachers for Our Nation's Schools*, chapters 8 and 9.

36. Frank Brainard, "Professional Development Schools: Status as of 1989," Occasional Paper No. 9, Center for Educational Renewal (Seattle, WA: College of Education, University of Washington, 1989).

37. Roger Soder, "Viewing the Now-Distant Past: How Faculty Members Feel When the Reward Structure Changes," *Phi Delta Kappan* 71 (May 1990): 702-709.

38. Zhixin Su, "School-University Partnerships: Ideas and Experiments (1986-1990)," Occasional Paper No. 12, Center for Educational Renewal (Seattle, WA: College of Education, University of Washington, 1990).

Name Index

Alexander, Robin, 136, 150
Alperson, Philip, 48, 49
Amabile, Teresa M., 190
Ames, Carole, 190
Ames, Russell E., 190
Angelico, Fra, 57
Anson, C. M., 149
Applebee, Arthur N., 17, 18
Arangio, S., 122
Arendt, Hannah, 69
Aristotle, 105, 122, 170
Armstrong, Michael, 150
Arnheim, Rudolf, 58, 94, 104, 105, 107, 110, 120, 122, 123, 191
Asante, Molefi Keti, 69
Ausubel, David D., 68
Ayer, Alfred J., 190

Baensh, Otto, 50
Barker-Lunn, Joan, 150
Ball, Deborah, 91
Bamberger, Jeanne, 132, 149
Barkan, Manuel, 74, 75
Bartholomae, David, 19
Battin, Margaret P., 168
Beardsley, Monroe C., 49, 50, 58, 59, 60, 64, 68, 74, 78
Beattie, Olga, 189
Beckett, Samuel, 47
Beethoven, Ludwig van, 37
Bellini, Giovanni, 57
Bentzen, Mary M., 312
Berenson, Bernard, 163
Beukhof, G., 190
Binet, Alfred, 4
Blatchford, Peter, 150
Bloom, Benjamin S., 49
Botts, Roderick, 18
Boyer, Ernest L., 196, 211
Brahms, Johannes, 37
Brainard, Frank, 212
Breuer, K., 191
Britain, W. Lambert, 120
Broudy, Harry S., 11, 12, 13, 18, 19, 48, 50, 63, 74, 75
Bruner, Jerome S., 10, 11, 18, 75, 97, 98, 113, 116, 121, 130, 131, 148
Bull, Dale, 131, 148
Burckhardt, Joseph, 163

Burke, Jessica, 150
Burnett, Joe R., 11, 18
Burton, Judith, 123
Bush, George, 192, 202

Calderhead, James, 150
Callen, Donald M., 68
Campbell, Donald T., 189
Canfield, Richard L., 121
Caravaggio, Michelangelo Merisi de, 163, 164
Carli, Massimo, 190
Carothers, Thomas, 107, 108, 122
Carrier, David E., 163
Case, Robbie, 121
Cassirer, Ernest, 12, 15, 18, 51, 55, 67
Cezanne, Paul, 37
Chang, Hsing-Wu, 131, 148
Chomsky, Noam, 97, 98, 120
Chubb, John E., 211
Cizek, Franz, 17
Clark, Kenneth, 64, 68, 69
Clifford, Geraldine J., 186, 189, 191
Cohen, David K., 91, 211
Cole, Michael, 121
Coleman, James S., 211
Collingwood, Robert, 189
Coltrane, John, 30, 31, 44
Colwell, Richard J., 191
Conant, James B., 201, 212
Connell, J. P., 190
Constable, John, 57
Cork, C., 135, 150
Cortazzi, Martin, 136, 150
Cowie, Helen, 130, 131, 134, 148, 149
Cox, Maureen V., 133, 148, 149
Cremin, Lawrence A., 16, 17, 18, 211
Croll, Paul, 150
Csikszentmihalyi, Isabella, 190
Csikszentmihalyi, Mihaly, 169, 171, 183, 189, 190, 191
Cunningham, Merce, 30, 31

d'Amico, Victor, 122
Danto, Arthur, 49, 68, 78, 80, 82, 91
Darwin, Charles, 20
Davidson, Lyle, 132, 134, 148, 149
Davis, Jessica, 92, 123
Deci, Edward L., 177, 190

213

DeKooning, Willem, 81
Delamont, Sara, 141, 150
Delespaul, Philip, 190
Dennis, Sonja, 121
Descartes, René, 15
Deutsch, Diana, 148
Dewey, John, 4, 11, 12, 17, 18, 28, 36, 50, 56, 57, 68, 190
Dickie, George, 49
Dienstbier, Richard A., 190
Dowling, W. Jay, 148, 149
Duchamp, Marcel, 80
Dufrenne, Mikel, 38, 40, 50

Eaton, Marcia Muelder, 50, 69, 151, 168
Ebel, Robert L., 191
Ecker, David, 122
Ecob, Russell, 150
Edmundson, Phyllis, J., 212
Efland, Arthur, D., 17, 48, 91
Eisner, Elliot W., 18, 19, 49, 74, 122, 123, 191, 204, 212
Engel, Martin, 123

Farquhar, Clare, 150
Farrar, Eleanor, 211
Feldman, David H., 90
Feldman, Edmund B., 68
Fenstermacher, Gary D, 18
Feyerabend, Paul, 28
Fischer, Kurt W., 121
Fisher, D., 122
Fisher, John, 69, 168
Fowler, Charles, 206, 212
Freeman, Norman H., 121, 148, 149
Freud, Sigmund, 4
Friedman, Sarah, 101, 121
Fry, Roger, 32, 49

Galton, Maurice J., 124, 141, 144, 150
Gardner, Howard, 16, 19, 67, 73, 90, 91, 92, 107, 108, 109, 110, 120, 121, 122, 123, 127, 132, 148, 149, 189, 204, 212
Garfunkel, G., 122
Geahigan, George, 1
Gehlbach, Roger D., 191
Gendlin, Eugene, 190
Gerberich, J. Raymond, 191
Getzels, Jacob, 171, 189
Giotto, 57
Goldberg, Jill, 121
Golomb, Claire, 90, 121
Gombrich, Ernst H., 58, 103, 104, 122
Goodlad, John I., 18, 192, 211, 212

Goodman, Nelson, 15, 16, 19, 49, 50, 58, 68, 72, 78, 90, 104, 105, 106, 122
Goodnow, Jacqueline J., 101, 121, 130, 148
Greene, Harry A., 191
Greenfield, Patricia, 121

Hall, G. Stanley, 4
Hanesian, Helen, 68
Hansen, Forest, 48
Hargreaves, Andy, 135, 150
Hargreaves, David, 124, 135, 136, 144, 148, 149, 150
Hargreaves, Linda, 147
Harris, D. B., 121
Harrow, Anita J., 49
Harter, Susan, 190
Hastie, W. Reid, 18
Hausman, Jerome J., 212
Heckman, Paul E., 211
Hegel, Georg Wilhelm Friedrich, 53
Hemingway, Ernest, 37
Henry, Nelson B., 18
Hidi, S., 190, 191
Hirsch, E. D., Jr., 53, 68
Hirst, Paul H., 11, 12, 18, 67
Holbein, Hans, 57
Housen, Abigail, 111, 123
Houston, W. Robert, 191
Howard, Vernon A., 19, 90
Howey, Kenneth R., 212
Hudelson, Earl, 17
Hurtwitz, A., 122

Ingres, Jean Auguste Dominque, 57
Inhelder, Barbel, 121, 150
Isaacs, Nathan, 136, 137
Isaacs, Susan, 136, 137, 150
Isenberg, Arnold, 159, 168
Ives, S. William, 107, 109, 122

Jackson, Philip W., 191
Jasman, A., 138, 150
John-Steiner, Vera, 121
Jones, Beverly J., 191
Jones, Philip M., 149
Jorgensen, Albert N., 191
Joyce, James, 171, 189
Jung, Carl Gustav, 171, 172, 190

Kaelin, Eugene F., 50
Kandinsky, Wassily, 92
Kant, Immanuel, 98, 102
Karmiloff-Smith, Annette, 121
Kaufmann, Walter, 69
Keating, Pamela, 211

Kellogg, Rhoda, 94, 120
Kelly, Hope, 122
Kierkegaard, Søren, 80
Kilpatrick, William, 4
Kircher, Mary, 132, 149
Klee, Paul, 92, 112
Klein, M. Frances, 211
Kliebard, Herbert M., 18, 48
Knieter, Gerard L., 48, 189
Koroscik, Judith, 85, 91
Korzenik, Diana, 109, 122
Kozulin, Alex, 121
Kramer, Hilton, 69
Krapp, A., 190, 191
Krathwohl, David R., 49
Kroll, B. M., 149
Kubey, Robert, 189
Kuhn, Thomas, 20
Kwalwasser, Jacob, 17

Lakatos, Imre, 28
Langer, Susanne K., 12, 15, 18, 36, 50
Lanier, Vincent, 18
Larson, Reed, 190, 191
Lederman, Arlene, 123
Leondar, Barbara, 19
Leonhard, Charles, 191
Levi, Albert William, 51, 53, 54, 60, 62, 66, 68
Lewis, David, 150
Lewis, Hilda P., 120
Locke, John, 15
London, Peter, 123
Lortie, Dan C., 212
Lovana-Kerr, Jessie, 90
Lowenfield, Viktor, 95, 120
Lucquet, G. H., 149

Madeja, Stanley S., 48, 189, 191
Mann, Horace, 5
Marini, Zopito, 121
Mark, Michael L., 48
Martin, Diane, 149
Masia, Bertram B., 49
Mason, Rachel, 69
Massimini, Fausto, 190
Matisse, Henri, 80
McFee, June K., 191
McKeough, Anne, 121
McKernon, Patricia, 148, 149
Meier, Norman C., 17
Mendelsohn, E., 122
Miller, George, 97, 98, 120
Mills, Janet, 147
Miró, Joan, 116

Moe, Terry M., 211
Mondrian, Piet, 30, 31
Moog, Helmut, 130, 148, 149
Moore, John H., 211
Moore, Ronald, 69, 155, 168
Mortimore, Peter, 138, 150
Mozart, Wolfgang Amadeus, 30

Nahrstedt, W., 189
Newell, Allen, 96, 98, 120
Newton-Smith, W. H., 28
Nias, Jennifer, 136, 150
Nicholls, John G., 190
Niles, Olive, 19
Nixon, J., 150
Nochlin, Linda, 85, 91
Nodine, C., 122
Nolen, Susan B., 190
Novak, Joseph D., 68

Oakes, Jeannie, 211
Olds, Clifton, 123
Olson, David R., 19, 90, 121
Olver, Rose R., 121
Osborne, Harold, 50, 60, 68, 74, 75, 78
Ott, R., 122

Pariser, David, 123
Parker, Francis W., 4, 17
Parsons, Michael J., 19, 70, 91, 111, 123, 132, 148, 149
Patashnick, Michael, 190
Patrick, Helen, 150
Perkins, David N., 19, 90
Perry, Martha, 112, 123
Pestalozzi, Johann Heinrich, 1
Peterson, Penelope, 91
Petrosky, Anthony R., 19
Pflederer, Marilyn, 133, 149
Phenix, Philip H., 11, 12, 18, 67
Phillips, D. C., 28, 49
Piaget, Jean, 10, 72, 98, 99, 100, 102, 106, 113, 117, 121, 125, 126, 127, 128, 130, 133, 136, 143, 147, 150, 189
Picasso, Pablo, 37, 74, 81, 92, 112
Pieters, J. M., 191
Pintrich, Paul R., 191
Plato, 27, 28, 35, 40, 56, 98
Plewis, Ian, 150
Poussin, Nicolas, 57
Powell, Arthur, 198, 211
Prenzel, M., 191
Purves, Alan C., 19, 48, 68

Rabinow, Paul, 91
Radford, John, 148
Raphael, 57
Rathunde, Kevin, 190
Ravitch, Diane, 69
Read, Herbert, 56, 57, 68
Reid, L. A., 67
Reimer, Bennett, 13, 19, 20, 49, 50, 123
Remarque, Erich Maria, 84, 85
Rembrandt, 32, 57
Renninger, K. A., 190, 191
Ricci, Corrado, 92, 116
Robinson, S., 144, 150
Roblin, Ronald, 49
Rochberg-Halton, Eugene, 189
Rogers, D. R., 121
Rorty, Richard, 65, 69
Rosenblatt, Elizabeth, 122
Rosenstiel, Anne K., 109, 122
Ross, Malcolm, 150
Rousseau, Jean Jaques, 4
Ruisdael, Jacob van, 57
Rush, Jean, 90
Ryan, R. Michael, 177, 190

Salomon, Gavriel, 121
Sammons, Pamela, 150
Schaefer-Simmern, Henry, 95, 120
Scheffler, Israel, 97, 98, 121
Schiefele, Ulrich, 169, 184, 190, 191
Schiller, Friedrich von, 56, 68
Schilpp, P. A., 189
Schlick, Moritz, 190
Schubert, William, 212
Sclafani, Richard, 49
Scribner, Sylvia, 121
Scripp, Lawrence, 132, 149
Serafine, Mary Louise, 149
Sergiovanni, Thomas, 211
Setton, T., 135, 150
Seurat, Georges, 85
Siegler, Robert, S., 121
Silk, Angèle M. J., 148
Silverman, Jen, 122
Silverman, Ronald, 18
Silvers, Anita, 69, 168
Simon, Brian, 150
Simon, Herbert, 96, 98, 120
Simons, P. R. J., 190, 191
Sirotnik, Kenneth J., 208, 211, 212
Sloboda, John A., 121, 149
Smith, B. Othanel, 11, 18
Smith, Peter K., 130, 148
Smith, Ralph A., 13, 18, 48, 49, 50, 51, 62, 68, 74, 75, 91

Socrates, 168
Soder, Roger, 212
Souberman, Ellen, 121
Sparshott, Francis, 33, 49
Spencer, Herbert, 2, 17, 20, 21, 22, 25, 48
Squire, James R., 19
Stallings, Jane, 48, 189
Stern, William, 94, 95, 116, 118, 119, 120, 123
Stevens, G., 122
Stokes, W. Ann, 50
Stoll, Louise, 150
Strauss, Sydney, 123, 149
Su, Zhixin, 211, 212
Sullivan, William, 91
Swanwick, Keith, 130, 132, 134, 148, 149

Taylor, Charles, 76, 91
Tellstrom, A. Theodore, 17
Terman, Lewis, 4
Thomas, Glyn V., 148
Thorndike, Edward, 4
Thorpe, Leigh A., 131, 148
Tickle, Les, 150
Tillman, June, 130, 132, 134, 148, 149
Timar, Thomas, 212
Tizard, Barbara, 138, 150
Tolstoy, Leo, 104, 105, 119, 122
Travers, Robert M. W., 191
Trehub, Sandra, E., 131, 148

Velázquez, Diego Rodriguez de Silva, 57
Van Gogh, Vincent, 57
Vygotsky, Lev, 72, 86, 99, 100, 110, 121

Walk, R., 90
Webster, Noah, 152
Welsh, Patricia, 134, 149
Werner, Heinz, 121
Westbury, Ian, 48, 68
Whalen, Samuel, 190
Whipple, Guy M., 17
Wilkinson, Elizabeth W., 68
Willcocks, John, 150
Willis, George, 212
Willoughby, L. A., 68
Winner, Ellen, 107, 108, 122, 123, 132, 149
Wittgenstein, Ludwig Josef Johan, 170, 189
Wittkower, Rudolf, 163
Wittrock, Merlin C., 191

Wold, Stanley G., 18
Wolf, Dennie, 73, 91, 110, 112, 121, 122, 123, 126, 132, 134, 148, 149
Wang, Marian, 183, 190
Wood, David, 136, 150

Wreen, Michael J., 68

Zimmerman, Marilyn, 126, 148
Zimpher, Nancy L., 212

Subject Index

Academic reform movement, outcomes of, for arts curriculum, 8-14

Aesthetic activity: description in, 161-63; interpretation in, 163-65

Aesthetic education: definition of, 35, 38-39; functions of, 31, 38-39, 42-45, 56-57; growing interest in idea of, 13, 26-27; recommendations for general and specialized curricula in, 45-48; see also, Arts education

Aesthetic experience: knowledge of history as crucial component of, 164; features of, 58-60; function of, 15; nature of, 160

Aesthetic knowing, dimensions of, 29-45

Aesthetic learning: cumulative nature of, 55, 60; pedagogical considerations important in, 61-67; phases in development of, 61-67

Aesthetics, impact of cognitive revolution on, 103-6

Art: use of puzzles in teaching of, 153-54, 155-57, 159-68; view of, as a basic form of human understanding, 51-52; see also, Arts

Art medium, conception of, as a symbol system, 72

Art objects, lack of clarity in definition of, 77-78

Art works: aesthetic relevance of intrinsic features of, 165-66; constitutive values of, 56; critical questions for understanding, 54; revelatory powers of, 67

Artistic development: phases of, 127-35 (table, 129); usefulness of generalized description of, 143-48; views of stages in, 127

Artists, as makers of meaning, 104-6; "knowings how" needed by, 39-41

Arts: aesthetic education as justification for, 25-27; cognitive function of, 12, 15; functionality as justification for, 22-23; impact of "new" cognitivism on, 71-72; potential contributions of, 204; reasons for rethinking the place of, in education, 169-70; Spencerian view of place of, in education, 20-21, 25; talent development as justification for, 24-25;

view of, as distinct symbol systems, 15; view of, as sources of knowledge, 12

Arts curriculum: conferences on, 13; difficulties of effecting changes in, 14; projects for improvement of, 13; proposals for, 12-13; theories regarding, 11-13

Arts education: effect of cognitive revolution on, 113-16; criticisms of, 151-52; impact of child-centered movement on, 6-7; impact of cultural pluralism on, 78-79; impact of social efficiency movement on, 4-6; impact of social reconstruction movement on, 7-8; necessity for, 67; objectives for, 52-53; percipience in art and culture as goal of, 52; purpose of, 55

Arts educators: changed perceptions of, regarding their subjects, 13-14; concerns of, about arts curriculum in post-Progressive period, 8-10

Arts products of children, research on teacher assessment of, 144-45

Arts programs in schools: isolation of, from other school programs, 209; lack of time and resources for, 194; reasons for scant attention to, 195; variability among, 194

ARTS PROPEL program, features of, 115-116

Arts subjects, in the curriculum: ambivalence of educators toward, 2; effects of progressive reforms on teaching of, 5-8; introduction of, 1; proposals for implementing new view of, 12-13; teaching of, in pre-Progressive period, 3-4; theories regarding role of, 11-13

Behaviorism, inadequacy of, in accounting for important behavioral and mental phenomena, 96

Carnegie Forum on Education and the Economy, 209

Child-centered movement, impact of, on arts education, 6-7

Children's drawings: cognitivist interpretation of constant features in, 116-20;

constant characteristics of, at various ages, 93-94; developing differentiation in, 108-10; developmental portrait of, 111-13; differing perspectives on stages in, 94-95; intention in, 107-8; stages in development of, as impacted by culture, 109; use of, as symbolic language, by young children, 110

Classroom practices, in arts (in United Kingdom): examples of, in secondary schools, 141-42; research on, in primary grades, 139-41

Cognition: equation of, with rational conceptualization, 27-28; inadequacy of traditional conceptions of, 25-26; interpretive aspects of, in language and in mathematics, 86-88; relation of, to perception, 73; symbol-systems approach to understanding of, 101-3

Cognitive movement, in arts education: philosophical aspects of, 70-73; psychological aspects of, 74-76

Cognitive revolution: beginnings of, in mid-1950s, 96-97; contributions of various researchers and theorists to, 96-103; interdisciplinary nature of, 104

Cognitive science: core assumptions of, 97; de-emphasis of content and affect in, 97-98; interdisciplinary nature of, 98; roots of, in philosophical issues, 98

Critical thinking skills, use of, in study of art, 154-60

Cultural pluralism, impact of, on arts education, 78-79

DELTA project (University of Leicester), 126, 144, 146-47, 153

Discipline-based art education, 75, 188; critique of, 42-43, 114-15; four content areas as components of, 114

Early childhood, aesthetic learning in, 110

Education: impact of instrumental model of, on curriculum, 195; impact of structural changes in (in United Kingdom), on teaching of creative arts, 137-38; utilitarian view of, 21

Education Summit (1989), 192, 202

Elementary schools: effects of use of special arts teachers in, 203; instructional hours per week in, 196-97; variability among, in time for school subjects, 195-96

Emotions: distinction between feeling and, 37-38; words as categorical symbols of, 36

Flow experience: conditions required for, 182; model for describing, 181 (figure, 183); nature of, 181-82; study of, in talented students, 182-83

Holmes group, 209

Humanities, definition of, 53

Humanities (percipience) curriculum: critical analysis in, 66-67; design for (figure), 62; importance of multicultural dimension of, 64-65; pedagogical considerations in, related to phases of aesthetic learnings, 61-67

Individual development, function of arts-related activities in, 171-73

Information processing, application of, to children's drawings, 100-1

Interpretation of arts objects: dependence of, on language, 75-76, 82-83; examples of need for language in, 79-86; implication of model of, for curriculum and assessment in arts education, 88-90; increasing need for, 78; meaning of, 76-77

Journal of Aesthetic Education, 26

Junior high school, account of efforts to redesign program for, 205-6

Language: as most important developmental acquisition, 99; dependence of interpretation upon, 75-76, 79-86; inadequacy of, to express quality of feeling, 36

League of Cooperating Schools, 208, 209

Moral education, function of aesthetic education in, 56-57

Multiple intelligences, theory of, 16, 73, 102-3, 204

National curriculum (United Kingdom), components of, 124

National Network for Educational Research, 210

Notationality, theory of, 15

ORACLE (Observational Research and Classroom Learning Evaluation), 138-41

Perception, stages in development of, 111-12

Percipience: interpretive character of, 75; nature of, as goal of education, 74-75

Percipience (humanities) curriculum, design for (figure), 62

Piagetian stage theory, 98-99; postulates of, 126; problems with, in artistic development, 126-27

Plowden Report (1967), 136-37

Primary teachers (in United Kingdom): predominance of "horticultural metaphor" among, 136-37; use of impressionistic judgments by, in assessing students' creative work, 138; views of, on their role in informal learning, 136

PRISMS (Curriculum Provision in Small Primary Schools), study by, of classroom practices in art in United Kingdom, 139, 141

Progressive movement, impact of, on arts education, 2-8

Project Zero (Harvard University): interest of, in arts education, 16; investigation of, into children's drawings, 106-40; research of, on art media as symbol systems, 72; work of, on spontaneous singing of preschool children, 131

Puzzles: nature of, 152-53; use of, in aesthetics and art education, 153-54; 155-57; 159-68

Quality of experience: as valid predictor of engagement and school achievement, 183-84; case studies showing high level of, for talented arts students, 174-77; factors contributing to, 181; implication of research on, for arts education, 187-88; relationship of, to interest, 185-86; study of, in talented students in arts/music and math/science, 177-80; use of Experience Sampling Method to get descriptions of, 173-74

Rational cognition: aesthetic cognition, as complementary alternate to, 171; constraints of, in dealing with human affairs, 170; important function of, as tool for adaptation, 170

Rationality, role of, in making value judgments, 155-60

Science, centrality of, in Spencerian view of education, 21

School reform: importance of linking reform in teacher education to, 201-2; individual school as most promising unit for, 201; obstacles encountered in, 207-9

School-university partnerships: necessity for, in preparation of teachers, 209-10; obstacles to establishing, 210-11

Secondary schools, in United States: curriculum tracks in, 198-99; neglect of arts in, 197-99; proposals for allocation of time for, to various subjects, 200; variability in allocation of teachers in, to various subjects, 197-98

Symbols, functions of, 101-2

Symbol systems research: concerns of, with décalage, 102; contributions of, to development of theory of multiple intelligences, 102-3; longitudinal studies in, 102

Teacher education: deficiencies in, 201-2; failure to tie reforms in, to school reform, 201; necessity for school-university partnerships in programs for, 209-210; separation of the arts from other programs for, 186-87

Teachers: difficulty of, in translating theory into practice, 143; "working theories" of, 143

Teachers (of art), need of, for more study in the humanities, 67

Teaching (in the arts), lack of research on, 186-87

Universal schooling, centrality of idea of, in U. S., 194-95

Visual arts, perception and production as aspects of, 111-13

Woods Hole Conference (1959), 10, 37; outcomes of, regarding the arts, 13

INFORMATION ABOUT MEMBERSHIP IN THE SOCIETY

Membership in the National Society for the Study of Education is open to all who desire to receive its publications.

There are two categories of membership, Regular and Comprehensive. The Regular Membership (annual dues in 1992, $25) entitles the member to receive both volumes of the yearbook. The Comprehensive Membership (annual dues in 1992, $48) entitles the member to receive the two-volume yearbook and the two current volumes in the Series on Contemporary Educational Issues. For their first year of membership, full-time graduate students pay reduced dues in 1992 as follows: Regular, $21; Comprehensive, $43.

Membership in the Society is for the calendar year. Dues are payable on or before January 1 of each year.

New members are required to pay an entrance fee of $1, in addition to annual dues for the year in which they join.

Members of the Society include professors, researchers, graduate students, and administrators in colleges and universities; teachers, supervisors, curriculum specialists, and administrators in elementary and secondary schools; and a considerable number of persons not formally connected with educational institutions.

All members participate in the nomination and election of the six-member Board of Directors, which is responsible for managing the affairs of the Society, including the authorization of volumes to appear in the yearbook series. All members whose dues are paid for the current year are eligible for election to the Board of Directors.

Each year the Society arranges for meetings to be held in conjunction with the annual conferences of one or more of the major national educational organizations. All members are urged to attend these sessions. Members are also encouraged to submit proposals for future yearbooks or for volumes in the series on Contemporary Educational Issues.

Further information about the Society may be secured by writing to the Secretary-Treasurer, NSSE, 5835 Kimbark Avenue, Chicago, IL 60637.

RECENT PUBLICATIONS OF THE NATIONAL
SOCIETY FOR THE STUDY OF EDUCATION

1. The Yearbooks

Ninety-first Yearbook (1992)

Part 1. *The Changing Contexts of Teaching.* Ann Lieberman, editor. Cloth.
Part 2. *The Arts, Education, and Aesthetic Knowing.* Bennett Reimer and Ralph A. Smith, editors. Cloth.

Ninetieth Yearbook (1991)

Part 1. *The Care and Education of America's Young Children: Obstacles and Opportunities.* Sharon L. Kagan, editor. Cloth.
Part 2. *Evaluation and Education: At Quarter Century.* Milbrey W. McLaughlin and D. C. Phillips, editors. Cloth.

Eighty-ninth Yearbook (1990)

Part 1. *Textbooks and Schooling in the United States.* David L. Elliott and Arthur Woodward, editors. Cloth.
Part 2. *Educational Leadership and Changing Contexts of Families, Communities, and Schools.* Brad Mitchell and Luvern L. Cunningham, editors. Paper.

Eighty-eighth Yearbook (1989)

Part 1. *From Socrates to Software: The Teacher as Text and the Text as Teacher.* Philip W. Jackson and Sophie Haroutunian-Gordon, editors. Cloth.
Part 2. *Schooling and Disability.* Douglas Biklen, Dianne Ferguson, and Alison Ford, editors. Cloth.

Eighty-seventh Yearbook (1988)

Part 1. *Critical Issues in Curriculum.* Laurel N. Tanner, editor. Cloth.
Part 2. *Cultural Literacy and the Idea of General Education.* Ian Westbury and Alan C. Purves, editors. Cloth.

Eighty-sixth Yearbook (1987)

Part 1. *The Ecology of School Renewal.* John I. Goodlad, editor. Cloth.
Part 2. *Society as Educator in an Age of Transition.* Kenneth D. Benne and Steven Tozer, editors. Cloth.

Eighty-fifth Yearbook (1986)

Part 1. *Microcomputers and Education.* Jack A. Culbertson and Luvern L. Cunningham, editors. Cloth.
Part 2. *The Teaching of Writing.* Anthony R. Petrosky and David Bartholomae, editors. Paper.

225

Eighty-fourth Yearbook (1985)

Part 1. *Education in School and Nonschool Settings.* Mario D. Fantini and Robert Sinclair, editors. Cloth.

Part 2. *Learning and Teaching the Ways of Knowing.* Elliot Eisner, editor. Paper.

Eighty-third Yearbook (1984)

Part 1. *Becoming Readers in a Complex Society.* Alan C. Purves and Olive S. Niles, editors. Cloth.

Part 2. *The Humanities in Precollegiate Education.* Benjamin Ladner, editor. Paper.

Eighty-second Yearbook (1983)

Part 1. *Individual Differences and the Common Curriculum.* Gary D Fenstermacher and John I. Goodlad, editors. Paper.

Eighty-first Yearbook (1982)

Part 1. *Policy Making in Education.* Ann Lieberman and Milbrey W. McLaughlin, editors. Cloth.

Part 2. *Education and Work.* Harry F. Silberman, editor. Cloth.

Eightieth Yearbook (1981)

Part 1. *Philosophy and Education.* Jonas P. Soltis, editor. Cloth.

Part 2. *The Social Studies.* Howard D. Mehlinger and O. L. Davis, Jr., editors. Cloth.

Seventy-ninth Yearbook (1980)

Part 1. *Toward Adolescence: The Middle School Years.* Mauritz Johnson, editor. Paper.

Seventy-eighth Yearbook (1979)

Part 1. *The Gifted and the Talented: Their Education and Development.* A. Harry Passow, editor. Paper.

Part 2. *Classroom Management.* Daniel L. Duke, editor. Paper.

Seventy-seventh Yearbook (1978)

Part 1. *The Courts and Education.* Clifford B. Hooker, editor. Cloth.

Seventy-sixth Yearbook (1977)

Part 1. *The Teaching of English.* James R. Squire, editor. Cloth.

The above titles in the Society's Yearbook series may be ordered from the University of Chicago Press, Book Order Department, 11030 Langley Ave., Chicago, IL 60628. For a list of earlier titles in the yearbook series still available, write to the Secretary, NSSE, 5835 Kimbark Ave., Chicago, IL 60637.

2. The Series on Contemporary Educational Issues

The following volumes in the Society's Series on Contemporary Educational Issues may be ordered from the McCutchan Publishing Corporation, P.O. Box 774, Berkeley, CA 94702.

Boyd, William Lowe, and Walberg, Herbert J., editors. *Choice in Education: Potential and Problems.* 1990.
Case, Charles W., and Matthes, William A., editors. *Colleges of Education: Perspectives on Their Future.* 1985.
Eisner, Elliot, and Vallance, Elizabeth, editors. *Conflicting Conceptions of Curriculum.* 1974.
Erickson, Donald A., and Reller, Theodore L., editors. *The Principal in Metropolitan Schools.* 1979.
Farley, Frank H., and Gordon, Neal J., editors. *Psychology and Education: The State of the Union.* 1981.
Fennema, Elizabeth, and Ayer, M. Jane, editors. *Women and Education: Equity or Equality.* 1984.
First, Patricia F., and Walberg, Herbert J., editors. *School Boards: Changing Local Control.* 1992.
Griffiths, Daniel E., Stout, Robert T., and Forsyth, Patrick, editors. *Leaders for America's Schools: The Report and Papers of the National Commission on Excellence in Educational Administration.* 1988.
Jackson, Philip W., editor. *Contributing to Educational Change: Perspectives on Research and Practice.* 1988.
Lane, John J., and Epps, Edgar A., editors. *Restructuring the Schools: Problems and Prospects.* 1992.
Lane, John J., and Walberg, Herbert J., editors. *Effective School Leadership: Policy and Process.* 1987.
Levine, Daniel U., and Havighurst, Robert J., editors. *The Future of Big City Schools: Desegregation Policies and Magnet Alternatives.* 1977.
Lindquist, Mary M., editor. *Selected Issues in Mathematics Education.* 1981.
Murphy, Joseph, editor. *The Educational Reform Movement of the 1980s: Perspectives and Cases.* 1990.
Nucci, Larry P., editor. *Moral Development and Character Education.* 1989.
Peterson, Penelope L., and Walberg, Herbert J., editors. *Research on Teaching: Concepts, Findings, and Implications.* 1979.
Pflaum-Connor, Susanna, editor. *Aspects of Reading Education.* 1978.
Purves, Alan, and Levine, Daniel U., editors. *Educational Policy and International Assessment: Implications of the IEA Assessment of Achievement.* 1975.
Sinclair, Robert L., and Ghory, Ward. *Reaching Marginal Students: A Prime Concern for School Renewal.* 1987.
Spodek, Bernard, and Walberg, Herbert J., editors. *Early Childhood Education: Issues and Insights.* 1977.
Talmage, Harriet, editor. *Systems of Individualized Education.* 1975.
Tomlinson, Tommy M., and Walberg, Herbert J., editors. *Academic Work and Educational Excellence: Raising Student Productivity.* 1986.
Tyler, Ralph W., editor. *From Youth to Constructive Adult Life: The Role of the Public School.* 1978.

Tyler, Ralph W., and Wolf, Richard M., editors. *Crucial Issues in Testing.* 1974.

Walberg, Herbert J., editor. *Educational Environments and Effects: Evaluation, Policy, and Productivity.* 1979.

Walberg, Herbert J., editor. *Improving Educational Standards and Productivity: The Research Basis for Policy.* 1982.

Wang, Margaret C., and Walberg, Herbert J., editors. *Adapting Instruction to Student Differences.* 1985.

Warren, Donald R., editor. *History, Education, and Public Policy: Recovering the American Educational Past.* 1978.

Waxman, Hersholt C., and Walberg, Herbert J., editors. *Effective Teaching: Current Research.* 1991.